Jesus in the Victorian Novel

NEW DIRECTIONS IN RELIGION AND LITERATURE

This series aims to showcase new work at the forefront of religion and literature through short studies written by leading and rising scholars in the field. Books will pursue a variety of theoretical approaches as they engage with writing from different religious and literary traditions. Collectively, the series will offer a timely critical intervention to the interdisciplinary crossover between religion and literature, speaking to wider contemporary interests and mapping out new directions for the field in the early twenty-first century.

Series editors: Emma Mason and Mark Knight

ALSO AVAILABLE IN THE SERIES:

The New Atheist Novel, Arthur Bradley and Andrew Tate
Blake. Wordsworth. Religion, Jonathan Roberts
Do the Gods Wear Capes?, Ben Saunders
England's Secular Scripture, Jo Carruthers
Victorian Parables, Susan E. Colón
The Late Walter Benjamin, John Schad
Dante and the Sense of Transgression, William Franke
The Glyph and the Gramophone, Luke Ferretter
John Cage and Buddhist Ecopoetics, Peter Jaeger
Rewriting the Old Testament in Anglo-Saxon Verse, Samantha Zacher
Forgiveness in Victorian Literature, Richard Hughes Gibson
The Gospel According to the Novelist, Magdalena Mączyńska
Jewish Feeling, Richa Dwor
Beyond the Willing Suspension of Disbelief, Michael Tomko
The Gospel According to David Foster Wallace, Adam S. Miller
Pentecostal Modernism, Stephen Shapiro and Philip Barnard
The Bible in the American Short Story, Lesleigh Cushing Stahlberg and Peter S. Hawkins
Faith in Poetry, Michael D. Hurley
Jeanette Winterson and Religion, Emily McAvan
Religion and American Literature since the 1950s, Mark Eaton
Esoteric Islam in Modern French Thought, Ziad Elmarsafy
The Rhetoric of Conversion in English Puritan Writing, David Parry
Djuna Barnes and Theology, Zhao Ng

FORTHCOMING:

Marilynne Robinson's Wordly Gospel, Ryan S. Kemp and Jordan M. Rodgers
Weird Faith in 19th Century Literature, Mark Knight and Emma Mason
Christian Heresy, James Joyce and the Modernist Literary Imagination, Gregory T. Erikson

Jesus in the Victorian Novel

Reimagining Christ

Jessica Ann Hughes

BLOOMSBURY ACADEMIC
LONDON • NEW YORK • OXFORD • NEW DELHI • SYDNEY

BLOOMSBURY ACADEMIC
Bloomsbury Publishing Plc
50 Bedford Square, London, WC1B 3DP, UK
1385 Broadway, New York, NY 10018, USA
29 Earlsfort Terrace, Dublin 2, Ireland

BLOOMSBURY, BLOOMSBURY ACADEMIC and the Diana logo
are trademarks of Bloomsbury Publishing Plc

First published in Great Britain 2022
This paperback edition published 2023

Copyright © Jessica Ann Hughes, 2022

Jessica Ann Hughes has asserted her right under the Copyright, Designs
and Patents Act, 1988, to be identified as Author of this work.

For legal purposes the Acknowledgements on pp. vi–vii constitute
an extension of this copyright page.

Cover design: Eleanor Rose
Cover image © Bridgeman

All rights reserved. No part of this publication may be reproduced or
transmitted in any form or by any means, electronic or mechanical, including
photocopying, recording, or any information storage or retrieval system,
without prior permission in writing from the publishers.

Bloomsbury Publishing Plc does not have any control over, or responsibility for,
any third-party websites referred to or in this book. All internet addresses given
in this book were correct at the time of going to press. The author and publisher
regret any inconvenience caused if addresses have changed or sites have
ceased to exist, but can accept no responsibility for any such changes.

A catalogue record for this book is available from the British Library.

A catalog record for this book is available from the Library of Congress.

ISBN: HB: 978-1-3502-7815-8
PB: 978-1-3502-7819-6
ePDF: 978-1-3502-7816-5
eBook: 978-1-3502-7817-2

Series: New Directions in Religion and Literature

Typeset by Integra Software Services Pvt. Ltd.

To find out more about our authors and books visit www.bloomsbury.com
and sign up for our newsletters.

Contents

Acknowledgements	vi
Introduction	1
1 The Narrative Consequences of Theology	11
The Backstory: Conversion Narratives and the Novel	11
Grace Abounding… To Me	18
Union with Jesus	26
2 Popular Piety and Jesus of Nazareth	39
The Romantic Incarnation	45
Jesus and Domesticity	52
Jesus and Myth	60
3 Jesus the Revolutionary King	67
Kingsley and the Incarnation	69
The Re-formed Conversion Narrative	79
4 Jesus the Reconciling High Priest	101
The Jesus of Faith and the Jesus of History	105
Justice, Mercy, and Reconciliation	114
5 Jesus the Moral Prophet	131
Imitating Jesus	136
The Failed Prophet	158
A New Hope	162
Conclusion	169
Bibliography	174
Index	185

Acknowledgements

This book began one May morning in graduate school, when Mark Noll asked me, "What do the Victorians think of Jesus?" Truth be told, I fumbled for an answer that morning because I had learned only an hour earlier that I was pregnant with my second child. But even amid all the expectations and foreboding and excitement that go with such knowledge, Professor Noll's question intrigued me, particularly given the novels I had been reading. Since then, many patient and generous mentors, colleagues, and friends have come alongside and helped make this book what it is today.

I am profoundly thankful for the guidance of Sara Maurer, Chris R. VandenBossche, David Thomas, and of course Mark Noll in the early stages of this research. Their expertise directing various lines of inquiry and reading early drafts was foundational to this book. Since graduate school, Tim Larsen deserves special thanks for his ongoing support of this project, particularly in generously sharing his own research. Thanks also go to my colleagues at George Fox University, particularly Brooks Lampe, Guadalupe Garcia McCall, and Paul Anderson, for their advice, suggestions, and encouragement along the way.

The American Association of University Women's (AAUW) funded much of the research on Eliot and Ward through a generous fellowship, for which I am very grateful. Special thanks go to the *Victorians Institute Journal*, which published an earlier version of the material on *Adam Bede* and granted permission for that material to be republished here. Thank you to Ben Doyle and the team at Bloomsbury who have taken this book and helped bring it into this final form. The helpful feedback from their readers and Ben's encouragement made this a much better book.

Many people have encouraged me, read drafts, braved asking about my research, advised me on all manner of academic and publishing topics, and cared for me during the writing process, but particular thanks go to: John G. Stackhouse, Kristen Kobes du Mez, Han-luen Kantzer Komline, David Komline, Danae Jacobson, Michael Yankoski, Meagan Simpson, Emma Argall, Beth Graybill, and Linda and Stephen Boyle. Thank you all for the particular ways you have helped shape this book. I am so deeply thankful for B. E. Bruning, who has come alongside me as a partner, critic, and friend. His thoughtful conversation, pesky questions, and pedantic precision—all delivered with real kindness—were a tremendous gift.

Finally, my deepest thanks go to Andrew, Abi, and Danny, who have given me so much time and space to write this book. Andrew, thank you for your generosity in listening to Victorian minutia, your insightful theological questions, your ability to see and handle all the areas of life that escape me, and for all the life we share outside my research. Our adventures together inspire my curiosity and energize my writing. Abi, thank you for all the meals you have cooked, rooms you have vacuumed, and stories you have read to your brother so that I could finish this book. But most of all, thank you for your love of stories and writing, which remind me again and again why my work matters. And Danny, this book has grown up alongside you—from the day I first learned of your existence, to starting the very first draft two weeks after your birth, to finishing the dissertation version as you started preschool, to writing these words just as you finish these strange years of kindergarten and first grade, spent largely at home and blurred together due to Covid-19. Thank you for so many lovely memories that mark the passages of this book with your life.

Introduction

John Bunyan's late seventeenth-century allegory, *The Pilgrim's Progress*, details the spiritual progress of the emblematic Christian (named simply "Christian") as he journeys toward the Celestial City. In such a story—particularly one penned by one of England's most famous Baptist ministers—one might expect Jesus to be a central character or narrative focus. As an allegory, there is no reason why Jesus could not appear under some guise, no generic insistence on what Margaret Doody has called Prescriptive Realism that banishes "fantasy and experiment, and severely limits certain forms of psychic and social questioning."[1] Yet, Jesus is largely missing from the narrative. Some readers point to Good-Will as Jesus because he pulls Christian through the wicket gate just as he is about to step through himself, is addressed as Lord by Christian and later Christina, and pardons Christina and Mercie's sins. Yet, as J. H. Alexander has argued, "there is no unambiguous suggestion... that Good-Will is specifically a figure representing Christ."[2] Good-Will's identification with Jesus is also rejected because, while Good-Will aligns with Jesus in some ways, he also talks about Jesus as someone else, someone who he is not. Furthermore, other characters and objects are also recognizable as Christ figures; the Wicket Gate itself is a specific allusion to the saying of Jesus in Mt 7:13-14. While readers can identify hints of Christ's presence throughout the allegory, identifying any one of its characters or features with Jesus is impossible. Part of the difficulty in finding Jesus within the story owes to the fact that references to him are always through past events that no longer represent Jesus's contemporary presence, such as the allusion to his historical life through his former "country-house" in the "valley of humiliation." Rather, as exemplified by Christian's conversation with Hope, the narrative characterizes Jesus Christ as the risen, ascended, and exalted savior who atones for Christian's sins. Because these glimpses of Jesus emphasize his

---

[1] Margaret Anne Doody, *The True Story of the Novel* (New Brunswick, NJ: Rutgers UP, 1996), 294.
[2] J. H. Alexander, "Christ in the Pilgrim's Progress," *Bunyan Studies* 1, no. 2 (1989): 23.

divine character, saving work, and ascended state, he remains a distant, elusive personality. What matters in the narrative are Christian's journey, the Book that guides him, and the community of people who sustain him on his journey.

Fast-forward nearly two centuries to another immensely popular narrative that details the spiritual journey of an individual drawn to Jesus, Mary Augusta Ward's *Robert Elsmere*, and the contrast with Bunyan and his portrayal of attaining knowledge of Jesus reflect a much altered English social, political, and epistemic landscape. The nineteenth-century narrative of secularization is well rehearsed and nearly as well challenged.[3] Secularization altered the location for administrative authority, with control of vital records, education, social services, and burial grounds all having been transferred from the church to the state between 1830 and 1880. Scientific discoveries began to erode faith in the biblical narrative. In 1830 Lyell's *Principles of Geology* argued persuasively for the slow, uniform, and evolutionary development of the planet by forces still at work, putting pressure on traditional interpretations of the creation narrative. In 1859 Darwin's *Origin of the Species* put further pressure on traditional readings of the creation accounts in Genesis by claiming that species were not fixed and suggesting that humanity was not a unique species in creation. As disturbing as these ideas could be for Victorian Britons, developments in biblical scholarship coming out of Germany were far more disturbing for some Victorian believers. David Frederich Strauss's work on the historical Jesus in the 1830s argued that the Gospel accounts reflect mythological development of a historical person. Furthermore, the work of so-called higher criticism continued to challenge the historicity and reliability of the Old Testament, leading to Julius Wellhausen's 1883 formulation of the Documentary Hypothesis—that four different sources from four widely separated periods had been compiled to make the Torah/Pentateuch, a hypothesis that seemed to cut straight through the notion that the Bible was divinely inspired. Within this shifting worldview, Mary Augusta Ward's immensely popular *Robert Elsmere* sees its title character come to understand Jesus with a very different emphasis from the Jesus hinted at in Bunyan. Whereas Bunyan's Jesus is exalted and divine, Elsmere's Jesus is thoroughly and exclusively

---

[3] The nineteenth century was very much both an epoch of belief and an epoch of incredulity, an era of religious power and an era of secularization. For a comprehensive overview of the "continual slippage" between sacred and secular across nineteenth-century literature, see Mark Knight and Emma Mason, *Nineteenth-Century Religion and Literature: An Introduction* (Oxford: Oxford University Press, 2006). For more on both the persistence of religious belief and the growth of religious doubt in the nineteenth century, see Christopher Lane, *The Age of Doubt: Tracing the Roots of Our Religious Uncertainty* (New Haven: Yale University Press, 2012); Sebastian Lecourt, *Cultivating Belief: Victorian Anthropology, Liberal Aesthetics, and the Secular Imagination* (New York: Oxford University Press, 2018).

human, one of history's great teachers and moral inspirations. In fact, Elsmere's driving passion is "to transfer to [people's] minds that image of Jesus of Nazareth which thought, and love, and reading have left upon my own."[4]

Whereas Christian's journey to heaven guided by the Book is emblematic of Puritanism's Bible-centered and believer-centered Christianity, Elsmere's central obsession with the reliability of the Bible as it reveals Jesus's identity is emblematic of a changing understanding of Jesus across Victorian England. From this observation numerous questions arise: What do Victorians think about Jesus? Why does Jesus become so important to Victorian culture? How is Jesus the historical man treated differently than the idea of Christ?

No single book can answer all these questions, and a few monographs are already tackling some aspects of Jesus within fiction, particularly in the nineteenth century. Theodore Ziolkowski's 1972 work, *Fictional Transfigurations of Jesus* has long been the starting point for considering fictional representation of Jesus. Ziolkowski defines four categories: the fictionalized biography, the historical Jesus novel, the imitation of Christ, and the *Jesus redivivus*. Each category presents its own challenge in wrestling with the life of Jesus. Fictionalized biographies—ranging from Victorian Lives of Jesus that harmonize the gospels (such as Renan's *Vie de Jesus* or Seeley's *Ecce Homo*, Fararr's *The Life of Christ*) to works dubbed "fifth gospels" that tell new stories about Jesus (such those Wilde's "Doer of Good," and "The Master")—offered readers fresh narratives of the Nazarene's life, reflecting both denominational convictions and scholarly doubt.[5] Historical Jesus novels, most famously represented by the American novel *Ben Hur*, participate in historical realism through the framework that surrounds Jesus, but offer only what Jefferson Gatrall calls "literary portraits" of Jesus. These portraits give us passing glimpses of Jesus as he is observed through other characters but do not delve into the particularities of his personality.[6] Similarly, Sebastian Lecourt has considered how keeping Jesus largely offstage marks the very secularization of the novel, as Lukács and many since have argued, by placing Jesus "at the very boundary of the representable."[7] While the

---

[4] Mary Augusta (Mrs. Humphry) Ward, *Robert Elsmere* (Urbana, IL: Project Gutenberg, 2008), 362.

[5] For a complete look at fictional biographies in the Victorian period, see Daniel L. Pals, *The Victorian "Lives of Jesus"* (San Antonio, TX: Trinity University Press, 1982). For work on later fifth gospels and particularly Oscar Wilde, see Jennifer Stevens, *The Historical Jesus and the Literary Imagination: 1860–1920* (Liverpool: Liverpool University Press, 2010).

[6] Jefferson J. A. Gatrall, *The Real and the Sacred* (Ann Arbor: University of Michigan Press, 2014), 28. Also see Ellis Hanson, *Decadence and Catholicism* (Cambridge: Harvard University Press, 1997), particularly chapter 4.

[7] Sebastian Lecourt, "Prophets Genuine and Spurious: The Victorian Jesus Novel and the Ends of Comparison," *Representations* 143 (Spring 2018): 37.

significant work of such scholars on historical Jesus novels and fifth gospels tells us much about the intersections of historiography, empire, race, and fiction in the Victorian period, these studies do not consider other "transfigurations" of Jesus, most notably those where the historical Jesus makes appearances in the modern world.

Unlike fictionalized biographies and historical Jesus novels, imitations of Christ and *Jesus redivivus* novels are not set in the first century of the common era. Imitations of Christ abound in Western literature, and to some extent every "Christ-figure" participates in this category. Imitations of Christ and Christ figures bear traditional markers of Jesus's life, particularly those that reflect his salvific self-sacrifice and subsequent vindication as "Christ" or "Messiah." Included in this category are characters who sacrifice their lives for others, either literally or in a more prolonged life of selflessness. While Ziolkowski takes steps to separate every Christ figure from a true imitation of Christ, the barriers between typological Christs and real imitators are hard to maintain, especially in the Victorian period.

Recent scholarship on "Christ" in the Victorian period attests to the popularity of such imitators of Christ and the intellectual and cultural work such visions of Christ do. Be it female Christs, Catholic Christs, elisions of Mary and Christ, or sexuality and Christ, the idea of Christ—that is an anointed, self-sacrificing savior—provides a fundamental archetype for Victorian thinking. Not surprisingly, a number of works on Christ imitators and Christ figures in the Victorian period pertain to gender. Sue Zemka's *Victorian Testaments* draws attention to higher criticism's influence on Victorian Christology by separating the carnal Jesus from the example of Christ, while simultaneously creating space to consider the gender dynamics of Christ in the works of Irving, Coleridge, Nightingale, Dickens, and Kingsley.[8] Kimberly VanEsveld Adams and Carol Engelhardt Herringer consider how imagery associated with Christ intersects with Marian typologies in the writings of Victorian feminists like Elizabeth Gaskell and George Eliot.[9] In considering imitations of Christ, scholarship on Florence Nightingale's *Cassandra* is particularly instructive in understanding both how imitations use typology to recharacterize Christ and how these same

---

[8] Sue Zemka, *Victorian Testaments: The Bible, Christology, and Literary Authority in Early-Nineteenth-Century British Culture* (Stanford: Stanford University Press, 1997).

[9] Kimberly VanEsveld Adams, *Our Lady of Victorian Feminism: The Madonna in the Work of Anna Jameson, Bargaret Fuller, and George Eliot* (Athens: Ohio University Press, 2001); Carol Engelhardt Herringer, *Victorians and the Virgin Mary: Religion and Gender in England, 1830–85* (Manchester: Manchester University Press, 2008).

works apply the Christ narrative to modern women.[10] In analogous ways, work on English Catholicism has challenged dominant narratives about Protestant Britain as such texts reclaim Christ and the Virgin Mary to imagine alternative visions of both Christianity and Britishness.[11] More recently, Jeffrey F. Keuss's *The Poetics of Jesus* examines how the ideals of Christ become re-embodied in later Victorian literature, rendering art—and particularly fiction—an incarnational, sacred space.[12] Similarly, Charles LaPorte's *Victorian Poets and the Changing Bible* considers how poetry in the mid- to late Victorian period draws on the ideals of higher criticism to render poetry a form of scripture, particularly as poetry reworks and re-inscribes biblical ideals.[13]

Differing from all these imitations of Christ and Christ figures is what Ziolkowski dubs *Jesus redivivus*, a subgenre of speculative fiction that imagines what Jesus would be like if he were to reappear as himself in the modern world. Unlike imitations of Christ, where a clear separation remains between the imitator and ideal archetype of Christ, *Jesus redivivus* stories introduce a character who elides with the historical Jesus in peculiar ways and is sometimes recognized as Jesus himself. Although Jennifer Stevens addresses such Jesuses in her work on Wilde and others, little scholarly attention has been given to instances of Jesus reappearing in Victorian fiction, in part because such stories are relatively uncommon until the twentieth century. Even in overtly religious novels of the nineteenth century, characters rarely encounter a living character who is also a historicized Jesus. Evangelical novels, where one might expect to find such supernatural encounters, tend to present potential converts with a formal biography of Jesus. This biographical Jesus is not a character but a highly determined historical person being related through another character. And while Catholic novels occasionally include a mystical encounter with Jesus, such experiences of his real presence are mediated through the Eucharist. The

---

[10] See Christiana De Groot and Marion Ann Taylor, *Recovering Nineteenth-Century Women Interpreters of the Bible*, Society of Biblical Literature Symposium Series (Leiden; Boston: Brill, 2007); Hilary Fraser and Victoria Burrows, "The Feminist Theology of Florence Nightingale," in *Reinventing Christianity* (Aldershot: Ashgate, 2001); Ruth Y. Jenkins, *Reclaiming Myths of Power: Women Writers and the Victorian Spiritual Crisis* (Lewisburg, PA: Bucknell University Press, 1995); George P. Landow, "Aggressive (Re)Interpretations of the Female Sage: Florence Nightingale's Cassandra," in *Victorian Sages and Cultural Discourse: Renegotiating Gender and Power*, ed. Thais E. Morgan (New Brunswick: Rutgers University Press, vii, 1990); Mary Poovey, *Uneven Developments: The Ideological Work of Gender in Mid-Victorian England* (Chicago: University of Chicago Press, 1988).

[11] See Maria LaMonaca, *Masked Atheism: Catholicism and the Secular Victorian Home* (Columbus: Ohio State University Press, 2008); Patrick R. O'Malley, *Catholicism, Sexual Deviance, and Victorian Gothic Culture* (Cambridge: Cambridge University Press, 2006).

[12] Jeffrey F. Keuss, *A Poetics of Jesus: The Search for Christ through Writings in the Nineteenth Century* (Aldershot: Ashgate, 2002).

[13] Charles LaPorte, *Victorian Poets and the Changing Bible* (Charlottesville, VA: University of Virgina Press, 2011).

divine is present in the elements, but not in the historical body of a first-century Galilean.

The Figure of Christ in the Long Nineteenth Century, a collection of essays edited by Elizabeth Ludlow, draws together these many representations of Jesus himself and other Christ figures in nineteenth-century literature.[14] Overturning tidy divisions between the sacred and secular, the volume considers Christ in the work of Blake and later romantics, popular culture, Tennyson's poetry, Tractarian theology, pre-Raphaelite painting and poetry, Chartist writings, and in mid- and late Victorian fiction. One particularly helpful contribution of the essays in this volume is to show that, even when dealing with imitators of Christ or Christ figures, the nineteenth-century imagination is always still wrestling with the historical person of Jesus. And yet, even in this seminal collection, the contributions pay scant attention to some significant literary representations of Jesus of Nazareth understood as a historical, first-century man who maintains active agency in the world, that is, as a character who serves as more than a frequently self-sacrificing influence upon other characters. Because realist representations of Jesus perform a particular sort of theological work, the Nazarene of *Jesus redivivus* tales deserves greater and more focused attention, both on his own and as distinguished from other literary Christ figures and Christ imitators.

This book addresses precisely such representations of Jesus—instances in realist novels where Jesus appears as himself to characters in the Victorian period, even if simultaneously embodied in other characters—to further elucidate how mainstream Victorian writers understand Jesus and imagine others relating *to* Jesus. Of course, such encounters with Jesus are highly problematic, but not (as Lukács and those coming after him have argued) because the realist novel is an inherently secular form. If there is one thing that much of the work on Jesus in novels has already demonstrated, it is that the novel is a versatile form making room for all sorts of experimentation, including experimentation with the supernatural and Jesus himself. In fact, the realist novel would seem to offer an ideal form for encountering Jesus as an empirically absent but vibrant personality because novels foster the sensation of an intimate acquaintance between readers and characters. But challenges to traditional Christologies, pieties, and even decorum inevitably arise when Jesus is dislocated from the theological and philosophical systems that define the incarnation and placed

---

[14] Elizabeth Ludlow, *The Figure of Christ in the Long Nineteenth Century*, ed. Elizabeth Ludlow, Palgrave Studies in Nineteenth-Century Writing and Culture (London: Palgrave Macmillan, 2020).

instead amid the novel's messy representations of human life. Through this very messiness literary encounters with Jesus offer fascinating insights into changing Victorian theology and Victorian understandings of Jesus as a character. For some writers such an experiment was its own act of devotion. For many writers these novelistic explorations were an attempt to reimagine Jesus. And for more than a few writers, experimenting with Jesus in a novel offered desirable disruptions to traditional orthodoxies and received tradition.

This book, then, considers characterizations of Jesus among a particular group of leading nineteenth-century writers—writers who engaged science and biblical scholarship, who were well read in traditional Christian theologies, and who were invested in high realism. In particular, it examines how they used the novel to explore what an encounter with Jesus as a real, present, embodied character might look like, how that experience might be possible in Victorian England, and how people might respond to him if he showed up in nineteenth-century society. Although such representations of Jesus become increasingly common in the twentieth century, they are only just beginning in England in this period as previously noted, Evangelical novels do not tend to represent Jesus in this way but prefer to present Jesus's life as a closed biography. Catholic novels do not represent Jesus this way either, preferring to present Jesus as present in the Eucharistic elements.[15] Rather, these representations turn up in novels of writers who are deeply conversant with a broad range of Christian theologies and biblical scholarship, but who are more readily identified with humanism and atheism. That said, the writers considered in the following chapters are responding to the particular influence of Evangelicalism and biblicism within Victorian culture and, at times, championing the sorts of "broad church" theologies published in 1860 in *Essays and Reviews*, a widely read and furiously debated collection that made public the "gap between Christian doctrine and the real beliefs of educated men."[16] Consequently, the analysis of this book does at times consider the popular piety of the Established Church, along with the influence of Evangelicalism to which the idea of the "broad church" was in part a response. The analysis does not, however, address Catholic theologies, emerging Catholicisms, or Catholic writers, except when they intersect with the matter at hand: novelistic representations of a historical Jesus in the modern world.

---

[15] For a look at how the incarnation gets reasoned through the Eucharist and the tensions this creates between Protestant and Catholic understandings of the New Testament and British identity, see Jan-Melissa Schramm, *Censorship and the Representation of the Sacred in Nineteenth-Century England* (Oxford: Oxford University Press, 2019), particularly chapter 4.

[16] Owen Chadwick, *The Victorian Church, Part 2, 1860–1901*, 2 vols. (Oxford: Oxford University Press, 1970), 76.

Despite the broad-church, humanist, and even atheist commitments of writers like Charles Kingsley, George Eliot, Eliza Lynn Linton, and Mary Augusta Ward, their representations of Jesus rework traditional understandings of his "threefold office," an ancient typological schema ascribing the fulfillment of three "anointed" roles from the Christian Old Testament—prophet, priest, and king—to the life and work of Jesus as the definitive Anointed ("Messiah," "Christ"). Their novels provide valuable insight into the relationship between literature and innovations in religious thought, all the more so because these writers were all highly successful and celebrated in their own era, even if today (with the exception of George Eliot) they are largely forgotten by readers outside the literary classroom. Within their own historical context, these novels offer yet more evidence that narratives of secularization are simplifications of a more complex cultural process, part of which involved reimagining Jesus in light of a rapidly changing world. For example, while Eliot's and Ward's demythologizations of Jesus can be construed as secularization, their works are better understood as innovative heterodox engagements with Jesus, German higher criticism, and the biblicism that marks many Protestant traditions.

Apart from Victorian conversations about secularities and secularizations, these novels serve as insightful literary theologies. By removing the idea of God incarnate from the traditional theological and philosophical systems of Christian theology and placing him in the messy realities of human life represented in realist fiction, these novels disrupt received ideas about both divinity and humanity. Studying these novels helps us to better understand the ways in which traditional theologies have sanitized—and even silenced—the biblical text's representation of Jesus by rendering the Bible and some of the most basic traditional interpretive schemas like the threefold office unfamiliar and thus new. While the novelistic representations explored in these pages will have their own challenges, they ultimately open up new understandings of the enigmatic man at the heart of the Gospels.

To understand why Jesus begins to make appearances in nineteenth-century realist fiction and why that is both to be expected and why it creates complications for many traditional Christian theologies, it is helpful to understand how Christian theologies generally—and Protestant theologies in particular—encode specific narratives and characterizations in the minds of believers. The first chapter begins in the eighteenth century, as Protestant theology in England becomes especially focused on atonement due to the influence of the evangelical revival, at once centering evangelical preaching and cultural practices around conversion narratives and at the same time (albeit inadvertently) sidelining Jesus. With the narrative consequences of theology in place, the second chapter explores the nineteenth century's development of the sentimental Jesus of domestic ideology and Christmas celebrations, and the concurrent rise in interest in the life of Jesus. When this popular piety intersects with scientific developments and biblical criticism, the life of Jesus comes under increased scrutiny, rendering the Galilean both more and less familiar. From there, this book turns to the unique attempts by Victorian novelists to write Jesus into the nineteenth-century world. Chapter 3 examines how Jesus the cosmic king is reimagined in terms of revolutionary politics and kingly brotherhood in Charles Kingsley's *Alton Locke*. Chapter 4 considers Jesus as the high priest who brings about reconciliation through tolerance, pity, and even love in George Eliot's *Adam Bede*. Finally, Chapter 5 considers Jesus as the inspirational prophet calling society to a potentially impossible moral standard in Mary Augusta Ward's *Robert Elsmere* and Eliza Lynn Linton's *The True History of Joshua Davidson: Christian and Communist*.

1

The Narrative Consequences of Theology

The eighteenth century's evangelical revival underscored Great Britain's self-understanding as not only largely Christian but as specifically Protestant. In such a context, one might expect Jesus to occupy a position of cultural centrality, and yet nineteenth-century poetry, popular piety, and biblical criticism bring Jesus—and an inherited lack of clarity about his identity—into far greater focus. So, how did it come about that figure of Jesus came to be relatively neglected in the eighteenth century, leaving the gap the nineteenth century rushed to fill? And, why in the world would writers think that the novel offered a way to resurrect Jesus from the fog of familiarity that rendered his character both ubiquitous and a complete mystery? To answer these questions, one must first understand how the widespread theology of substitutionary atonement preached by eighteenth-century evangelicals encoded a particular narrative structure that re-centered the narrative of faith on the believer rather than Jesus. At the same time, one must also understand how the relational procedures of the novel offered a means by which readers might "relate" to Jesus.

The Backstory: Conversion Narratives and the Novel

To say that narratives contain theology is obvious. Both in terms of content and in the ideologies that shape narrative structure, stories communicate ideas about God and the world, in other words, theology. But Christian theology, and in particular Protestant theology, is at its very foundation narrative in its form. While it is easy to lose sight of this reality when staring at shelf-after-shelf of multivolume systematic theologies, all these systematizations are, at their core, systematic explications of the biblical narrative. But theology is not essentially narrative because it examines a story any more than literary criticism is narrative because it engages stories. Theology's narrative power lies in the way that theology shapes the retelling of the Bible and the telling of the life of the believer in preaching and practice.

Beginning with Peter's sermon at Pentecost, Christian preaching frequently articulates a two-fold narrative. One is the narrative of God's actions (especially as manifest through Jesus). The other is the narrative of those listening, the narrative of believers and potential believers as their lives intersect—and potentially become a part of—this divine drama. Both these narratives are always present in the communication of Christian doctrine across traditions and denominations, and these narratives serve as the basis for Christian theology across traditions and denominations. But whether the divine or human narrative is emphasized changes with time and place, culture, circumstance, and the central theologies preferred by a particular body of Christians. Moreover both narratives exist in a constant hermeneutic circle with theology, where the text or the experience of reading communities or individuals gives rise to interpretation, even as previous interpretations (also called theology) always shape a reading of the text or of the community's or individual's experience. These formative interpretations frequently force particular structures, assumptions, focal points, characterizations, and themes to become dominant within the believer's or community's worldview, such that other concerns become virtually invisible. One fraught theology that encoded a particularly powerful narrative form in the eighteenth century is the idea of the atonement: the idea that God and the world are somehow reconciled through Jesus's death on the cross.

For the first thousand years of Christian history, the majority of Western theologians frequently understood the atonement achieved through Jesus's death and resurrection in terms of either a divine ransom or a heroic champion.[1] The ransom theory of the atonement maintained that Satan enslaved humanity along with the whole earth through Adam and Eve's fall in the Garden of Eden. In order to buy humanity back, God paid a ransom to Satan through Jesus, whom Satan was then free to kill. In doing so, God essentially tricked Satan because Jesus, being himself God the Son, could not be held by death (which Satan somehow did not know). After Satan's defeat, there remains the project of restoring order amid the chaos Satan left behind. In this version of the atonement, God is the classic literary trickster who uses his wily cunning to defeat the villain.

---

[1] For a complete treatment of different theories about the atonement discussed here, see Gustaf Aulen, *Christus Victor: An Historical Study of Three Main Types of the Idea of the Atonement*, trans. A. G. Herber (New York: Macmillan, 1969).

In the heroic, or *Christus Victor*, model, the earth becomes occupied by the forces of evil at the fall. Jesus battles with Satan through his life, passion, and death, finally defeating Satan through his resurrection. Because Jesus is "fully human," he is the single-combat champion for humanity and thus, in defeating Satan, he frees humanity from Satan's occupying forces. While this model casts Jesus as the triumphant military victor at the Resurrection, his victory is followed by a long period of ridding the earth of Satan's remaining strongholds. Both the ransom theory of the atonement and *Christus Victor* frequently appear side-by-side in the writings of the early church and through the middle ages, and the two are not in fact exclusive. Both traditions involve a period of ridding the world of evil after Jesus's victory, and both offer similar characterizations of God (and of God through Jesus). In both, God is presented in traditional heroic terms: like Odysseus or Jacob, God is a trickster; like Achilles, Romulus, or David, Jesus's victory is victory for all.

By the late seventeenth century a different model of the atonement became influential in Protestant theology in England. English Puritans, like many other Protestants of the time, had developed a Calvinistically inflected way of understanding the atonement known as penal substitution. While substitutionary atonement generally is not unique to Protestantism (in fact it was influentially theorized Anselm in the eleventh century), the nuances of penal substitution were central to Protestantism's self-definition against Catholicism, particularly in Britain where Protestantism became central in constructions of national identity.[2] Penal substitution depicts humanity as alienated from God because all creation was marred through the fall. To reconcile God and the world, God in Jesus takes the place intended for sinners, thereby paying for humanity's crimes against divine holiness with his own death. In his construction of penal substitution, Calvin allegorizes the ritualistic understanding of the Israel's priesthood and aligns it with juridical language, equating not only sacrifice and debt-repayment but also roles of priest with mediator or advocate. Thus, "because Christ now bears the office of priest" he "not only that by the eternal law of reconciliation... may render the Father favourable and propitious to us, but also admit us into this most honourable alliance."[3]

In penal substitution, then, humanity's debt is not owed to Satan but to God. As such, God becomes the narrative all-in-all. God is both the offended party

---

[2] For a detailed account of penal substitution in context, see *Christus Victor: An Historical Study of Three Main Types of the Idea of the Atonement*.

[3] John Calvin, *Institutes of the Christian Religion*, trans. Henry Beveridge (Edinburgh: Calvin Translation Society, 1845), 2:15: 6.

and the means by which restitution is made. Consequently, all the narrative drama—the struggle between good and evil, between the hero and villain—is collapsed into God's own being. God is offended, but God wants to redeem his people; God satisfies his own wrath with the bloody execution of God the Son, and God chooses whom he will save. In this tradition God's emotional life appears deeply contradictory and even potentially illogical. If God is the one who is offended, why does he need blood to satisfy his own wrath? Can't he just let it go? If God is so loving, why does he only choose to save some people? Particularly within the Calvinistic version common among Puritans, the individual human's only role in the story is to search for signs of divine election for salvation. As such, the individual has little actual agency in the divine drama.

Because substitutionary atonement locates the core problem driving narrative and the dramatic tension within God, traditions like Puritanism and later evangelicalism minimize the narrative of cosmic battle between good and evil. The battle instead is between God's love and God's justice. Accordingly, Jesus's victory is a foregone conclusion scripted by God and contained within an unchanging (albeit emotionally complicated) God. Such divine sovereignty produces two connected narrative consequences. First, any element of Jesus as an active hero striving against cosmic evil or oppression is erased from Jesus's narrative action. While Jesus may oppose the injustice that humans wreak on each other, he is not personally engaged in the conflict. Rather, his role on earth is to be a perfect human and satisfy God the Father's wrath, all of which he will always, certainly do. The second consequence is that God's character becomes impossible to narrate. Because he is unchanging, it is heretical to say that God changes from wanting justice to preferring mercy through the events of the cross. Because he is all-knowing, God cannot wrestle with contradictory emotions and then, after long and hard thought, develop the solution of the cross. And because he is outside of time, God cannot respond to human action in a way that produces narrative tension within his own being. While it may look to humans like God suddenly responded to their prayers or sins or righteous actions, from the perspective of the timeless and unchanging God, he has always and will always be aware of human action and be responding to it out of his justice and mercy. Thus, in this theological tradition, the divine narrative becomes a bit like watching a mediocre, well-known, and highly predictable dramatic movie with badly acted, flat characters from the past. Not only is the ending obvious, the journey to that conclusion is utterly free of dramatic tension and human emotion. The story does not even offer the action-packed close calls, near misses, real temptations, and questionable heroic actions that make watching other well-known films fun.

While the Calvinist, Puritan, and later evangelical tradition of the atonement precludes the possibility of Jesus as an epic hero, this tradition does maintain the epic sense of a closed past. From the earliest days of the Reformation, Protestants made clear that Jesus's sacrifice on the cross exists in an absolute past because of theological polemics regarding the manner in which Jesus might be present in the Eucharist. Whereas Catholics argued that the Eucharist draws believers into the eternally present, ongoing sacrifice of Jesus, many Protestant traditions insisted his death was not an ongoing act taking place during the mass or communion. Even though the Eucharistic theology of both Luther and Calvin allows for Jesus to be "present" in communion, neither casts his presence in terms of present, narrative action: Jesus's death is a finished act in history.

This insistence on a closed, finished past also has important narrative consequences. In such Protestant theologies, Jesus is no longer passively suffering on the cross. In his present state, Jesus is the triumphant, risen Son of God, ascended into heaven and seated at the right hand of the Father. Because believers understand Jesus to be exalted in heaven—and watching each person from on high—he is at present distant from the believer. In Protestant eucharistic theology, Jesus's life story and his suffering become "an absolute distanced image, beyond the sphere of possible contact with the developing, incomplete and therefore re-thinking and re-evaluating present."[4] Particularly for Puritans and evangelicals, Jesus is able to break through to the sphere of developing present, but not in the eucharistic enactment of his sacrificial death. Instead, Jesus can break into the present via the subjective experience of the believer. As such, the realm of dramatic action is no longer the historical narrative of Jesus's life, death, and resurrection but the story of the believer as he or she comes to understand and respond to the Jesus narrative.

One place we see the narrative implications of substitutionary atonement inscribed is in eighteenth-century hymns. During the evangelical revival, hymnody emphasizes the triumphant and ascended Jesus, whose past work provides the context for the individual believer's experience. The Methodist hymnody of the era, which became popular throughout English-speaking Protestant congregations, borrows heavily from the church and the stage,

---

[4] Bakhtin says this about the epic hero, but the description is completely appropriate to the Jesus of Protestant tradition. See M. M. Bakhtin, *The Dialogic Imagination: Four Essays*, ed. Michael Holquist, trans. Vadim Liapunov and Kenneth Brostrom (Austin: University of Texas Press, 1982).

alluding to the emotional and sexual intensity of the pleading lover, as Misty Anderson argues.[5] The dramatic scope of these hymns frequently includes a meditation on the crucifixion and passion, drawing on the Moravian tradition of contemplating the suffering body of Jesus. And yet, such hymnody always presents Jesus's suffering as taking place in a narrative and temporal past, even if not explicitly a historical or historicized past. Tense is a small grammatical detail but, by consistently presenting Jesus's bloody and broken body in the past or past perfect tense, such hymns reinforce the past and completed nature of Jesus's narrative of suffering. Jesus is not currently bloody and broken. Rather, in the words of "Amazing Love," Jesus "*left* his Father's throne," "*Emptied* himself of all but love, And *bled* for Adam's helpless race." Though his suffering was great, it is over. In the words of Charles Wesley's enduring Easter hymn, "Christ the Lord Is Risen Today," "Love's redeeming work is done." Jesus has "fought the fight" and "the battle won." The finished nature of Jesus's suffering is reinforced in hymns like Wesley's "Lo! He Comes with Clouds Descending," "Soldiers of Christ Arise!" and "Love Divine," all of which position Jesus currently in heaven. His heavenly position is reinforced in such hymns by his ability to rule this life, either in the heart of the believer or over the earth as the eschatological king. As one would expect, in these hymns Jesus's triumphant descent is expressed in either the present, future, or imperative tenses, reinforcing the conviction that his current state is that of the triumphant, ascended God-Man in heaven.

Within Methodist hymnody, the narrative significance of Jesus's past suffering and current glory lies in the salvation and sanctification of the believer. Wesley's celebratory "O For a Thousand Tongues to Sing" captures this narrative force particularly well. Depicting Jesus as the "gracious master and... God" who has redeemed humanity and conquered death through his atoning work on the cross, the hymn details the speaker's salvation and his desire to spread the message of Jesus's sacrificial death and victorious resurrection throughout the world (hence the need for "a thousand tongues"). Even in the stanza beginning, "Jesus, the name that calms our fears," when the hymn appears as if it might turn away from the speaker's own religious concerns, the speaker consistently celebrates Jesus in terms of services rendered and concludes with the personal testimony that "his blood availed for me." The proclamatory final verses call the dead, the guilty, the sinners, the lame, and the dumb to Jesus. Appearing in the context of the speaker's desire to preach the gospel, these final stanzas may very well be the speaker's dreamed-of sermon. In a similar vein, Wesley's "Jesus, Lover of

---

[5] Misty G. Anderson, *Imagining Methodism in Eighteenth-Century Britain: Enthusiams, Belief and the Borders of the Self* (Baltimore: Johns Hopkins University Press, 2012), 172.

My Soul"—which would seem to promise a more emotionally engaged Jesus—again emphasizes Jesus as the sinner's refuge and comfort, circumscribing Jesus's characterization in terms of the sinner's salvation. On the whole, Wesley's hymns present Jesus as powerful and good. He is the one who "breaks canceled sin" and whose "eye defused a quickening ray," all so that the believer can be set free. Yet, this good and powerful Jesus is not a complicated, complex personality with his own set of dreads and sorrows. Although there is biblical precedent for Jesus experiencing all these emotions, such dynamic material is ascribed to the believer in most evangelical hymnody.

Sermons of the period illustrate the same tendencies when characterizing Jesus, with John Wesley and George Whitefield's sermons speaking of Jesus as the good and loving ascended Lord. Of course, the purpose of evangelical sermons is not to present a complex vision of Jesus; the purpose is to bring sinners to Jesus. Consequently, when talking about Jesus both Wesley and Whitefield point frequently to what Jesus can do for the listener, the ways in which he can "help" the lost sinner. Whitefield, in one sermon collection, designates Jesus as a "help" to his listeners seventy-five times in as many sermons.[6] While Jesus's act of rescuing the world from sin is assumed in these sermons, the focus is not on Jesus's personal, historical narrative, nor really on his work. Rather, the focus is on the listener's spiritual need. Focusing on the sinner's need to convert reduces Jesus's narrative to the backstory that enables the believer's own narrative to reach an important moment of self-awareness resulting in rebirth. Thus, eighteenth-century evangelical preaching typically culminates with the story of the individual believer, his or her own narrative of salvation and individual faith, rather than with a lengthy development of Jesus's character and history.

Within the context of such preaching and singing it is no surprise that eighteenth-century characterizations of Jesus emphasize his exalted and perfected status: he is Savior and Lord of all, endlessly loving and seeking the lost. What Bakhtin writes about characters in the closed history of the epic is an exact description of this characterization of Jesus: "he coincides with himself, he is absolutely equal to himself .... There is not the slightest gap between his authentic essence and its external manifestation. All his potential, all his possibilities are realized utterly in his external social position."[7] In fact, such perfect correspondence is the point of the ascended image of Jesus. The gap between Jesus's identity as God and the humiliation of the cross is rendered a passing state over which Jesus triumphed. Despite Jesus's love and eternal desire for the

---

[6] See George Whitefield, *Sermons on Important Subjects* (London: Thomas Tegg, 1841).
[7] Bakhtin, *The Dialogic Imagination: Four Essays*, 34.

sinner's repentance, the eighteenth-century emphasis on the risen Jesus leads to a static, unchanging, divine character. Against the static, unchanging center of help that Jesus offers, the believer's personality—along with the individual's need and/or desire to be untied to the resurrected and ascended Jesus—becomes the dynamic narrative focal point of evangelical conversion narratives, sermons, and even hymns, frequently at the expense of Jesus's characterization.

Grace Abounding... To Me

In eighteenth-century evangelicalism—and, spreading from there, in many Protestant denominations in England—Jesus's characterization is grounded in the theology of substitutionary atonement, a theology that represents divine narrative action as complete and completed by a God stripped of a narratable character. This drives the narrative interest and energy to the salvation of the individual human as told from the human perspective. Such a believer-centered story is an open-ended narrative because the individual's ultimate standing within the community of the saved is an open question in most Protestant theologies. The shift of narrative energy to the individual is particularly important in the Arminian evangelical tradition, which emphasizes the individual's free will in responding to God's offer of forgiveness through Jesus.[8] Because free will gives agency to human beings, the eighteenth-century evangelical tradition created a new space for drama within the narrative inscribed by substitutionary atonement. An exciting story is possible with substitutionary atonement—but it is the story of the individual's conversion, not the story of the God who saves.

Perhaps because the believer's story was the only new story left to tell, conversion became a hallmark and normative prototype of authentic faith, first among Puritans and especially during the evangelical revival. Unlike earlier Protestants who "more or less took for granted the enfolding of individual believers into the corporate structures of Christendom," Puritanism placed "a new stress on personal conversion... emphasiz[ing] the need for a deliberate, personal response to God's provision of salvation" offered through Jesus Christ.[9]

---

[8] John Wesley's preaching, in particular, emphasized the believer's free will in choosing to receive salvation and the resistible nature of grace. This was opposed to the Calvinist doctrine of irresistible grace, in which people chosen by God for the life of faith are unable to resist that decision of the divine will. While Wesley's theology did emphasize that a prevenient grace made it possible for a person to choose God, the believer's own will was necessary to either accept or reject God.

[9] Mark Noll, *Protestantism: A Very Short Introduction* (Oxford: Oxford University Press, 2011), 34.

In this narrative of personal conversion, Puritans understood the life of each believer to be "a recapitulation in themselves" of the biblical story of human fall and redemption.[10] Thus, their writings traced "the story of Everyman Adam, from temptation and fall, through reconciliation, restoration, and renewal. They were interested in the stages of the redeemed soul's progress: election, vocation, justification, sanctification, glorification."[11] As a result, Puritans placed less emphasis on the historical narrative of Jesus's life, a tendency that, coupled with an anti-Catholic reflex, led them to forego celebrations of Christmas and Easter. As historian Horton Davies puts it, "the birth [that the Puritan] cared for was the rebirth of the soul, his own regeneration. The crucifixion he bothered about was the crucifixion of the old Adam in him by the power of the new Adam, Christ."[12] Somewhat ironically, the need for a deliberate and personal response to Jesus actually marginalized the Jesus narrative within Puritan practice.

With the evangelical revival in the eighteenth century, the Puritan emphasis on the believer's journey from sin to salvation combined with the evangelical emphasis on a personal experience of salvation fostering an ongoing "relationship" with God. Such faith was frequently described in terms of "experimental" and "vital" religion because of this emphasis on the experience of the believer. Evangelicals often went so far as to legitimize their experiences of God in terms of a sixth sense: because they experienced a divine stimulus to a spiritual faculty as akin to experiencing any other stimulus to one of the physical senses, they argued that such an experience constituted an empirical knowledge of God grounded in Lockean epistemology.[13] What developed within the evangelical community as it narrated conversion experience was a contradiction between content and form. The content of evangelical preaching and conversion narratives insisted upon substitutionary atonement, emphasizing the completed sacrifice of Jesus and the agency of God to bring the believer to faith. But in the conversion narrative's form, evangelicals continued to place Jesus's work in a finished past and to focus the narrative action on the life of the believer.

Because of the emphasis placed on the life of the individual believer, it is no surprise that Puritan spiritual autobiography and evangelical conversion narratives help shape—and are shaped by—the novel.

---

[10] Horton Davies, *Worship and Theology in England, Vol 1: From Cranmer to Hooker, 1534–1603* (Princeton: Princeton University Press, 1970), 68.
[11] Davies, *Worship and Theology in England, Vol 1: From Cranmer to Hooker, 1534–1603*, 68.
[12] Davies, *Worship and Theology in England, Vol 1: From Cranmer to Hooker, 1534–1603*, 68.
[13] David Bebbington, *Evangelicalism in Modern Britain* (Boston: Unwin Hyman, 1989), 49–52.

While Lukács, Levine, Hillis Miller, Moretti, and others have argued that the novel is inherently secular, replacing the gods of epic with the arbitrary force of history and insisting on representation grounded in the verifiable realities of empiricism, much work has challenged this scholarly analysis, both in terms of the origins of the novel and the nature of the novel itself.[14] As Susan Colón has argued, such constructions of the secular "implicitly... posit as 'religion' an impossibly pure and rarefied realm of spiritual being, and thus... give over to 'the secular'... everything short of the supernatural, that is, everything material."[15]

Given the problematic nature of such sweeping constructions of "secular," it is more helpful to consider the idea of secularity in terms of the novel's origin. Michael McKeon has argued that the genre itself is secularized and fictionalized from the genre of religious life writing. Accordingly, the novel does in fact maintain particular religious narrative structures, despite arguments to the contrary. The plot structures of both religious life writing and the emerging novel emphasize interiority and share "the basic biographical dynamic between individual life and overarching pattern through a more subtle narrative balance between present action and retrospective narration."[16] But it is not simply that religious writing shaped the novel. During the eighteenth century, the plots, tone, and characterization of religious life writing change along with the novel, suggesting an ongoing interplay between the two genres. For example, whereas Puritans emphasize the "authority of tradition, reason, and exegesis,... eighteenth-century letters and magazines reflect... an appeal to experiences and a new confidence about discerning the hand of God in history."[17] This emphasis on history as a driving force in parallels the historical consciousness that Lukács and Morreti in particular identify as a hallmark of the novel, especially as the genre

---

[14] The novel as secular form tradition continues to have its proponents, for example, Susanna Lee, *A World Abandoned by God: Narrative and Secularism* (Lewisburg: Bucknell University Press, 2005); Vincent P. Pecora, *Secularization without End* (Notre Dame: University of Notre Dame Press, 2015). Much work is being done challenging this narrative, too. See Miriam Elizabeth Burstein, *Victorian Reformations: Historical Fiction and Religious Controversy, 1820–1900* (Notre Dame: University of Notre Dame Press, 2014); Susan E. Colón, *Victorian Parables* (New York: Bloomsbury, 2012); LaPorte, *Victorian Poets and the Changing Bible*; Lecourt, *Cultivating Belief: Victorian Anthropology, Liberal Aesthetics, and the Secular Imagination*; J. Russell Perkin, *Theology and the Victorian Novel* (Montreal and Kingston: McGill-Queen's University Press, 2009). See also Michael Tomko, *Beyond the Willing Suspension of Disbelief: Poetic Faith from Coleridge to Tolkien* (New York: Bloomsbury, 2015).

[15] Colón, *Victorian Parables*, 34.

[16] Michael McKeon, *The Origins of the English Novel, 1600–1740*, 2nd ed. (Baltimore: Johns Hopkins University Press, 2002), 95.

[17] D. Bruce Hindmarsh, *The Evangelical Conversion Narrative: Spiritual Autobiography in Early Modern England* (Oxford: Oxford University Press, 2005), 71.

becomes ascendant during the late eighteenth and early nineteenth centuries.[18] Significantly, Moretti takes the English novel to task for not being appropriately historical enough and for lacking the complications and ambiguities of the emerging modern world. Perhaps it is not that history and revolution are absent from the English novel (especially the *Bildungsroman*), or that the English are only capable of thinking in terms of "fairytale" justice with its clear sense of right and wrong. Instead, it may be that Moretti has misjudged the arena of revolution in nineteenth-century England, assuming a comparative European framework for the cultural work of the English *Bildungsroman* that neglects its development from the eighteenth-century entanglement with religious life writing in which McKeon situates the emergent English novel. In the "Christian culture" of Britain described by Mark Knight and Emma Mason, "Theological debate was almost inseparable from philosophical, scientific, medical, historical, and political thought in the eighteenth and nineteenth centuries."[19] Viewed in this light, the English novel's revolutionary energy manifests itself in a religious rather than political or material sphere of life, reflecting the theological revolutions taking place in England during the nineteenth century. If so, then Moretti's criticisms of the English novel as "fairytales" concerned with moral uprightness serve to highlight the profound influence of religious life writing on the English novel and on the narrative expectations of novel readers in the eighteenth and even nineteenth centuries.

The mutual influence of novel and conversion narratives extends beyond the moral concerns of both genres and the potential discernment of God within the forces of history. By emphasizing the knowability of God through individual experience, evangelical narratives (like the novel) drew increasing attention to the unique life of each and every believer, not just significant leaders within the community. As D. Bruce Hindmarsh explains, unlike the New Testament conversion narratives that are generically more akin to the Hebrew tradition of the prophetic "call" or the medieval conversion narratives that characterize life as a process of religious transformation centered on the desire for conversion, the evangelical conversion narrative is characterized by a single, intense emotional experience that cuts across the boundaries of class, race, and gender and that every individual believer is expected to identify and narrate within their own life.[20] Previously, even in Puritan autobiographies, the subject of the narrative

---

[18] For Moretti's full argument, see Franco Moretti, *The Way of the World: The Bildungsroman in European Culture*, New ed. (New York: Verso Press, 2000), 183–212.

[19] Knight and Mason, *Nineteenth-Century Religion and Literature: An Introduction*, 3.

[20] Hindmarsh, *The Evangelical Conversion Narrative: Spiritual Autobiography in Early Modern England*, 59.

was typically a notable or exemplary Christian, not an everyman. Even when Puritan autobiographies focused on a less famous figure, the "proper syntax" for conversion involved a "family tree" of church leaders that led to knowledge of God and the self.[21] Later evangelical autobiographies, however, were produced by both the leaders of the revival and the populace, foregrounding the voices of more diverse individuals.[22] As Hindmarsh explains, the narratives (which differ slightly between Methodist, Moravian, and Calvinist evangelicals) represent not only educated individuals, but also "artisans, craftsmen, skilled and unskilled labourers, apprentices, [and] domestic servants."[23] This popular orientation combined with the widespread practice of writing, publishing, and reading these narratives strongly suggests that particularly evangelical conversion narratives contributed to the growing emphasis on nontraditional plots, particular people, and individual circumstances represented by unique names and identities, features that Ian Watt identifies as the basic outlines for realist novels.[24]

The evangelical sense that personal experience provides reliable insight into God's purposes in the believer's life creates two additional links between religious writing and the realist novel. First, because evangelical conversion narratives draw attention to the material ways God works in history to bring about a conversion, the material world including letters, books, paintings, carriage rides, and other human beings becomes integral to the unity of the narrative and the formation of the believer's consciousness. Materiality exists not just as a setting for the narrative action but as a participant in shaping characters and subsequent narrative action. As in realism, materiality in these conversion narratives "makes vivid [the] systems in which objects play a part."[25] While moments of such materiality exist in earlier autobiographies (of which there are not nearly as many), the sense of God working ceaselessly and almost exclusively through the believer's particular material circumstances becomes a new emphasis of conversion stories in the early eighteenth century.

Second, and more significantly, because the narrator has the confidence to discern the divine purposes working through the material world, interpretive authority shifts toward the narrator. Such interpretive authority does not mean that the narrator sees herself as the primary agent in her own self-fashioning. Whereas the realist novel presents identity in the naturalized

---

[21] Hindmarsh, *The Evangelical Conversion Narrative: Spiritual Autobiography in Early Modern England*, 35.
[22] Hindmarsh, *The Evangelical Conversion Narrative: Spiritual Autobiography in Early Modern England*, 90.
[23] Hindmarsh, *The Evangelical Conversion Narrative: Spiritual Autobiography in Early Modern England*, 324.
[24] See Ian Watt, *The Rise of the Novel*, 2nd ed. (Berkeley: University of California Press, 2001).
[25] Harry E. Shaw, *Narrating Reality: Austen, Scott, Eliot* (Ithaca: Cornell University Press, 1999), xi.

terms of Lockean epistemology, with an individual's identity grounded in the memory of his own experiences over time, conversion narratives maintain a supernatural intelligence orchestrating the material world and other people over time.[26] The realism of the conversion narrative is thus a prime example of Auerbach's "figural realism," in which the material world is part of a divine system infused with "cosmic importance," as opposed to a "modern realism" in which the material world is part of a historical system and only significant in light of history.[27] Because conversion narratives present God as sovereign over the material world, evangelical narrators disavow their own authority, thereby "qualify[ing] the notion of self-fashioning" with the sense of an identity "bestowed supernaturally" upon the believer.[28] Despite these disavowals of personal authority and the subsequent ideology of a qualified self-fashioning, believers remain the sole voices interpreting their experiences amid a narrative in which their unique experiences take center stage.

While conversion narratives do not create the novel, the narrative shape encoded in evangelical preaching and hymnody—and narrated by believers as they experience and appropriate a Puritan influenced version of the atonement for their salvation—leads to many shared characteristics between conversion narratives and the realist novel, particularly those identified in some way as *Bildungsromane*. The most notable similarity between the realist novel and spiritual autobiography is the split consciousness in the narrative between narrator and character in first person narration. A similar dynamic divide exists in third person narration between characters as presented at the beginning of a narrative and the narrator's implication of who characters will become, but the division within narrated characters as they progress through time is less pronounced and frequently diffused into the narrative in myriad ways. For the sake of clarity, I will focus on first person narration in considering the structural parallels between the realist novel and the conversion narrative, but will further consider third person narration in later chapters.

In both first person realist novel and conversion narrative, the narrator and character remain discrete presences until the final section of the narrative. Uniting this split consciousness is the express work of the narrative. In a *Bildungsroman*, the divide within the psyche is a direct threat to the very notion

---

[26] Watt, *The Rise of the Novel*, 22–4.
[27] Shaw, *Narrating Reality: Austen, Scott, Eliot*, 93.
[28] Hindmarsh, *The Evangelical Conversion Narrative: Spiritual Autobiography in Early Modern England*, 6, 10.

of identity; in a conversion narrative, this same divide is the manifestation of a person who remains separate from God—a person who is "unsaved." In both genres, it is only through the course of the narrative that "the dangerous gap between Character and Narrator gradually diminishes through vertical narrative intrusions, until the two are finally one."[29]

Michael McKeon's description of this narrative process as "the narrative equivalent of atonement" is particularly helpful in crystalizing one of the key areas of narrative and ideological difficulty in evangelical conversion narratives, and moreover suggests further how religious narratives and the novel interrelate.[30] McKeon draws on a general definition of *atonement* as the perfect reconciliation and joining together of the divine and human consciousness, regardless of the method by which that union is achieved. Thus, in literature atonement occurs when the character and narrator become one, a unified consciousness, or when characters become unified to their ideal selves and their communities. When a novel deals only with a human character represented through first person narration, this process is largely straightforward: the character gradually becomes the narrator as a result of personal growth fostered by the story's events. Within eighteenth-century evangelical conversion narratives, the narrative "atonement" between character and narrator is complicated by the simultaneous need for theological atonement between the believing narrator and Jesus on which the literary atonement of narrator and character depends. While an explicitly three-way narrative atonement between the character (believer), narrator, and Jesus is rare, it is a feature of some mid-nineteenth-century novels dealing with religious faith, such as *Alton Locke,* as we will see in Chapter 3. That said, a desacralized version of this three-way atonement structure, in which the character/narrator union is contingent upon the restoration of character's relationships with other characters, is a pronounced feature of the nineteenth-century novel. For example, the character Jane Eyre becomes the narrating Jane only after she is also brought into union with her long-lost extended family and married to Rochester. Likewise, in *Great Expectations* Pip the narrator and Pip the character become a unified consciousness only once Pip has also made peace with Magwitch.

When reconciliation is necessary across multiple character planes (and particularly in evangelical conversion narratives), the first step toward literary and spiritual atonement between the character, the narrator, and Jesus typically involves an intellectual understanding of evangelical teaching. While the

---

[29] McKeon, *The Origins of the English Novel, 1600–1740*, 95.
[30] McKeon, *The Origins of the English Novel, 1600–1740*, 95.

character's intellectual understanding is aligned to the belief that Jesus's death makes reparation for her sins, her psycho-spiritual being is not yet transformed by this knowledge. In terms of McKeon's narrator/character divide, this interim period is when the gap between the narrator and character is largely minimized, but some definitive action remains to be taken. It is the period between Jane Eyre returning to the injured Rochester and the declaration, "Reader, I married him," that marks the final union of the narrating consciousness with the character Jane.

Another way to understand this limbo state between intellectual knowledge and union with Jesus is to consider the difference between reading a biographical summary of a life and a novelized version of that life. The biography provides information, might inspire new thinking and revised actions; but the novelistic account requires the reader's personal sympathetic investment in the character, in which the boundaries between the self and the character are somewhat porous. This first step toward intellectual knowledge is relatively easy to represent in a novel, and it frequently appears as a short biography of Jesus in a sermon or a religious tract to which a character responds. This intellectual encounter with the other allows the character/believer to become more fully known, then he or she can make the final transition into the narrating self.

The second step of atonement, where the character, narrator, and Jesus are somehow made one, is more difficult to represent. If the first step toward representing atonement is similar to reading a biography, the second step is like reading a novel. It requires a transformative process in which the boundaries between oneself and the other are minimal, yet maintained. In this porous relational state, the relationship with Jesus remains a relationship; there is a union between Jesus and the believer but also a differentiation. The self is not Jesus, but the self is related to and is "in Christ." In this moment, the believer's identity is revealed, constituted, and transformed by a relationship to Jesus much like a novel reader's identity can be constituted and transformed through his or her experience of a novel character.[31] Explaining this experience of union between the believer and Jesus is difficult enough. Narrating this type of encounter, such that the reader experiences the character being united to Jesus in a believable way, is well-nigh impossible. And yet, this sort of conversion experience is commonly reported among eighteenth-century evangelicals, later evangelicals,

---

[31] As Deidre Lynch has argued, eighteenth- and nineteenth-century novel readers would intentionally imagine themselves as exemplary novel characters to better identify with them and thus help foster personal character formation. See Deidre Shauna Lynch, *The Economy of Character: Novels, Market Culture, and the Business of Inner Meaning* (Chicago: Chicago University Press, 1998), 252–4.

and even among other Christian traditions. And because this is a recognized part of evangelical religious experience, it is no surprise that some nineteenth-century novelists do try their hand at representing such encounters on the page. Narrating such encounters involved two distinct issues: narrating union with Jesus and narrating Jesus as a character with whom other characters might have a relationship. The rest of this chapter will consider the evangelical tradition and narrative dynamics of narrating union between a believer and Jesus.

Union with Jesus

As eighteenth-century life writers and nineteenth-century novelists work through the identity and structural issues raised by these conversions, they must find ways to represent the experience of a divine encounter for readers who may not believe in such encounters, while rendering that encounter believable in the real world. Failure to make this divine encounter narratively successful threatens both fictional and nonfictional conversion stories in three significant ways. Obviously, the theological aims of such narratives are weakened when a work fails to represent a character's encounter with God in ways that believably bring about atonement and restoration between the human and God. Secondly, if the representation of an encounter with God through Jesus does not work, it threatens to undermine the union of character and narrator on which the story's resolution depends. If the narrator is not reconciled to God, then the gap between narrator and character may remain unbridged and the narrative may also remain unresolved. Finally, a narrator claiming union between the character self and the narrating self through a questionably represented encounter with Jesus threatens that narrator's reliability, potentially rendering the entire narrative suspect.

When a novel's theological content requires atonement between the individual and Jesus, writers are faced with a unique set of representational challenges. In an epistemological framework grounded in empiricism (as in Europe since the late eighteenth-century), any claim about an encounter with an invisible God that takes place in the believer's mind or imagination, thereby altering the individual's metaphysical state and drastically changing his or her life, will be treated with skepticism. But Western epistemology is not the only reason that writers might struggle to represent a divine/human encounter. Traditional language for explaining a believer's encounter with Jesus presents its own set of narrative challenges.

Atonement and conversion, whether through baptism as an infant or at a tent revival as an adult, have always been understood as a profound transition. This movement "from death to life" represents the essential event that separates the saved from the unsaved in many Christian traditions. Earlier Christians and non-evangelical Christians often understand this transition as an ongoing process, sacramentally occurring at the moment of baptism and continually renewed through the Eucharist, prayer, the reading of Scripture, and the like. Such ongoing salvation beginning with a baby's reception of baptism is the sort of enfolding into the Christian community common to pre-evangelical Christianity.[32] Evangelicals rejected this model of the believer saved passively through a world imbued with sacramental power. Instead, evangelicals (particularly Wesleyan ones) insisted upon an adult's conscious decision to be joined to Jesus in order for a person to be truly "saved." Emphasizing the believer's conscious decision transfers the medium through which salvation is received from the material world of water, voice, and text to the psychological realm of emotional, intellectual, and spiritual experience. As such, the movement from unsaved to saved moves beyond ritual acts and even an intellectual acceptance of theological propositions. Instead, salvation requires a thorough reimagining of the self, generated by an encounter with Christ and empowered by his sacrificial death and resurrection.

This reconception of salvation as an event in the conscious mind of the believer complicates the simultaneous pursuit of clear, simple language to explain such a reconciliation and subsequent reimagining of the self. In the eighteenth-century many evangelical believers (along with other British Protestants influenced by evangelicalism) invoke the vocabulary of Scripture, stating that they have been "united" to Christ, "made new," "saved," "made alive," "forgiven," or "crucified with Christ." When evangelical leaders talk about this transformation, particularly in their professional capacity as preachers and pastors, their language is also largely biblical. When Wesley discusses what it means for a believer to be "in Christ" (a notoriously difficult phrase to unpack in theology), he uses the language of being "grafted" onto Christ and being "made conformable" to Jesus.[33] In his *Explanatory Notes* Wesley speaks of Jesus being "united" to the Father when discussing the Gospel of John and then uses the same language for the relationship between the believer and Jesus when discussing Paul's epistles.[34] Two generations later,

---

[32] See Noll, *Protestantism: A Very Short Introduction*, 34.
[33] John Wesley, *Explanatory Notes upon the New Testament* (New York: J. Soule and T. Mason, 1818), 295, 486.
[34] Wesley, *Explanatory Notes Upon the New Testament*, 233, 43, 65, 517.

the evangelical preacher Charles Simeon uses the language of being "captive" to Jesus and "infused" with him, of being made "analagous" to Jesus, and of the "in-dwelling operation of Christ" directing the actions of the believer.[35] In hymnody, Charles Wesley describes this process in terms of Jesus "dwell[ing] within" the believer, Jesus's "Nature [being] impart[ed]" to the believer, and the believer being made "a copy" of Jesus.[36] In one of his most widely anthologized hymns, "Amazing Love," Wesley writes, "Jesus, and all in him, is mine; / Alive in him, my living Head," expressing this transformation through the paradox of the believer's possession of Jesus and simultaneous enfolding into Jesus. At the end of the eighteenth century, the *Evangelical Magazine* argues that believers should "appropriate" Jesus, and not remain mere observers of Christian faith, reiterating this sense of making Jesus one's own.[37]

More helpful than these phrases are the metaphors evangelicals repeatedly employ to describe their experience of union with Jesus. Apart from cultic imagery of being washed in the blood of Jesus, marriage is the most common metaphor for this spiritual union in evangelical sermons and hymnody. Of course, the marriage metaphor is both biblical and widespread.[38] The Hebrew Scriptures that Christians read as the Old Testament frequently depict Israel as the chosen bride for the divine, and consequently the prophets condemn unfaithfulness as adultery. In Christian readings—in biblical commentaries, hymns, sermons, and the very structure of Christian thought—the "church" frequently supersedes Israel as the Bride of Christ. And even a long history of interpretation dating back to the Church Fathers explains the eroticism of the Song of Songs in terms of Christ's relationship to the church. But in all these examples, ranging from the biblical text through the first 1,500 years of Western, Christian interpretation, such metaphors are typically (although

---

[35] Charles Simeon, *Horae Homileticae*, 21 vols. (London: Hodsworth and Ball, 1832–33), 17:58, 61.

[36] These particular expressions come from "Father, at Thy Footstool See," "Come Thou All-Inspiring Spirit," "O Unexhausted Grace," and "O for a Heart to Praise My God." Wesley's hymns are replete with such sentiments, so similar language is used throughout his hymnody.

[37] Zebedee, "List of the Improper Phrases Sometimes Used in the Pulpit," *Evangelical Magazine*, December 1795, 502.

[38] Eighteenth-century evangelicals also occasionally employ the metaphor of the vine and its branches. In chapter 15 of the Gospel of John, Jesus explains the relationship between God the Father, Jesus, and believers through an extended horticultural metaphor in which Jesus is the vine and the believers are the branches. In this telling metaphor that eighteenth- and nineteenth-century evangelicals use to express the experience of being united to Jesus and their continuing dependence upon Jesus, the believer's identity becomes a part of Jesus's identity. The metaphor requires that believers understand themselves as existing only as a part of Jesus because, as extended metaphor makes clear, if they are cut off from the vine, they will wither, die, and be burned in the flames.

not always) treated as expressions of God's relationship to a particular human *community*.[39]

These marriage metaphors are occasionally appropriated for the individual's experience by mystics in Western tradition, but in the late seventeenth century they begin to become a common way for individual Protestants to talk about their personal experience of God. When John Bunyan writes of his "union" with Jesus, he writes of being "joined to Him," of being made "flesh of His flesh, and bone of His bone," in the same language used in Gen 2:23 for the creation of woman from man and pointing to their subsequent union as "one flesh." In the same passage he states, "He and I were one."[40] In the eighteenth century, the earliest Methodist narratives lack the same emphasis on bridal language as their Moravian counterparts, but the idea of being married to Christ increasingly shapes evangelical language through hymnody, sermons, and eventually conversion narratives.[41] John Wesley's journals reflect this tradition, particularly in the conversion narratives of others that he collected and that were subsequently published embedded within his own narrative of ministry. In December of 1738 Wesley received two letters from followers in London that he thought worthy of including in his journal. One letter describes the writer's relationship to Jesus as being "bone of his bone and flesh of his flesh" in a vein similar to Bunyan. In the second, a young woman describes "The Love of God" as:

> a flame kindled [in the heart], with pains so violent, yet so very ravishing, that my body was almost torn asunder. I loved,... I sweated, I trembled, I fainted, I sung, I joined my voice with those that excel in strength.... I was dissolved in love. My Beloved is mine, and I am his. He has all charms. He has ravished my heart. He is my Comforter, my Friend, my All. He is now in his garden, feeding among the lilies. O I am sick of love. He is altogether lovely, the chiefest among ten thousand. O how Jesus fills, Jesus extends, Jesus overwhelms the soul in which he dwells![42]

---

[39] This mystical tradition is best represented by Teresa of Avila, Margery Kemp, and others. See Rabia Gregory, *Marrying Jesus in Medieval and Early Modern Northern Europe* (Abingdon: Routledge, 2016).

[40] Religious Tract Society, *Christian Biography; Containing the Lives of John Bunyan, John Owen, Rev. Thomas Halyburton, Rev. George Herbert*, 15 vols., vol. 13 (London: Religious Tract Society, 1832), 1.56.

[41] Hindmarsh, *The Evangelical Conversion Narrative: Spiritual Autobiography in Early Modern England*, 180–2.

[42] John Wesley, *An Extract of the Rev. Mr. John Wesley's Journal from His Embarking for Georgia to His Return to London* (London: Printed for G. Whitefield, 1797), 3:27.

This erotic language functions as the ecstatic conclusion to a story of religious longing, which represents atonement or union with Jesus through explicitly sexual references. By including these particular passages, Wesley reinforces the tendency to think of conversion and union with Jesus in terms of marriage. Moreover, these passages are reproduced with authorial commentary in Robert Southey's 1820 biography of Wesley, reinforcing the imagery and language of marriage as characteristic of Methodism.[43]

The marriage metaphor is also particularly explicit in one of George Whitefield's anthologized sermons, "Christ the Believer's Husband."[44] In this sermon, Whitefield asks, "Need I tell my married persons in this congregation, that they must go to the university, and learn the languages, before they can tell whether they are married or not?... And... cannot you tell me the rise and progress, and consummation of the spiritual marriage, between Jesus Christ and your souls?" Whitefield speaks of Jesus "woo[ing]," "stripp[ing]" the believer of his or her "fig-leaves." In this allusion to Genesis, in which Adam and Eve devise clothes of fig leaves to cover their nakedness, Whitefield omits God's subsequent dressing with animal skins, moving instead to Jesus "forc[ing]" the believer "from the embraces of [his or her] old husband" and "mak[ing]" the believer "willing to embrace him."[45] The passage culminates in the believer "captivate[d], and fill[ed]," in a "rapture of holy surprise, and ecstasy," crying out "My Maker is my husband!"

This individual appropriation of marriage metaphors is also encoded through eighteenth-century hymnody. The hymnist Isaac Watts draws heavily on the Song of Songs when describing the believer's relationship to Jesus in "When Strangers Stand and Hear Me Tell," and for Charles Wesley, Jesus is the "lover of [his] soul." In fact, Wesley's use of sexually laden language leads J. R. Watson to characterize his hymns as "tak[ing] over secular images and us[ing] them to indicate the love of God."[46] This exchange between the language of romance and religion does not run just one direction; some nineteenth-century Christians applied (or re-applied) the passionate language of hymns to human love. Thus, observes Valentine Cunningham, the Brontës "deceived the world" into thinking they wrote "naughty books" by "appropriating Methodism's love of God,

---

[43] Southey comments on the young woman's "ravings," linking them to medieval Catholicism and prurient priests in order to suggest that such language is inappropriate for a person to use in reference to Jesus. See Robert Southey, *The Life of Wesley; and the Rise and Progress of Methodism*, in Two Volumes, vol. 1 (London: Longman, Hurst, Rees, Orme, and Brown, 1820).

[44] Whitefield, *Sermons on Important Subjects*, 158–9.

[45] Whitefield, *Sermons on Important Subjects*, 159.

[46] J. R. Watson, *The English Hymn: A Critical and Historical Study* (Oxford: Oxford University Press, 1997), 246–7.

exploiting the language of divine love for earthy love."[47] The exchange of sexual language between romance and devotion points to the ubiquitous (if frequently only implied) understanding of union with Christ as akin to the marital bond expressed through sexual intercourse.[48]

Characterizations of Jesus as one's lover make it difficult to narrate an encounter between Jesus and an individual in a believable way. Accounts such as those Wesley includes in his journal would likely undermine the reliability of any narrator in a realist novel, not to mention create awkward content in nineteenth-century fiction that carefully avoids explicit sexual content. In addition, making Jesus a leading character with whom another character might experience such amorous salvation runs counter to the narrative dynamics embedded in theologies of substitutionary atonement. As explained above, the Protestant interpretation of substitutionary atonement places Jesus's action in a finished past, transferring the dramatic action from Jesus's death and resurrection to the believer's life and experience of Jesus. While the stated theology of most Protestant traditions emphasized the totality of divine providence and agency, evangelical narrative practices in particular made each believer's life the dramatic narrative worth telling. Thus, novelists who want to use fiction to explore the experience of knowing Jesus are faced with two distinct challenges. First, they must reimagine the traditional language of marriage for the relationship between the believer and Jesus. Second, they must figure out how to best embed Jesus, whose own narrative locates him at present in heaven, within the novel's various character networks such that he seems "real" to readers. It is to this question of "real" novel characters and networks of character relationships that we now turn.

While Jesus as lover can be awkward when depicted literally, as in Wesley's journal, the idea of marrying Jesus is particularly significant to the nineteenth-century novel, in terms of both ideology and the novel's practices around characterization more generally. Victorian domestic ideology viewed marriage as the primary location for human sympathy in its most idealized form. The psycho-spiritual results of the evangelical experience of salvation—that is, perfect communion with the other, a satiation of longing, and the revelation of one's true self—are all easily translated into the Victorian vision of human

---

[47] Valentine Cunningham, *Everywhere Spoken against: Dissent in the Victorian Novel* (Oxford: Clarendon Press, 1975), 125.

[48] For some, like Laurence Sterne, the use of double entendre and innuendo served satirical purposes, but Evangelicals like John Wesley took issue with such "uncouthness" and later evangelical William Wilberforce blamed Sterne for "lowering the standard of manners and morals" in England, suggesting a more earnest use of marital metaphors. For more on Sterne, see Ryan Stark, *Biblical Sterne: Rhetoric and Religion in the Shandyverse* (New York: Bloomsbury, 2021).

marriage. But these ideological parallels also point to important narrative parallels. In terms of characterization, the evangelical habit of emphasizing personal experience and structuring conversion narratives around relationships, both human and divine, establishes relational networks as the means through which characters' true selves are both constituted and revealed. These relational networks are key to unlocking the novel's attempt to characterize Jesus because such networks suggest a unique habit of thought that is different from the self-constituting thought typically associated with characterization.

Novels frequently tell us more than what a character thinks; they show us a character thinking in real time, recreating the experience of human thought for the reader. There is a well-established relationship between the process of thinking and modern notions of what it means to exist as a "self." As Charles Taylor explains, ever since Descartes, to be a "self" is more than simply being a thinking being. Being a "self" is being a radically reflexive being, a being who is not just aware of the process of thinking but actually constituted by the process of thinking.[49]

Part of what renders novel characters dynamic (and somehow "real" in the mind of the reader) is the two-fold access to characters that novels offer. Novel characters, be they fictional or what Catherine Gallagher has called "counterfactual," offer readers a chance to "be" a different self because readers participate in the imaginative act of self-creating-thought along with novel characters.[50] As readers think along with characters—particularly through narrative structures like free indirect discourse—the character is constituted in the reader's mind as a thinking being who is aware of his or her own thinking. Being aware of a self who is thinking and creating an identity through such thought-awareness is the same cognitive process through which the reader's own self is constituted. As Charles Taylor explains in modern constructions of selfhood, "The self is both made and explored with words."[51] Whether thinking about one's own self or reading a novel, this self-making through words takes place in the same physiological location: the reader's mind. As a result, the reader's mind creates and inhabits the character's identity, just as if it were the reader's own identity.

---

[49] See, in particular chapters 8–9 in Charles Taylor, *Sources of the Self: The Making of the Modern Identity* (Cambridge, MA: Harvard University Press, 1989).

[50] For a discussion of counterfactual characters, see Catherine Gallagher, "What Would Napoleon Do: Historical, Fictional, and Counterfactual Characters," *New Literary History: A Journal of Theory and Interpretation* 42, no. 2 (2011): 36.

[51] Taylor, *Sources of the Self: The Making of the Modern Identity*, 183.

This process of actively imagining the self in light of another consciousness has historically been used for the express purpose of self-fashioning along moral, social, and even economic lines. As Deidre Lynch argues, the "deep" or psychologically complex character that emerges with Austen and flourishes in the nineteenth century is a template of human identity and action that middle-class readers can use to reshape themselves.[52] As a result of this personal reformation, middle-class readers are then able to assert their moral superiority when they become the people they first aspired to be through their encounter with a novel character. As Lynch demonstrates, the reading public can then exercise their moral authority by deciding which books are worthy sources of such self-fashioning, thereby influencing canon formation.[53] Novel-reading and self-formation, then, become significant sites of cultural power for the middle class, further reinforcing the value of novel reading. In literary studies, mapping of the self onto a fictional identity is not necessarily given a moral value tied to some vision of self-improvement. But the practice remains the foundational model for reader-character interaction known as "identification," in which readers see themselves as the fictional identity through the process discussed above. But such theories about identification and the novel overlook an important point: access to self-forming thought is not something humans experience only when constituting our own identities.

Being privy to self-constituting thought through language is not for the individual alone. While the self is made through words, the best constructions of identity, Taylor explains, come through "the words spoken in the dialogue of friendship. In default of that, the debate with the solitary self comes limping far behind."[54] In other words, we form intimate personal relationship through self- and other-constituting language. Human intimacy is largely about being let into the process of another person's thought coupled with shared experience over time, and the centrality of time should not be underestimated here. In real life, those rare, lifelong friends and partners hold a particularly intimate place in our psyche because we grow as they do. We are privy to their process of self-constituting language, just as our friends are privy to our own self-constituting thought throughout the years as we share hopes, dreams, fears, and insecurities. Importantly here, intimacy is not limited to friendliness. As epitomized in

---

[52] Lynch, *The Economy of Character: Novels, Market Culture, and the Business of Inner Meaning*, 252–4.
[53] Lynch, *The Economy of Character: Novels, Market Culture, and the Business of Inner Meaning*.
[54] Taylor, *Sources of the Self: The Making of the Modern Identity*, 183.

Holmes and Moriarty (and so many other literary pairs), relationships between enemies are often more intimate than those among friends.

The links between novel characters and real-life relational intimacy should be obvious at this point. Novel characters are identities whose self-constituting thoughts are shared with the reader and with whom the reader shares experiences through time—both the real time of reading a book and the story-world time of plot. Rae Greiner makes essentially this argument when considering the formal structures of sympathy in the nineteenth-century novel: realism is not only constituted by subjective individualism or mimesis but by "the sentimental and rhetorical dimensions" that novels encode through the character-constituting language of free indirect discourse that positions readers to "go along with" novel characters.[55] Using the lens of intimate relationships (be that intimacy friendly or not) opens up a helpful way of understanding why characters seem "real" to the minds of readers. Novelistic realism is not about characters who are kindred spirits, or characters who readers experience as extensions of themselves. Realism is grounded in characters who share the same subject positions as readers' friends, enemies, families, and neighbors. Characters seem real because readers experience them as other people with whom they share the intimacy of self-constituting thought coupled with experiences shared over time.

The argument I am putting forth here about realist characters is embedded (albeit overlooked) in nineteenth-century literary thought. In her treatise on realism in the middle of *Adam Bede*, George Eliot articulates the values and tendencies of realist art by the middle of the nineteenth century as a form that records—and by recording ennobles—the commonplace. Much has been said about Eliot's anti-heroic emphasis in favor of commonplace communities, historic belief structures, and rural language when she writes that the work of the novelist is to "avoid any... arbitrary picture, and to give a faithful account of men and things as they have mirrored themselves in [her] mind."[56]

What Eliot implies next is that realist art is essentially relational. For Eliot, realism's "faithful account" is valuable as an aesthetic form because the genre models good, bad, and problematic human relationships. By viewing characters in relationship to each other, readers see misunderstandings, human folly, and harsh judgments leading to unfair treatment. Because readers have watched characters wrestle with each other, readers have seen what courses of action

---

[55] Rae Greiner, *Sympathetic Realism in Nineteenth-Century British Fiction* (Baltimore: Johns Hopkins University Press, 2012), 11. See also chapter 1, "Going along with others" for her overview of sympathetic realism.

[56] George Eliot, *Adam Bede* (Oxford: Oxford University Press, 2008), 159.

lead to understanding and sympathy. Through this process readers learn (in theory) to appreciate the beauty in even the most difficult personalities, leading readers to live lives "of forbearance... [and] outspoken, brave justice."[57] But, in order for realism to achieve this telos of vibrant, just, and sympathetic human relationships, the unspoken requirement is that the characters themselves seem "real" to readers. If characters merely reflect personality types, archetypes, or stock characters, then forbearance with "real" people is never practiced.

This requisite appearance of reality raises the question, what then are the novelistic procedures of characterization that make characters seem real? The procedures of characterization that make characters and the worlds they inhabit real are found in the novelistic forms that encode relational networks. On the microlevel these procedures include conversation, the shifting gaze of characters from themselves to others, free indirect discourse that moves from character to character, and first person narration. These relational networks are also at work on the macrolevel of the marriage plot that governs so much nineteenth-century fiction, and even the self-centered *Bildungsroman* in which the narrating self merges with the character self through a matrix of other human relationships.

In terms of the relational structures just described, there is no reason that Jesus should not be a prime candidate for inclusion in a novel. Accounts of his life are replete with human relationships, including friends, foes, and family. More importantly, many strands of traditional Christian spirituality emphasize the reality of a highly prescribed relationship between Jesus and believers frequently, though not exclusively, mediated through a text. Such conditions prepare the way for the notion that a text besides the Bible might also be able to mediate Jesus's presence. Through such texts, believers could potentially experience intimacy with Jesus, and he could become their "friend," despite being empirically absent.

The distinction between real-life, historical characters and fictional characters does not fundamentally alter these narrative dynamics. Catherine Gallagher has argued that a character's fictionality is essential for making the character seem real to readers because subtle textual admissions signal to readers that fictional characters have no bodies and can thus be "universally appropriated" by readers.[58] As a result, historical figures can never be novel protagonists since narrating such people always admits their material existence and with these admissions

---

[57] Eliot, *A.B.*, 160.
[58] For Gallagher's original argument, see Catherine Gallagher, *Nobody's Story: The Vanishing Acts of Women Writers in the Marketplace, 1670-1820* (Berkeley; Los Angeles: University of California Press, 1994), 165–74. More recently, she has argued for counterfactual characters as part of realism, see "What Would Napoleon Do: Historical, Fictional, and Counterfactual Characters."

the impossibility of their appropriation by readers. The primary problem with Gallagher's argument is the assumption that novel characters are experienced as "real" by readers because they are identities that readers "appropriate." By understanding characters as identities with whom readers share intimate relationships rather than as alter-egos of the reading self, readers do not need to encounter characters as identities that can be "universally appropriated." Characters merely need to be knowable to readers, as the flourishing of biofiction since the late 1990s suggests. I am not suggesting that biographies are essentially the same genre as novels here, only that the fact/fiction divide is not the key feature in rendering characters "real."

Even though Jesus and novel characters occupy a structurally similar situation in relationship to the believer and the novel reader, respectively, with the obvious caveat that believers understand Jesus to be nonfictional both in history and in the current moment via his spiritual presence, there were challenges to placing Jesus in a novel during the eighteenth century. The Puritan and evangelical emphasis on substitutionary atonement in a closed past precluded his inclusion in a novel because all of Jesus's narrative action and its meaning had been predetermined and all the narrative drama rendered static due to God's timeless and unchaining character. Jesus was further removed from the realm of the novel because both Protestant theology and anti-Catholic polemics emphasized the triumphant and ascended aspects of Jesus's personality. Locating Jesus in heaven further excluded him from the realm of self-constituting thought that defines novel characters. The narrative consequences of these beliefs meant that the believer's story became the primary drama that people recounted, effectively decentering Jesus from the Christian narrative. Jesus was known factually in history and at times experienced mystically, but his narrative was not where narrative interest lay by the end of the eighteenth century.

By the end of the eighteenth century, atonement theology had so foregrounded the believer's own narrative that Jesus was pushed to the narrative margin. Furthermore, traditional Christologies that present Jesus as a perfect character in a closed past rendered him an implausible choice for a novel character. And yet, evangelically influenced Protestants in England narrated their religious relationship with Jesus in ways that bear structural resemblance to the relationship a reader experiences with a novel character. Jesus is, after all, an empirically absent character whom believers are meant to know in a relationship mediated through a text. So who is this Jesus that one ought to know? And how does one get to know him?

As the next chapter will demonstrate, a number of significant cultural forces—including aesthetic movements, popular piety, and biblical scholarship—brought renewed attention to Jesus's identity as a historical human character. The subsequent chapters will examine how, during the second half of the nineteenth century, the realist novel experimented with its own attempts to answer questions regarding the knowability of the character of Jesus.

2

Popular Piety and Jesus of Nazareth

During the early part of the nineteenth century, Jesus and the idea of the incarnation was moving to the forefront of both theology and popular piety.[1] Unlike piety focused on theories of the atonement, which emphasize one past event in Jesus's life (his death on the cross), the incarnation is explicitly about Jesus's character: what does it look like when a person is completely God and completely human? To better understand how some English novelists wrestled with the question of Jesus's identity—and what he would have been like as a real person in history—it is helpful first to understand some of the cultural trends that brought Jesus's character into focus.

At the turn of the nineteenth century, England was home to many religious communities, but as Linda Colley and many other since have argued, "Protestantism was the foundation that made the invention of Great Britain possible."[2] This official story of Britain's Protestant identity served to smooth over myriad divisions within that Protestantism along with other forms of belief and non-belief in Britain at the time. At the turn of the nineteenth century, Britain was home to diverse Christian denominations, but most fell into one of three groups: the Church of England, Roman Catholicism, and

---

[1] This claim is intended as a qualification and correction to Boyd Hilton's seminal work *The Age of Atonement*, which has convincingly argued evangelicals (and with them a large swath of British Christianity) focused on the incarnation as their core doctrine *after* the mid-nineteenth century. As part of his argument, he focuses on the role atonement theology played in economics and politics in the first half of nineteenth century in Britain. As Hilton's own work shows, important theological influencers, such as Edward Irving, began emphasizing the incarnation in their works as early as the 1830s. More importantly, popular piety across Protestant denominations shows evidence of an increasing focus on the incarnation prior to 1850. For Hilton's look at Irving's influence, see *The Age of Atonement: The Influence of Evangelicalism on Social and Economic Thought, 1785–1865* (Oxford: Oxford University Press, 1988), 284–97.

[2] Linda Colley, *Britons: Forging the Nation, 1707–1837* (New Haven: Yale University Press, 1992), 54. Since Colley many scholars have furthered the thesis that Britain imagined itself as Christian and Protestant, even as those definitions were both diverse and contested. See Burstein, *Victorian Reformations: Historical Fiction and Religious Controversy, 1820–1900*; Joshua King, *Imagined Spiritual Communities in Britain's Age of Print* (Athens, OH: Ohio University Press, 2015); William R. McKelvy, *The English Cult of Literature: Devoted Readers, 1774–1880*, Victorian Literature and Culture Series (Charlottesville: University of Virginia Press, 2007).

Old Dissent.[3] Dissent in England was a long and proud tradition that included Protestant denominations ranging from non-conforming Puritans like John Bunyan and Richard Baxter to progressive Unitarians like Isaac Newton, Joseph Priestley, and Mary Wollstonecraft. Similarly, the Church of England encompassed low and high church practice, Arminian and Calvinist theologies, sacramentalism and biblicism, and even Romanticism and Classicism. As Jasper Cragwall has explained, in the Established Church, "Wesleyans and Anglicans debated the terms of 'Romanticism' more ferociously than any poet, struggling over the character and even existence of inspiration, prophecy, the moral and Providential significance of the natural world, and the value of autobiographical and lyrical forms."[4] Such divisions over worship traditions, theologies, aesthetics, and epistemology, eventually led to the Methodist movement separating from the Established Church.[5]

The split between Methodism and Anglicanism in 1795 marked, as well, a split in the evangelical revival that had been taking place for the better part of seventy years.[6] Evangelicalism had always harbored a significant internal division between George Whitefield's Calvinism, which endorsed Reformed doctrines like election, and John and Charles Wesley's Arminian theology, which emphasized the individual's free will in choosing to embrace salvation. Through Wesley's publications of journals and hymns, print culture helped create and shape a virtual evangelical community identity across traditional denominational lines.[7]

---

[3] While dissent within English Christianity could easily be traced to the Lollards, it flourished after the Reformation and again after the Act of Uniformity in 1662. Horton Davies offers a nuanced look at the myriad forms of Christianity that developed in England tracing both practice and belief. Isabel Rivers also provides a helpful examination of the intellectual context that allowed dissent to flourish during and shortly after the Act of Uniformity. See Horton Davies, *Worship and Theology in England, Vol 3: From Watts and Wesley to Maurice, 1690-1850* (Princeton: Princeton University Press, 1961). Also Isabel Rivers, *Reason, Grace, and Sentiment: A Study of the Language of Religion and Ethics in England, 1660-1780: Whichcote to Wesley*, 2 vols., vol. 1 (Cambridge: Cambridge University Press, 1991).

[4] Jasper Cragwall, *Lake Methodism: Polite Literature and Popular Religion in England, 1780-1830* (Athens, OH: Ohio University Press, 2013), 4.

[5] For a detailed look at the history of Methodism in England, see David Hempton's seminal, *Methodism: Empire of the Spirit* (New Haven: Yale University Press, 2005).

[6] A number of helpful works on the evangelical revival have detailed the history of the movement within the English church. The standard starting point remains Bebbington, *Evangelicalism in Modern Britain*. This chapter will continue to reference a number of the more recent works on evangelical history as they pertain to particular subjects.

[7] Joshua King's praiseworthy study on imagined spiritual communities attends to print culture beginning around 1800, examining its power to create, in essence, virtual communities existing within, across, alongside, and in opposition to traditional institutional structures. What King identifies in the nineteenth century appears in no small way to develop what had already begun in the 1700s with the Wesleys who, through their publication of conversion narratives, sermons, and hymns, formed a "connexion" that united some British Protestants from within and without the Established Church, while reinscribing divides within the Church of England. See King, *Imagined Spiritual Communities in Britain's Age of Print*.

The result was that evangelicalism in Britain existed both "within the church of England *and* [as] a pan-denominational Christian movement."[8] The dynamics of evangelical self-perception as a pan-denominational movement grounded in revival and experiential conversion helped underscore church evangelicals' self-perception as a reforming force within the Established Church. Believing the national moral character and Protestant identity of the Church of England to be under threat, church evangelicals placed a very high emphasis on the Bible, personal faith, and individual morality, while being at best ambivalent toward liturgy and sacramentality with their suggestions of Roman Catholicism.[9]

Despite such narratives of Protestant identity, continuing anxieties about the unstable category of Protestantism and the ongoing influence of Roman Catholicism within England and even the Established Church led to what Miriam Burstein has described as the "national pastime" of "writing about and debating the Reformation."[10] Embedded within such writing are ongoing debates and polemics about the nature of the Eucharist, papal authority, the status and proper interpretation of the biblical text, and what forms of faith observance and theological reasoning were most "authentic" to the historical church and thus most legitimate—but none are preoccupied with Jesus as a historical person. As such works demonstrate, Britain might have been Protestant in its official self-conception, but this national identity was at best a convenient fiction that became increasingly tenuous through the nineteenth century.[11]

British anxieties about its Protestantism took very public form beginning in 1828, when the British Parliament repealed the Test and Corporations Acts (1661 and 1673, respectively). By requiring all men serving in government to be communicants of the Church of England and to affirm a statement denying

---

[8] Mark Knight, *Good Words: Evangelicalism and the Victorian Novel* (Columbus: University of Ohio Press, 2019), 2.

[9] Although evangelicals may have perceived their own role as a moralizing influence, Christopher Herbert has argued that evangelicals actually lowered the moral tone in Britain. Herbert helpfully identifies a tendency in evangelical thinking and preaching that discounts all "works" and morality that are separate from an evangelical faith experience. Yet by over-emphasizing particular representations of evangelicals in Victorian novels, Herbert discounts the many types of evangelicalisms and evangelically influenced Protestantisms in Britain. For a helpful look at the diversity of Evangelicalism in nineteenth-century Britain, see the introduction in *Good Words: Evangelicalism and the Victorian Novel*.

[10] Burstein, *Victorian Reformations: Historical Fiction and Religious Controversy, 1820–1900*, 2.

[11] Much good work has been done on Catholicism in nineteenth-century literary culture. For example, see Hanson, *Decadence and Catholicism*; Ian Ker, *The Catholic Revival in English Literature, 1845–961* (Notre Dame: University of Notre Dame Press, 2003); LaMonaca, *Masked Atheism: Catholicism and the Secular Victorian Home*; O'Malley, *Catholicism, Sexual Deviance, and Victorian Gothic Culture*.

transubstantiation, these acts were designed to keep Catholics in particular from serving in the government. Their repeal in 1828 was followed by Catholic Emancipation in 1829, which further removed legal restrictions on Britain's Catholics. While these moves did not affect church governance within the Established Church or other Christian denominations, they challenged Britain's narrative about itself. The perceived "threat" of Catholics serving in Parliament, combined with a severe cholera outbreak in 1831 and the passing of the First Reform Act in 1832, led some British Christians to begin thinking that the end may very well be nigh. As Burstein explains, "as Catholicism made headway in English culture in the 1830s, apocalyptic speculations about the approaching end of days became common currency among all Protestant denominations. Although Protestants had long identified the pope with the Antichrist, Emancipation suggested that the millennium itself was at hand."[12] Such millenarianism gained particular traction among Dissent, with the influential Scottish clergyman Edward Irving's interpretation of the signs of the times leading to the formation of the Catholic Apostolic Church.[13] Other Christians re-embraced Calvinism, or a more fundamentalist approach to the Bible, or charismatic experience.

While the imagined "threat" of Catholics and even working-class voters put pressure on dominant narratives of British identity, a far more real ecclesiological threat to the Established Church came in the Oxford Movement. The roots of this movement can be traced back at least to Keble's 1827 publication of *The Christian Year* or perhaps as far back as the Reformation itself, but the event that officially began the larger Oxford Movement started with the publication of the *Tracts for Our Times* in 1833. These tracts insisted on the importance of apostolic succession and argued that the English Church is really the Catholic Church in England. While the movement at first focused on issues of church governance, such as what was necessary for a bishop's ordination to be "legitimate" as understood throughout Christian tradition, the tracts also addressed questions of church worship and sacramentality. These practical issues about the nature of the Communion, what constitutes proper worship, and the role of ritual in Christian spirituality have led to much confusion

---

[12] Burstein, *Victorian Reformations: Historical Fiction and Religious Controversy, 1820–1900*, 11.
[13] For a detailed theological and historical consideration of millenarianism in the 1830s, see Bebbington chapter 3 and Hilton, pages 285–97. Edward Irving became particularly influential through the work of F. D. Maurice, who "loved and revered" Irving and his emphasis on the humanity of Jesus (Hilton, 285).

around terms such as "high church," "low church," "broad church," "liberal," and "conservative."[14]

Because the Tractarians understood the sacraments as, in Augustine's words, "outward and visible signs of an inward and spiritual grace," they emphasized the frequent celebration of the Eucharist. They also emphasized "high" forms of worship, including ritual language and physical symbols in worship, such as candles, vestments, and flowers on the altar. As the century progressed, high church Anglicans would frequently embrace the aesthetics of the Tractarian movement and a mysticism adjacent to sacramentality, but the next generation of "high churchmen" were not conservative in their Christology in the same sense as the early Tractarians like Keble, Newman, and Pusey. This first generation of thinkers upheld ancient Christian doctrines, including miracles like the incarnation and bodily resurrection, and insisted on both the authority of the Bible as interpreted within church tradition and on the authority of the church as evidenced in church tradition. Thus, while they were revolutionary within the English church, they were deeply conservative in terms of Christian theology. Despite the theologically conservative nature of Tractarianism, the movement threatened the stability of the English Church and revealed a deep divide between the more sacramentally and liturgically minded Tractarians and the low church evangelicals who embraced the *solas* of the Protestant Reformation (particularly *sola scriptura* and *sola fides*), emphasized unadorned worship, and minimized the role—and the efficacy—of church sacraments.

While the Established Church wrestled with the nature of its historic identity along with its liturgical practice, and while English Dissent grew new denominational branches, a far more existential threat to biblicist Protestantisms was unleashed by Charles Lyell's *Principles of Geology* published in three volumes in the years 1830–3. Drawing upon and popularizing the work of James Hutton, Lyell's work confronted the British public with the reality that the earth's surface—from the rocks and dirt to the mountains and valleys—developed

---

[14] The theological and ritualistic associations with the terms "low," "high," "broad," "conservative," "liberal," and "orthodox" are frequently confusing in scholarship around the Victorian church, in part because theological convictions and ritual practice do not always align, and in part because uses of the same terms today muddy their nineteenth-century meaning. William Winn does an excellent job explaining the emergence of the term "broad church" in his essay "*Tom Brown's Schooldays* and the Development of 'Muscular Christianity'," *Church History* 29, no. 1 (1960). Valarie Dodd helps fill in this picture in her article, "Strauss's English Propagandists and the Politics of Unitarianism, 1841–1845," *Church History* 50, no. 4 (1981). Timothy Larsen carefully applies these terms in his examination of how Victorians across religious and political spectrums read the Bible in *A People of One Book: The Bible and the Victorians* (Oxford: Oxford University Press, 2012).

through natural processes over eons. For many, this notion that the earth was millions of years old challenged the apparent truth claims of the biblical text. In the years that followed, some British Protestants doubled down on literal readings of the Bible, repudiating any science that challenged such understandings of the natural world. Others, like Charles Kingsley, who will be discussed in the next chapter, embraced the discoveries of science and worked to bring the natural sciences and theology together.[15]

But Lyell was just the beginning. In the late 1830s rumors of a German work by David Friedrich Strauss began to rumble through England. The subsequent decades would bring in Darwin, Feuerbach, Wellhausen, and ultimately Schweitzer in 1906. This combination of natural science undermining literalistic readings of Genesis and German biblical scholarship challenging traditional understandings about the compositional history of the biblical text and the character of Jesus presented therein added fuel to the already smoldering religious doubts of many in Victorian Britain.

While Lyell is a convenient starting point, it is unfair to blame (or credit) him with igniting a crisis of faith. That responsibility more properly belongs to eighteenth-century Scottish philosopher David Hume. Hume's *Philosophical Essays Concerning Human Understanding* (1748) includes his well-known and highly influential treatise "Of Miracles," which undermined traditional belief in the miraculous and the intellectual respectability of such belief. In "On Miracles" Hume argues that it is always more rational to disbelieve the report of a miracle than to embrace it because we only have cause to believe that which we have personally, empirically experienced. By the nineteenth century, this argument was often repeated and glossed as "miracles can't happen." While Hume never directly addresses Christian doctrine or the traditional creeds in this section, the implications are obvious. If miracles are at best unbelievable, then the faithful have no rational basis for believing two central doctrines of the historic Christian creeds: the belief in Jesus's bodily resurrection and the belief that God the Son is incarnate in the person of Jesus. Hume's epistemology and his German descendants, from Kant, Hegel, and Goethe to Strauss, Feuerbach,

---

[15] Christopher Lane offers a particularly nuanced consideration of the intersection of Victorian scientific advances and religious faith in Lane, *The Age of Doubt: Tracing the Roots of Our Religious Uncertainty*. For detailed examinations of the intersection of science, ethics, and narrative, Anne DeWitt provides a helpful overview in *Moral Authority, Men of Science, and the Victorian Novel* (Cambridge: Cambridge University Press, 2013). For literature as a vehicle for considering religious doubt in light of Victorian science, see Elizabeth M. Sanders, *Genres of Doubt: Science Fiction, Fantasy, and the Victorian Crisis of Faith* (Jefferson, NC: McFarland & Co Press, 2017).

and the Tübingen School, would haunt much of British Christianity throughout the Victorian period.[16]

These changes to political, economic, religious, and intellectual life in Britain have often been characterized as an intellectual crisis of faith. But such a representation is problematic for a number of reasons. As Timothy Larsen, Mark Knight and Emma Mason, Joshua King, and many others have convincingly demonstrated, this "crisis" was significant because of the widespread presumption of vibrant Christian faith.[17] Moreover, these various challenges to Britain's hegemonic narrative of Protestant—and specifically Anglican—identity, all assume a particular construction of faith that would find all such developments—whether in philosophy, ecclesiology, science, or biblical scholarship—challenging. This is not to say that many forms of Christianity in Victorian Britain did not undergo profound changes in some form or other in the nineteenth century, but merely to observe that not all changes within a religious culture have a detrimental effect on "faith." As the Tractarian movement demonstrates, challenges to ecclesiology were not always challenges to Christology. Rather, as the conclusion to Newman's conversion novel, *Loss and Gain*, makes clear, sacramentality was for many a medium through which one might experience Jesus.

The Romantic Incarnation

Amid the changing religious climate of nineteenth-century Britain that put pressure on ecclesiastical and denominational structures, print culture offered a significant medium for fostering spiritual identities and communities within and across traditional forms of religious identification and governance.[18] In the eighteenth and even in the early nineteenth century, explicitly religious literature was often popular in orientation and frequently linked to evangelical or evangelical-adjacent communities. With an eye to education and catechesis,

---

[16] The history of Hume's influence on British thought, both directly and through continental thinkers, is helpfully traced in Peter Garratt's first chapter, "The Ghost of David Hume," in *Victorian Empiricism: Self, Knowledge, and Reality in Rusking, Bain, Lewes, Spencer, and George Eliot* (Madison: Fairleigh Dickinson University Press, 2010).

[17] See Larsen's *Crisis of Doubt: Honest Faith in Nineteenth-Century England* (Oxford: Oxford University Press, 2006). See also Knight and Mason, *Nineteenth-Century Religion and Literature: An Introduction*. The introduction is particularly helpful in King, *Imagined Spiritual Communities in Britain's Age of Print*.

[18] To understand the role of print culture in shaping religious communities, see *Imagined Spiritual Communities in Britain's Age of Print*.

devotionals, hymnals, evangelistic tracts, edifying tales, religious autobiographies, and religious fiction were written with workers and artisans in mind and were produced cheaply so as to be affordable to all members of society.[19] This popular impulse suggests such evangelical literature is an important precursor to Romanticism's emphasis on common language and the experience of common people. As Mark Noll argues, "if the literary world had heeded the hymns of the Wesleyan revivals, Wordsworth's proclamation would have caused hardly a ripple."[20] Cragwall has argued this point convincingly, explaining that "the Oxbridge poet could be heard harping the same tune as the ranting prophet," and only the "safely classical grammars and histories, and the politics of the ruling class they encoded," permitted enthusiasm to be "admitted as 'the Essence of Poetry.'"[21]

Despite the shared impulses of Romanticism and evangelicalism, writers like Hannah More, Sarah Trimmer, Mary Brunton, Laetitia-Matilda Hawkins, Harriet Corp, Amelia Opie, and Leigh Richmond seized upon the evangelistic and apologetic potential of cheaply produced tracts, religious stories, poems, and novels. Focusing more on converting readers than embracing Romantic aesthetics, such writers often "repackag[ed] the evangelical message for the minds of the less spiritually adept while ensuring that the kernel remained intact."[22] The best-known, earnestly evangelical novel from the period, More's *Cœlebs in Search of a Wife* embodied its religious instruction through lengthy sermon-like conversations geared at converting character and reader alike.[23] Such evangelistic fiction was applauded by none other than Wilberforce himself, who wrote to More from East-Bourne on July 15, 1809, that More has in *Cœlebs* provided "an introduction for opening the way to discussions on the most important topics, which otherwise would be hedged out from access."[24] Similarly, although Leigh Richmond's *The Dairyman's Daughter*

---

[19] D. Bruce Hindmarsh traces the ways in which structural changes in transport, industry, and urbanization all contributed to the popular accessibility and consequent populist impulse within the evangelical texts. For full details, see chapter 2, "The Revival of Conversion Narrative: Evangelical Awakening in the Eighteenth Century" of his *The Evangelical Conversion Narrative*.

[20] Mark Noll, "Romanticism and the Hymns of Charles Wesley," *The Evangelical Quarterly* 46 (1974): 198.

[21] Cragwall, *Lake Methodism: Polite Literature and Popular Religion in England, 1780–1830*, 10–11.

[22] Tim Killick, *British Short Fiction in the Early Nineteenth Century: The Rise of the Tale* (Hampshire: Ashgate, 2008), 76.

[23] Hannah More, *Cœlebs in Search of a Wife: Comprehending Observations on Domestic Habits and Manners, Religion and Morals*, ed. Patricia Demers (Peterborough, ON, Canada: Broadview Press, 2007).

[24] Robert and Samuel Wilberforce, *The Life of William Wilberforce*, 5 vols. (London: John Murray, 1838), 3:412.

(1814) offers vivid descriptions of rustic locations, relatable characters, and an engaging plot, it is clear that the narrative's only reason for existence is to inspire conversion.[25]

Unlike these conversion-driven narratives, John Keble in *The Christian Year* offers a new aesthetic direction by joining Christian devotion to Romanticism. Published in 1827, *The Christian Year* was wildly popular until the end of the nineteenth century across denominations, making it hard to overemphasize its influence on British piety. As Margaret Oliphant explains in her novel *Salem Chapel*, the "much-multiplied volume" was marketed to the full spectrum of Victorian Christians, ranging from "a tiny miniature copy just made to slip within the pocket of an Anglican waistcoat" to a "big red-leaved and morocco-bound edition" for use during family prayers.[26] Although Oliphant's description of both Masters Bookshop and the various versions of Keble's work suggests that evangelical and dissenting booksellers would never think to stock Keble, this was not the case. *The Christian Year* was so widely read within the Church of England and across denominational lines that, according to G. B. Tennyson, nearly all moderately educated Victorian households had a copy by the end of the century.[27] As Joshua King explains, "The immense popularity and wide reception of *The Christian Year*... provided a means for imagining private and domestic acts of reading as ways of participating in a print-mediated, national religious community."[28] Although Keble imagined that community to be Anglican, the "wide interdenominational circulation of *The Christian Year*" meant that Keble's devotional focus on the life of Jesus through the Book of Common Prayer exercised tremendous influence on British Christians across political, theological, and denominational spectrums.[29]

Reflecting the meditative, recollective habits of thought extolled in *Preface to the Lyrical Ballads*, *The Christian Year* emphasizes the contemplation of Jesus rather than conversion to Jesus. Thus, while Keble's poetry is popularly oriented in its emphasizing common experience and language like earlier evangelical literature, he uses folk language and commonplace experience to create a nondidactic, contemplative text characterized by "indirect expression

---

[25] Leigh Richmond, *The Dairyman's Daughter: An Authentic Narrative Containing an Account of Her Extraordinary Conversion, Godly Exercises, and Happy Death, with Serious Reflections on Death* (Kilmarnock: H. Crawford, 1817).

[26] Margaret Oliphant, *Salem Chapel* (Edinburgh: W. Blackwood and Sons, 1865), 49.

[27] G. B. Tennyson, *Victorian Devotional Poetry: The Tractarian Mode* (Cambridge: Harvard University Press, 1981), 226–32.

[28] King, *Imagined Spiritual Communities in Britain's Age of Print*, 130.

[29] King, *Imagined Spiritual Communities in Britain's Age of Print*, 131.

that includes allegory and other veiled modes of utterance."[30] While nature and the material world often serve as the initial occasion or subject of Keble's poetry, Jesus's historical life—albeit intermixed with his exalted governance of human history—frequently becomes a poetic focus. In the first Advent poem, we see this dual temporality as Jesus is both "pac[ing] through th' adoring crowd" and "keep[ing] silent watch from [his] triumphal throne" (19, 24). Similarly, in the poem for Good Friday, the speaker's attention remains focused on Jesus's physical suffering until the final two stanzas, in which the speaker begs to have his "sin and shame ... hid[den]" in Jesus's "wounded side." While the poem's final turn is to Jesus's function as an atoning sacrifice, the majority of the poem is focused on Jesus and not the speaker. As a result of spending so much time on Jesus's bodily suffering, Jesus's earthly life is given primacy of place over the benefits Jesus offers to believers. Even during the season of Trinity, which runs from after Pentecost until the start of the next Advent (often called "Ordinary Time" or "Kingdomtide" in other Christian traditions), the sustained attention of the poems remains on Jesus, in large part because Keble frequently focuses his poetic musings on the Gospel reading prescribed for each Sunday, each of which retells moments from Jesus's ministry.

The Christian Year is a watershed event in Britain's literary and religious thinking, not just because of its popularity or cultural influence, but because of the way Romantic aesthetics open up new Christological emphases. Jesus, according to the traditional creeds, is the prime example of God in the material world. As a result of this doctrine, Jesus frequently becomes the basis for seeing God within the rest of creation. Such theology makes Jesus an ideal bridge between Romanticism and Christian theology by providing the foundation for a "comprehensiveness" in which "'every part of life, every scene in nature' [is] an occasion of devotion, justify[ing] ... the writing of poetry."[31] Likewise, because the narrative of Jesus's life is encoded in the cyclical practices of the liturgy which joins a historic narrative to the material life and world of the observant community, the Book of Common Prayer serves as the perfect structure for Keble's poetic reflection and is amenable to both Romantic aesthetics and Christian theology. By bridging Christian devotion and Romanticism, *The Christian Year* also "restores the Prayer Book to its central place in mainstream culture of the age."[32] It also restores Jesus to his central place in Christian thinking, devotion, and theology.

---

[30] Tennyson, *Victorian Devotional Poetry: The Tractarian Mode*, 33.
[31] Tennyson, *Victorian Devotional Poetry: The Tractarian Mode*, 34.
[32] Sheridan Gilley, *Newman and His Age* (London: Darton, Longman, and Todd, 1990), 66.

Across party and even denominational lines *The Christian Year* moved religious thinking toward a greater interest in the life of Jesus as a narrative distinct from the narrative of the believer. With these poems, the central focus shifted from the story of the believer's spiritual progress to the story of God's action: becoming a specific man in a specific time and place in order to save the world. In terms of church history, Keble's focus on Jesus is particularly significant because most scholarship dates the Victorian interest in Jesus to Strauss's *Das Leben Jesu*, but Keble's poems predate the first, working-class translation of Strauss by over ten years and Eliot's better-known translation (1846) by almost twenty years.[33]

While Romanticism through Keble was essential in laying the groundwork for a shift in English piety and theology, Romanticism was not a straightforward influence on changing representations of Jesus. As M. H. Abrams argues in *Natural Supernaturalism*, Romanticism put new emphasis on the circular structure and themes of creation and recreation within the story of Jesus's life. By focusing on the narrative shape of creation and recreation in the Jesus story, the Romantic poets also secularized the narrative, making the "eschatological drama of [the] destruction of the old creation... and the emergence of a new creation" the archetype for each artist.[34] Taking the pattern of Jesus's life as a model for the growth of the artist also secularized the evangelical idea of union with Jesus, changing it from a mystical union to an imaginative union in which the protagonist sees his own rejection and suffering as a form of divine suffering.

Viewing Jesus as an archetype to be copied might seem to work against considering him as a historical human, but the opposite is true. As a historical archetype of humanity, Jesus's human life—his development, potential intellectual struggles, experiences of being misunderstood and unappreciated, and his willingness to suffer martyrdom for his ideals—all become important models to consider and follow. When Jesus functions as the archetype for the developing Recluse or the self-sacrificing Prometheus, the social prophet or the reconciling friend, the narrative tensions and nuances of personality embedded in the narratives of Jesus's life become areas for artistic exploration, free from theological restraints. While such uses of Jesus do not place him within the material world of first-century Palestine, they do place him solidly in

---

[33] For more on the English translation history of Strauss, see Dodd, "Strauss's English Propagandists and the Politics of Unitarianism, 1841–1845."
[34] M. H. Abrams, *Natural Supernaturalism* (New York: Norton, 1973), 35.

a human body and human mind, which lays the groundwork for more nuanced representations of his psychology, if not his historical embeddedness.

The impulse toward the commonplace and common experience that undergirds Keble's attention to Jesus also leads inevitably back to the novel. Religion aside, this trend is obvious in the nineteenth century generally: Romantic lyrics gave way to verse novels, dramatic monologues, and the ascendancy of the realist novel, which takes the now aesthetically respectable commonplace and embeds it within the structures of prose narrative. Following Bakhtin's understanding of the novel, the movement from Romantic poetry to the novel in the nineteenth century is inevitable. As Bakhtin argues, "the novelization of other genres... implies their liberation from all that serves as a brake on their unique development, from all that would change them along with the novel into some sort of stylization of forms that have outlived themselves."[35] By focusing on ordinary experience and ordinary language, Romantic poetry set in motion the very liberation of form and style that led to the centrality of the novel in the nineteenth century. In fact, later novelists like George Eliot and Mary Augusta Ward suggest their own aesthetic dependence on Romanticism. For both authors, Wordsworth serves as an aesthetic ideal and, by extension, a litmus test for characters. Characters who understand Wordsworth and his belief in the sacredness of the ordinary, like Ward's Robert Elsmere, prove to be good characters. Those who, like Arthur Donnithorne in *Adam Bede*, see Wordsworth as "twaddling stuff," prove deeply flawed.[36] Through such characterizations, Eliot and Ward affirm Romanticism and its concern for the ordinary, justifying their own high-realist art by aligning it to Romantic ideals. Similarly, Keble's Romantic aesthetics demonstrates that Jesus's life as recorded in the Gospels and Christian experience are appropriate subjects for art, while simultaneously encoding an inherently narrative emphasis on Jesus's life story through the lectionary prescribed in the Book of Common Prayer. Thus, while Keble is firmly grounded in lyrical poetry, the aesthetic and narrative dynamics of these poems lay important foundations for later religiously inflected novels.

Given the realist impulse of Romantic poetry, it is no surprise that the Romantic novel itself also played a particularly important role in shaping later nineteenth-century literature and in bringing the historical Jesus to the center of British Christianity. The Romantic novel, in its attention to the intrinsic nobility of materiality and history, encouraged a love for actual history while idealizing

---

[35] Bakhtin, *The Dialogic Imagination: Four Essays*, 39.
[36] Eliot, *A.B.*, 59.

the lost heroes of a past age. This double perspective on the past helped shape nineteenth-century religious practice. For example, by creating an appreciation for the ancient religious practices of English and Scottish culture, Scott's *Waverley* novels (1814–29) fostered liturgical renewal, including an emphasis on the liturgical year and the Eucharist.[37] As John Henry Newman explains in his autobiography, Scott's novels "stimulat[ed] [readers'] mental thirst, feeding their hopes, setting before them visions, which, when once seen, are not easily forgotten, and silently indoctrinating them with nobler ideas," thereby creating the religious imagination of the age.[38]

The twin impulses of the historical and "noble... ideas" in Scott's novels highlight the flexibility of the novel to create the imaginative structures necessary for thinking about the Jesus of the Christian creeds in literary terms. The love of history and the respect for the discrete consciousness and materiality of others that history teaches are necessary to thinking about the historical reality of Jesus. The lingering (and, according to literary critics like George Levine, fading) sense of heroic action in characters like Fergus and Flora Mac-Ivor creates a longing for an ennobled sense of human history and action, a longing for a material history that is significant on a grand scale, and a hope that such lives are possible.[39] Such hope is the narrative counterpart to the notion in Romantic poetry of the transcendent significance of the ordinary. The belief in the ennobled potential of history takes the metaphysical idea of divinity imbuing the ordinary and translates it into the chronological realm of historical significance. Such grand historical hope fosters the sort of imagination that can think about Jesus's divine nature in narrative rather than metaphysical terms, as a human being whose story shapes cosmic history.

The Romantic view of history, the ordinary, and the individual pushes English writers toward thinking about Jesus as a human being and as a novel character. Jesus, as a man in history or a novel character, is not to be confused with the "Christ figure," essentially any character who gives his or her life sacrificially on behalf of others. Christ figures and types of Christs abound in Victorian literature, even when they do not quite manage to die. For example, characters like Charlotte Yonge's Ethel in *The Daisy Chain* could be seen to inhabit the role

---

[37] Horton Davies, *Worship and Theology in England, Vol. 4: From Newman to Martineau, 1850–1900* (Princeton: Princeton University Press, 1962), 66–8.
[38] John Henry Newman, *Apologia Pro Vita Sua and Six Sermons*, ed. Frank M. Turner (New Haven: Yale University Press, 2008), 212.
[39] George Levine, *The Realistic Imagination: English Fiction from Frankenstein to Lady Chatterley* (Chicago: University of Chicago Press, 1981), 128.

of a Christ figure without dying. Similarly, Lizzie in "The Goblin Market" gives herself without actually dying, but the principle of sacrificing one's life remains intact for these characters. Such Christ figures fit comfortably with the Jesus of atonement theology, a Jesus whose main function is to die for the sake of others. In contract to these Christ figures, Romanticism through both poetry and the novel gives us something else. Romanticism gives us Jesus as a character defined by his historical materiality, his commonplace life, and his psychological struggles. Essentially, Romantic aesthetics open up the possibility of a Jesus who is not circumscribed by a definitive act of self-sacrifice.[40] The problem was (and is), who is Jesus when he is not dying for the sins of the world?

Even if the many strains of literary Romanticism did not clearly answer the question of who Jesus was for the rest of his thirty-three years, Romantic aesthetics did help create the imaginative circumstances for thinking about Jesus's life. Simultaneously, other cultural changes helped draw attention to Jesus's life, reinforcing the non-sacrificial aspects of his story. And perhaps no cultural change was as significant for the Jesus story than the development of modern Christmas celebrations.

Jesus and Domesticity

A second development that inevitably drew attention to Jesus's life with its material circumstances was the emergence of modern Christmas traditions in the 1830s and 1840s. Although Christmas observance in Britain had frequently involved attending church and family gatherings, the amount and quality of festive observances were perceived to have fallen off in the late eighteenth and early nineteenth centuries. In William Sandys 1833 introduction to *Christmas Carols, Ancient and Modern*, he laments the waning influence of the holiday, even in the northern and western regions where the holiday had been previously celebrated with "spirit."[41]

Yet, within a decade of Sandys's assessment, the expansion of Victorian Christmas festivities as both a sentimental and commercial endeavor was well

---

[40] This move away from thinking of Jesus in terms of self-sacrifice is indicative of a larger trend in Victorian literature toward altruism and mutuality. See Ilana M. Blumberg, *Victorian Sacrifice: Ethics and Economics in Mid-Century Novels* (Columbus: Ohio State University Press, 2013). Also Jan-Melissa Schramm, *Atonement and Self-Sacrifice in Nineteenth-Century Narrative* (Cambridge: Cambridge University Press, 2012).

[41] See William Sandys, *Christmas Carols Ancient and Modern* (London: Richard Beckley, 1833), l–li.

underway.⁴² Through the 1840s, idealized images of merry olde England (along with a host of other less obviously festive images) were marketed as Christmas cards and sent through the highly efficient British post. Traditions like the Christmas tree (from Prince Albert's German childhood) were highlighted in the press's coverage of the royal family's holiday observances, spreading such traditions to English families. Christmas was also a time for telling stories around the fire, with specialty publications like Dickens's *A Christmas Carol* (1843) encouraging generosity and reflecting practices like the Christmas feast. Dickens's Christmas stories also point to the Victorian practice of telling ghost stories at Christmas time. As Timothy Larsen reminds readers, "Victorian Christmases had affinities with our Halloween …. [Y]uletide was a time for stories about all sorts of creatures—weird and wondrous; sinister, supernatural, and mysterious; mythical, fantastical, and fabulous."⁴³ Tales of the supernatural do not at first seem particularly aligned with the more religious aspects of Christmas, but the fascination with the mythical and mysterious, the fantastic and fabulous offers intriguing parallels with the notion of a divine being entering the realm of human affairs. While this story of the domestic Victorian Christmas that emerged in the 1840s is well documented, what is often overlooked or mentioned as a sidenote is that Sandys collections of Christmas carols were published a full ten years before Henry Cole's first Christmas cards were sent or Dickens's "A Christmas Carol" was first published.

The early publication date of collections of Christmas carols points to the frequently invisible, buried, or compromised religious sensibility that underlies many Victorian attitudes and practices. While the Victorian Christmas was, certainly, as much due to sentimentality and consumerism as it was due to an interest in the incarnation of God in Jesus Christ, it is intriguing that Victorians are collecting and publishing songs reflecting on the birth of Jesus right when Keble's *The Christian Year* is being read in a significant portion of Victorian homes and as they being to tell ghost stories around the fire. Both Christmas carols and *The Christian Year* reflect domestic devotional practices that focus on Jesus's

---

[42] For an overview of nineteenth-century Christmas traditions, see Neil Armstrong, *Christmas in Nineteenth-Century England* (Manchester: Manchester University Press, 2010). Also see, Timothy Larsen, "The Nineteenth Century," in *Oxford Handbook of Christmas*, ed. Timothy Larsen (Oxford: Oxford University Press, 2020).

[43] Larsen, Timothy, *George Macdonald in the Age of Miracles: Incarnation, Doubt, and Reenchantment*, Hansen Lectureship (Downer's Grove: IVP Academic, 2018), 32.

life, and Victorian Christmas carols, in particular, focus on the infancy of Jesus. In considering representations of the infant Jesus, it is important to remember that the first half of the nineteenth century, which started to think about the baby Jesus, also created Victorian domestic ideology. This ideology celebrated marriage and the heteronormative family, placing the potentially compromised father within the public sphere, inscribing the angelic mother within the private sphere, and inventing a sentimentalized idea of innocent childhood within the home. Victorian Christmas even "taught us that children should be at the heart of our Christmas celebrations."[44] Placing the baby Jesus at the center of such family devotion might humanize him. It also permits rendering him another sentimental image of hearth and home.

To understand the shifting sensibilities and characterizations of Jesus, it is helpful to compare Charles Wesley's "Hark the Harold Angels Sing" (1739) with the early nineteenth-century carol "Angels from the Realms of Glory" (1816). "Hark" is the first of Wesley's hymns to be widely anthologized in the eighteenth century, and it appeared in edited form in Sandys 1833 collection. George Whitefield's changes to the opening couplet had become standard after the 1750s, but Wesley's original "Hark, How All the Welkin Rings" celebrates the nativity scene in terms of Jesus's eternal kingship.[45] The opening couplet gives "glory to the king of kings" and sets the tone of the entire hymn. While Jesus is "veil'd in flesh," Wesley quickly clarifies that it is "the Godhead [we] see." As the hymn continues, the emphasis lies firmly on Jesus's kingship and saving power, describing Jesus as the "Everlasting Lord," "heaven-born Prince of Peace," "desire of nations," "Son of Righteousness," and even "incarnate deity." His humanity is only referenced obliquely, insofar as he is "born," "in flesh," and the "offspring of the Virgin's womb." This third characterization actually marks him as less human, since most people are not offspring of virgins. In Wesley's original version, Jesus only "appear[s]" as man. Since this line borders on the heresy of Docetism, it was later changed to "dwell." Whether Jesus is "pleased as man with men to dwell" or "pleased as man with men t'appear," the point is essentially the same: Jesus's identity is more about being God than being human. As the first half of the hymn concludes, Wesley declares the purpose of Jesus's birth: "that men no more may die" and that he might "raise the sons of earth." The final two stanzas of the hymn, almost entirely unused today, turn from adoration to prayer.

---

[44] Larsen, Timothy, *George Macdonald in the Age of Miracles: Incarnation, Doubt, and Reenchantment*, 31.
[45] I am drawing on the text of Wesley's 1745 edition of these hymns found in *Hymns and Sacred Poems* (Bristol: Felix Farley, 1745), 142–3.

The hymn calls upon Jesus to "fix in us they humble home," "Display thy saving pow'r," and "in mystic union join" Jesus's "nature" to the community of believers by "form[ing] [himself] in each believing heart." Thus, while Wesley celebrates the incarnation, the hymn bears the stamp of the evangelical movement with its emphasis on the conversion of the believer, and its focus on Jesus's identity as an exalted savior. Despite the prayer for unity with Jesus, he is in no way presented as accessible, present, or personable.

James Montgomery, who "rescued hymns from the 'blood of the Lamb' school," presents a subtly different Jesus in his collection of hymns, *The Christian Psalmist*, published in 1825.[46] In "A Visit to Bethlehem in Spirit," which comes right after his well-known "Angels from the Realms of Glory," Montgomery imagines himself transported to Bethlehem to view Jesus's birth. The hymn reiterates many common themes found in carols, including the dark and silent night, celestial voices bearing good tidings, the birth of a kingly messiah, and God's love for humanity. But the language of the final two stanzas turns away from the kingly titles and promised "mercy" that has "begun" in the "poor shed." In the penultimate stanza the speaker questions if the stable can be the right place, as he sees the "infant," and then reflects on the "Stranger, meek and lowly." The subsequent hymn, "The Names and Offices of Christ" begins still at the manger and then takes up the proclamation of Isaiah 9:6 that "unto us a child is born... and the government shall be upon his shoulders, and his name shall be called wonderful, counselor, everlasting father, prince of peace."[47] Standing next to the promised messiah's manger, the speaker does not declare that Jesus *is* "bear[ing] / Power and majesty" but, following Isaiah's anticipation of what the birth promises, the speaker declares that Jesus "shall bear / Power and majesty." While Jesus is clearly royal and even divine in both hymns, here there is an implied narrative future. Mercy has only "begun," but has not yet completed its work. Jesus "*shall* bear / power and... names most high" (emphasis added)—but not yet. In the moment of the carol, the speaker is, like Isaiah, still looking for the promise to be fulfilled.

---

[46] Watson, *The English Hymn: A Critical and Historical Study*, 308. Montgomery's hymns are taken from *The Christian Psalmist, or Hymns, Selected and Original* (Glasgow: Chalmers and Collins, 1825), 389–91.

[47] The first Christmas performance of Handel's *Messiah*, which makes prominent use of these same texts, took place in 1818, in Boston. Given the early date of American Christmas Cards and this Christmas performance of Handel, more work on the influence of nineteenth-century American culture on English theology and piety might prove illuminating in understanding more the turn to emphasizing the incarnation in nineteenth-century Britain.

Montgomery's attention, albeit slight, to Jesus's birth as an event within a larger anticipated narrative becomes a hallmark of many Victorian carols, including "Once in Royal David's City" (1848), "What Child Is This" (1865), "Away in a Manger" (c. 1882, American), and "O Little Town of Bethlehem" (1865, American). The same impulse shapes Christina Rossetti's "In the Bleak Midwinter" (1872), which begins by reflecting on the infinitude of God but turns to the nativity scene. In a particularly confronting moment of materiality, the speaker muses that "A breastful of milk, / And a mangerful of hay" were sufficient for Jesus.

While Victorian carols certainly focus on Jesus as God, they also reflect on his humility in becoming human. Moreover, rather than explicitly calling sinners to repentance, Victorian carols call the whole of creation to adore the newborn Jesus. In this way, Victorian Christmas carols are representative of the larger trend in hymnody that J. R. Watson identifies as a transition from "salvation to adoration" (303). Of course, older hymns focusing on repentance, salvation, or an exalted Jesus never went out of fashion because such themes remain key aspects of Christian faith for many adherents. Additionally, Victorians were largely concerned with the development of the self, including conversion variously understood, and the great hymns of the evangelical revival (for Christmas and other times of year) express the psychology of the believer and the majesty of Jesus with a vigor and poetry that captures these concerns, ensuring their ongoing popularity. That said, it is telling that eighteenth-century hymnals are typically arranged around the life of the believer, moving through topics like repentance, salvation, and assurance, whereas the nineteenth century's *Hymns Ancient and Modern* are arranged around the life of Jesus as inscribed in the church year.[48]

If Christmas carols placed an infantilized Jesus at the center of a sentimentalized domestic feast, nineteenth-century Bible illustrations contribute to a somewhat different perception of Jesus. The tradition of depicting biblical scenes in art dates back to the earliest Christian iconography. Protestant Bibles

---

[48] For widely circulated examples, see Wesley's frequently reprinted *Hymns and Sacred Poems*, 4 ed. (Bristol: Felix Farley, 1743); see also *A Pocket Hymn Book, for the Use of Christians of All Denominations* (London: J. Paramore, 1787). Conversely, an 1820 Baptist hymnal published in Boston foregrounds the life of Jesus before turning to the life of the church. Midcentury Victorian hymnals that are organized around the life of Jesus include Henry Alford, *Psalms and Hymns Adapted to Sundays and Holidays Throughout the Year: To Which Are Added, Some Occasional Hymns* (London: Francis & John Rivington, 1844). See also *Hymns Ancient and Modern for Use in the Services of the Church with Accompanying Tunes* (London: Novello and Co., 1861). It is important to note that Wesleyan hymnals continued to be organized around the believer's narrative through the nineteenth century.

in the early modern period, beginning with Luther and Tyndale, include ornate woodcuts illustrating biblical stories that depict the characters and settings of the stories through the images of contemporary Europe and England. At times these illustrations even incorporate supernatural elements, such as angels looking down on the scene and breaking through the clouds to aid characters, or demons tempting humans. In the eighteenth century, biblical illustrations continued in the tradition of early modern illustrations with rare touches reflecting some historical awareness, such as dressing Caesar in robes rather than stockings.

It was not until the late eighteenth century that illustrated Bibles began to value the historical context and materiality of the biblical narratives. The expanding British Empire opened up international economic markets, making "Palestine comparatively near to… home" and facilitating artistic depictions of the biblical world's materiality.[49] In the 1830s publishers made the first attempt to bring artists' historicized renderings of biblical stories together with the biblical text in a way that encapsulates the new knowledge derived from empire and commerce. In 1838 Charles Knight and Company published the *Pictoral Bible illustrated with many hundred woodcuts representing the Historic events after celebrated pictures, the Landscape scenes, from original drawings, or from authentic engravings, and the subjects of Natural History, Costume, and Antiquities from the best sources, to which are added original notes, chiefly explanatory of the engravings, and of such passages connected with the History, Geography, Natural History and Antiquities of the Sacred Scriptures as require observation.* The *Pictoral Bible*'s long title makes clear that the illustrations, which were the chief selling-point for such Bibles, provide "factual" evidence of the historical, geographic, and cultural realities in which biblical stories are set. The implication is that, because the geographical, historical, and cultural contexts can be illustrated, the stories set within these contexts are also true. Somewhat ironically, the editors took incredible liberties with the illustrations. In one instance they changed a painting's title, so that an illustration that started its life as a painting of John the Baptist being beheaded became David beheading the Amalekite.[50] In another instance, the editors cropped a Middle Eastern landscape painting to focus on travelers in one section, and then titled the image Abigail Travelling to Meet David.[51] Despite these liberties, the implicit assumption of the *Pictoral Bible* is

---

[49] T.S.R. Boase, "Biblical Illustration in Nineteenth-Century English Art," *Journal of the Warburg and Courtauld Institutes* 29, no. 349–67 (1966): 356.
[50] Boase, "Biblical Illustration in Nineteenth-Century English Art," 356.
[51] Boase, "Biblical Illustration in Nineteenth-Century English Art," 356.

that the illustrations lend scholarly credence to the narratives within the text because they show the reader the "reality" of the place and people described in the text.

While the *Pictoral Bible* was an expensive, multivolume work not widely available, by 1845 illustrated Bibles were published by a number of publishers for the middle- and upper-class markets with "realistic" images. Subsequent illustrated Bibles—particularly in large, leather-bound editions designed to be family Bibles—showcased the highly detailed work of Friedrich Overbeck and Gustave Doré, along with the Daziel brothers' woodcuts of famous paintings. Just as materiality in the novel lends itself to realism, these illustrations connect materiality to the historical veracity of the narrative. Set alongside the texts they illustrate, such illustrations strengthen the idea that the Jesus of the gospel narratives is a historical, human figure by drawing attention to his physical body particularly in the passion narrative.

But depicting Jesus's body was not without complications for some Victorian Protestants. As a historical man, Jesus's body required artists to wrestle with Victorian constructions of masculinity that did not sit easily alongside claims about Jesus's divinity. As many scholars have demonstrated, masculinity in the nineteenth century was construed as tainted by the world of commerce, government and compromise, a taint removed by the purifying influence of the home.[52] But since Jesus was by definition perfect, he could not be morally tainted, thereby calling the nature of his masculinity into question. For other Victorians, such as William Holman Hunt, Jesus's perfection meant he would have to possess a balance between male and female characteristics, as seen in his much-reproduced work, *The Light of the World*.[53]

Squeamishness at depicting Jesus in masculine terms extended to any representation in which he is surrounded by poverty, squalor, or dirt. When Dickens reviewed Millais's painting *Christ in the House of His Parents* in the June 15, 1850, edition of *Household Words* he lambasted Millais for depicting the

---

[52] See "Preconditions" in John Tosh, *A Man's Place: Masculinity and the Middle-Class Home in Victorian England* (New Haven: Yale University Press, 2007). Elizabeth Langland, *Nobody's Angels: Middle-Class Women and Domestic Ideology in Victorian Culture* (Ithaca: Cornell University Press, 1995). See also the discussion on "healing masculinity" in chapter 2 of Tara MacDonald, *The New Man, Masculinity and Marriage in the Victorian Novel* (New York: Routledge, 2016).

[53] Leslie Parris discusses Hunt's blending of masculine and feminine qualities in *The Pre-Raphaelites* (London: Tate Gallery, 1984), 119. For more on the Victorian construction of gender that rendered masculinity morally compromised, see chapter 3 in Zemka, *Victorian Testaments: The Bible, Christology, and Literary Authority in Early-Nineteenth-Century British Culture*. For Hunt and the incarnation, see Andrew Tate's "'Real Visions of Real Things': The Light of the World, Incarnation, and Popular Culture," in Ludlow, *The Figure of Christ in the Long Nineteenth Century*, 85–98. Also Schramm, *Censorship and the Representation of the Sacred in Nineteenth-Century England*, 133–4.

"mean, odious, repulsive, and revolting" when placing Jesus in the carpenter's shop.[54] Dickens was not alone in his condemnation of Millais's painting. The pre-exhibition review in *The Morning Chronicle* described the painting as "utterly indefensible on any pretext whatsoever, either with regard to the offensiveness and repulsiveness of the subject… or the childish mode of treating it."[55] *The Standard* reported the painting to be "stiffer, worse drawn, and more ugly than the most grotesque [Medieval painting]."[56] The painting's "worst feature," according to the reviewer, is that "now-a-days,… it almost savors of impiety to depict the savior of mankind under such a mean and ridiculous aspect as is shown in this picture."[57] Likewise, *The Examiner* protests the "repulsive caricature" of the "tenderly elevated and sacred subject" of Jesus, Mary, and Joseph, going on to describe the painting as "the very anti-thesis of poetry, nature and art."[58] As these reviews make clear, Victorian art critics found the style of Millais's painting inappropriate because that style is applied to Jesus. To depict Jesus in unidealized terms—as a poor, dirty boy in a rude carpenter's shop—was an offense to Victorian sensibilities. This apparent tendency to associate piety with representing Jesus in an appropriate manner—as a nice, clean, aesthetically pleasing figure—points to the Victorian preference for an idealized Jesus, asleep in his mother's arms, dying meekly for the sins of the world, or ascending triumphant into heaven.[59]

In the first half of the nineteenth century, Jesus's life came into devotional focus through *The Christian Year*. Concurrently, a particular sort of historical imagination emerged with the Romantic novel, Christmas became a popular domestic holiday, Bibles joining "realistic" images of Jesus to Gospel passages were published, and leading artists wrestled with how to best depict Jesus on the canvas. All such works helped free Jesus from an identity circumscribed solely by his act of self-sacrifice and helped make him more human by focusing attention on his life. At the same time, these representations circumscribed Jesus within domestic piety, limiting his character to a highly idealized and divinized person,

---

[54] Charles Dickens, "Old Lamps for New Ones," *Household Words* 1, no. June 15 (1850): 265.
[55] "Exhibition at the Royal Academy," *The Morning Chronicle*, May 4, 1850, 5.
[56] "Royal Academy," *The Standard*, May 9, 1850, 1.
[57] "Royal Academy," 1.
[58] "Fine Arts: The Eighty-Second Exhibition of the Royal Academy," *The Examiner*, May 25 1850, 362.
[59] Dickens's *The Life of Our Lord*, written for his children in the late 1840s, offers a prime example of the sentimental and domestic Victorian Jesus. Because it was not published until 1934, it does not directly shape Victorian characterizations of Jesus but reflects them. For a treatment of Dickens's characterization of Jesus, see my own work, "Dickens's *The Life of Our Lord* and The Problem of Jesus," in *"Perplext in Faith:" Essays on Victorian Beliefs and Doubts*, ed. Julie Melnyk and Alisa Clapp-Itnyre (Cambridge: Cambridge Scholars, 2015), 268–303.

aligned with childhood and the domestic sphere. And debate about how to best represent Jesus only served to highlight the contested parts of Jesus's dual nature.

Jesus and Myth

While domestic ideology, popular piety, and visual representations of Jesus arguably made Jesus seem more human (albeit a very sentimentalized human), in the second half of the nineteenth century, scholarly texts took his character in the opposite direction by mythologizing his life. Before German biblical criticism became a widely feared threat among some British Christians, Victorians were already composing a great many retellings of the life of Jesus. In fact, from these retellings of the gospel narratives, Daniel Pals identifies a new subgenre that emerged, one that transformed the tradition of writing an account of Jesus's life by combining a scientific interest in history and anthropology with novelistic and biographic focus on plot and character to harmonize the Gospels and present a biography-like version of Jesus's life.[60] With these retellings developed a subset of the novel that Jefferson Gatrall dubs "the Jesus novel."[61] Beginning with Harriet Martineau's *Traditions of Palestine*, the Jesus novel is historical fiction that provides portraits and glimpses of Jesus through fictional first-century characters. The excitement comes in the novel's exploration of the life and times of Palestine and the drama within the fictional characters' lives. Because Jesus novels are not typically of the best literary quality, and perhaps because they are centered on Jesus, these novels remain an understudied subset of Victorian historical realism. Despite lacking in literary merit, literary retellings of Jesus's life and historical fiction set during his life and times became high-stakes genres because they brought into focus just how "real" or "unreal" Jesus might be to the imagination.

The sense of Jesus as a product of historical mythmaking is due, at least in part, to David Friedrich Strauss's *Das Leben Jesu*.[62] While scholars frequently talk about Strauss's effect on British Christianity in terms of Eliot's 1846 translation, editorials denouncing Strauss familiarized English readers with his arguments

---

[60] Daniel Pal's work remains the best examination of the genre he identifies in *The Victorian "Lives of Jesus."*

[61] For a detailed examination of the literary portraits of Jesus these novels provide, see Gatrall, *The Real and the Sacred.*

[62] David Friedrich Strauss, *The Life of Jesus, Critically Examined*, trans. George Eliot, 2nd ed. (New York: Macmillan & Co, 1892).

and offered counterarguments as early as 1840. In reality Eliot's translation did not sell well, and since both Strauss's arguments and their rebuttals had already appeared in the press, it made relatively little impact on popular opinion.[63] But at least part of Strauss's popular failure was due to the nature of *Das Leben Jesu*.

Despite its title, *Das Leben Jesu* is not really a retelling of the life of Jesus. In both form and content it is directed toward a scholarly audience concerned with the historical reliability of the gospel texts. It engages a wide range of eighteenth- and nineteenth-century German theological debates and dedicates a significant portion of each page to translation and philology, while developing a particular hermeneutic theory about how myth develops. When considering each pericope, Strauss begins with the biblical text, identifying textual contradictions, inexplicable miracles, or unbelievable supernatural appearances. Strauss then provides the best traditional solution to each issue he has identified, both from orthodox theology and from rationalist or naturalist readings of the text. As one might expect, the traditional answers prove unsatisfying and the rational or naturalist readings prove incomplete. Finally, he offers a new reading that interprets each pericope as a mythological narrative, using textual problems as evidence that events of Jesus's life evolved from natural events into stories of a great, divine ruler. This skeptical approach to Jesus made *Das Leben Jesu* a popular work for Victorians to denounce but not a popular work to sit down and read.

Whether Strauss was read or encountered solely through reviews, the work effectively undermined assumptions about the historical reliability of the gospel texts and, with them, the identity and character of Jesus. If the version of Jesus presented in the Bible is the product of years of pious editorializing and mythmaking, then how could anyone really know who the real, historical Jesus was in the first place? And thus, with Strauss, the quest for the historical Jesus was launched.

Nearly twenty years after Strauss's work appeared, Ernest Renan's *Vie de Jésus* (1863) became a popular sensation, shaping both the subject concerns and the literary form of future Lives of Jesus and Jesus novels.[64] Renan's detailed descriptions of the landscape and culture of first-century Palestine and speculation about Jesus's true motivations translated into spectacular sales, successful not only in France but in England and across the continent. Renan's Jesus is a highly compromised individual, ultimately characterized by

---

[63] Dodd, "Strauss's English Propagandists and the Politics of Unitarianism, 1841–1845," 418.
[64] Ernest Renan, *Vie De Jésus*, trans. Charles Edwin Wilbour (New York: Carleton, 1867).

weakness and deceit. Toward the end of *Vie de Jésus*, Jesus is "no longer himself .... [H]is conscience had lost something of its original purity. Desperate, and driven to extremity, he was no longer his own master. His mission overwhelmed him, and he yielded to the torrent."[65] While Renan's surprising interpretation of Jesus's narrative proved very popular and highly influential in subsequent years, his characterization of Jesus also challenged orthodox theology and traditional devotion.

Challenges to traditional characterizations continued in works like Sir John Robert Seeley's *Ecce Homo* (1866), the first significant English Life of Jesus to be published after Renan that also engaged German criticism.[66] *Ecce Homo* is haunted by the relationship between Jesus's humanity and his divinity, which both Strauss and Renan flatly rejected. The ambiguous Christology led some critics to laud it as a brilliant work of apologetics suggesting Jesus's divinity from beginning to end. Others disparaged the work as promulgating German skepticism and disbelief. In the June 1866 edition of *The Month*, John Henry Newman sums up the British response to Seeley, writing that it is impossible to tell whether the author "was an orthodox believer on his road to liberalism, or a liberal on his road to orthodoxy."[67] Not surprisingly, responses to *Ecce Homo*, such as Joseph Parker's *Ecce Deus* (1867), intended (as the title implies) to answer definitively the question of Jesus's identity.[68] *Ecce Deus* and Seeley's other respondents, with their predictable theology and unimaginative narratives, failed to capture the imagination of the reading public—at least as evidenced by their sales.

In the mid-1870s, Frederic W. Farrar's *The Life of Christ* (1874) was, by far, the most popular of the British "Lives" published in the nineteenth century.[69] Like Renan, Farrar situates his narrative firmly in the geography and culture of the Holy Land, introducing places and customs with the detailed descriptions common to travelogues of the period. Unlike Seeley, who separates his theological reflection from his scant retelling of the Jesus narrative, Farrar weaves religious reflection through the narrative events, such that the plot of Jesus's life provides both shape for the work as a whole and a narrative energy—but not narrative

---

[65] *Vie De Jésus*, 303.
[66] John Robert Seeley, *Ecce Homo: A Survey of the Life and Work of Jesus Christ* (Boston: Roberts Brothers, 1867).
[67] John Henry Newman, "Ecce Homo," *The Month* 4, no. 56 (1866): 564.
[68] Joseph Parker, *Ecce Deus, Essays on the Life and Doctrine of Jesus Christ. With Controversial Notes on "Ecce Homo"* (Boston: Roberts Brothers, 1867).
[69] F. W. Farrar, *The Life of Christ* (New York: E.P. Dutton & Co, 1894).

tension. From the beginning of the work there is no question about Jesus's holy character, no doubt where the story will end nor what conclusions might be drawn from the narrative. While some critics accused Farrar of being overly intimate with his subjects—in part because of his use of free indirect discourse where the biblical text reports thoughts—Farrar's training as a novelist does not lead him to overstep the bounds of popular piety with regard to Jesus's innermost thoughts. Instead, Farrar frequently pulls back when his narrative turns to Jesus, insisting that "we may not intrude too closely into this scene. It is shrouded in a halo and a mystery into which no footstep may penetrate."[70]

Farrar's training in philology helped create one of *The Life of Christ*'s notable narrative characteristics that further helps explain its popularity among many religiously committed Victorians. By providing key insights into the language and culture of first-century Judaism and problematic textual issues, Farrar's philological discussions give the text a scholarly aspect that defends British orthodoxy against the perceived threat of German scholarship. Despite its narrative and theological predictability, Farrar's holy, historical Jesus proved to be the perfect answer to the wholly historical Jesus of ongoing theological controversy. The work sold over twelve hundred copies in the first year and continued to be reissued in new editions, illustrated versions, leather-bound and gilded versions, pocket versions, and translations for markets in Russia and Japan for a quarter century following its initial publication.[71]

Following Farrar's success, other scholar-writers attempted to capitalize on interest in the life of Jesus. Cunningham Geikie's two-volume *Life and Words of Christ* sold well, with Charles Spurgeon reportedly calling him "one of the best religious writers of the age."[72] A few years later, Alfred Edersheim's *Life and Times of Jesus the Messiah* drew upon the author's education in the Talmud and Jewish history, along with extensive archeological research, to correct the "many erroneous and misleading statements" about Judaism and life in Palestine at the time of Jesus.[73] Edersheim, a Jewish convert to Christianity, was particularly concerned with illustrating that Jesus was the very real, material fulfillment of Jewish messianic expectations. While some criticized Edersheim's work as being anti-Semitic, he strongly denied such charges in the preface to the second and third editions, arguing both for the Jewishness of Jesus whom

---

[70] Farrar, *The Life of Christ*, 554.
[71] Pals, *The Victorian "Lives of Jesus"*, 79.
[72] Pals, *The Victorian "Lives of Jesus"*, 97.
[73] Alfred Edersheim, *Life and Times of Jesus the Messiah* (London: Longmans, Green, and Co, 1906), x.

he sought to make more real in the mind of his readers and for the historical development of Judaism, such that to find fault with particular practices in the first century says nothing about one's views of modern Judaism or the Jewish community. The same extensive knowledge of Judaism from which Edersheim criticizes his former tradition and distinguishes different traditions and schools within Judaism imbued his work with an ethos of scholarly rigor and cultural authenticity for English readers. Despite the relatively accessible prose, Edersheim never achieved the popularity of writers like Seeley, Farrar, or Geikie.

As the Lives of Jesus flourished in the mid- and late nineteenth century, so too did the Jesus novel. Jesus novels are typically set in the first century and center on fictional characters whose lives intersect with the life of Jesus in some way. Critical studies of Jesus novels (and fifth gospels that continue the life of Jesus or provide new narrative instances in Jesus's life) consider the relationships between these novels and a range of related phenomena: biblical hermeneutics, the reworkings of Christian theology, continental iconography, and race and nationality.[74] Such studies reveal that, within these Jesus-conscious novels, Jesus remains a distant image, a portrait glimpsed through the eyes of a work's other characters. Whereas the Lives of Jesus retell the Jesus narrative in some manner or other, Jesus novels like Martineau's—or (more famously) *Ben-Hur*—present the Jesus narrative by allowing the protagonist to observe or even briefly encounter Jesus at a few key moments in Jesus's life. Because such works do not focus on Jesus as a particular, conscious character in the novel, presenting him instead with in the "field" of minor characters, these literary portraits beg questions about how Jesus might appear as a central novel character.[75]

The first half of the nineteenth century brought Jesus into view as a historical character with a real life through Romanticism, print culture, and festive celebrations. But just as Victorians began to focus their attention on the life of Jesus, scientific advancements put pressure on literal readings of the biblical text, and biblical scholarship challenged the portrayal of Jesus found in the Gospels. The intersection of these cultural forces formed the perfect storm to challenge perceptions of Jesus, making him both the center of Victorian attention and a subject for scrutiny. While many writers engage the idea of Christ, far fewer

---

[74] See Gatrall, *The Real and the Sacred*; Keuss, *A Poetics of Jesus: The Search for Christ through Writings in the Nineteenth Century*; Stevens, *The Historical Jesus and the Literary Imagination: 1860–1920*; Theodore Ziolkowski, *Fictional Transfigurations of Jesus* (Princeton, NJ: Princeton University Press, 1972).

[75] For a discussion of how characterization functions for minor characters in realist fiction, see Alex Woloch, *The One vs. The Many: Minor Characters and the Space of the Protagonist in the Novel* (Princeton: Princeton University Press, 2003).

risk trying to narrate an actual encounter with Jesus because creating such an encounter on the page requires that Jesus exist as a relatable novel character.

The chapters that follow will focus on four major attempts at such narration—four novels in which Jesus appears as a sympathetic novel character whom other characters encounter—and the theological and narrative implications embedded in these characterizations of Jesus. It is historically and methodologically significant to note that George Eliot and Mary Augusta Ward are deeply engaged with Charles Kingsley's writing: Eliot both loving and hating Kingsley and Ward modeling the young rector Robert Elsmere on Kingsley. Eliza Lynn Linton's Joshua, with his concerns for urban social work and Jesus as a revolutionary, also reflects Kingsley's Parson Lot. Furthermore, all four novelists represent the enviable intersection of popular success, literary respectability, and theological savvy. Finally, these novels share a deep engagement with traditional characterizations of Jesus as prophet, priest, and king. As such they represent literary explorations, challenges, and reworkings of Jesus's character that are still deeply engaged with the broad stream of traditional Christianity, even as they inevitably challenge and nuance Christological traditions.

3

Jesus the Revolutionary King

The statement "Jesus is Lord" has always been a political statement. If Jesus is Lord, then the monarch is at best a surrogate and at worst a usurper, be that monarch Caesar or the Queen of England. While the claim of Jesus's cosmic rule has at times caused political trouble for a variety of Christian groups, by the nineteenth century most English subjects experienced no tension between loyalty to church and crown. But even with such loyalties in place, the question remained: how should a society respond to the king of the universe who became human? And if all people were under the rule of this God, whose very act of becoming incarnate renewed the divine image in each person, then how should this human family of divine image-bearers treat each other? Does the incarnation mean that Jesus's kingship extends beyond a heavenly kingdom in our political and social status quos? Despite the apparent peace between the monarch and the divinity, some nineteenth-century Christians reimagined Jesus's office as king through the incarnation, giving his lordship profound implications for life in the here and now. For the Anglican reverend and novelist Charles Kingsley, Jesus's divine kingship meant a revolutionary restructuring of society in terms of its both political and economic relationships.

In the particularly defensive Epilogue to the 1851 revised edition of *Yeast* (first published in 1848), Charles Kingsley acknowledges, "Readers will complain... of the very mythical and mysterious denouement of a story which began by things so gross and palpable as field-sports and pauperism. But is it not true that, sooner or later, *'omnia exeunt in mysterium'*?"[1] This mysterious conclusion involves Lancelot, the skeptical dilettante, coming to Christian faith, surrendering himself to belief in "Jesus Christ—THE MAN," a line that emphasizes Kingsley's theological emphasis on Jesus's humanity.[2]

---

[1] Charles Kingsley, *Yeast; Poems, The Works of Charles Kingsley* (Philadelphia: J. F. Taylor and Co., 1899), 335.
[2] Kingsley, *Yeast; Poems*.

Kingsley was correct about his readers' response to the novel's ending. On the whole, they did not like the ending to *Yeast*, or his mystical endings in general. *The Scottish Review* for April 1856 complains, "the dramatic world is dissipated into the thinnest shadows before the curtain drops."[3] *The Christian Remembrancer* describes all his novels through 1857 as characterized by "hurried composition: a haste, not only in putting thoughts into language, but in giving those thoughts utterance so soon as they enter the mind at all" and characterizes the denouement of *Yeast* as "a lame and impotent conclusion."[4] Similarly, the review for *Blackwood's Edinburgh Magazine* in 1855 suggests that in *Yeast* and *Alton Locke* Kingsley, "did not even pretend to have a plot to develop."[5] And *The National Review* (1860) comments, "It is difficult to believe that... he had laid his plot beforehand."[6]

While critics and readers alike were frustrated with Kingsley's endings, he repeatedly attempted to perfect a plot that culminates in a real-world encounter with Jesus. The reason for Kingsley's stubbornness about his endings is really quite simple: he sincerely believed that Jesus was the answer to Britain's class strife, the answer to science and scholarship's intellectual doubts, and the answer to every human being's personal longing. But such faith created a real literary difficulty for Kingsley. How could he make this understanding of Jesus (which always turns out to be his protagonist's understanding of Jesus) real for his readers? Simply stating that the ultimate answer is "Jesus Christ—THE MAN" did not work in *Yeast*, and (if his later epilogue is any indication) Kingsley knew this. In *Alton Locke* (1849), Kingsley expands the concluding encounter with Jesus, experimenting with the narrative structure and perspective embedded within first person narration in an attempt to recreate Alton's experience of Jesus, rather than simply reporting such an experience took place. The results are, admittedly, mixed. But Kingsley's attempt is helpful because it elucidates at least one Victorian understanding of social demands implicit in the very orthodox characterization of Jesus as a cosmic king. Moreover, Kingsley's experimentation with perspective in *Alton Locke* highlights some of the narrative difficulties embedded within evangelically influenced Protestant theology. To understand how Kingsley attempts to characterize Jesus within the novel, it is important to first understand Kingsley's thinking, both within the Victorian church and within broader Christian traditions, since his theological commitments shape his characterization of Jesus.

---

[3] "Mr. Kingsley's Imaginative Writings," *The Scottish Review*, April 1856, 102.
[4] "Yeast," *The Christian Remembrancer*, October 1857, 391, 411.
[5] "The Rev. Charles Kingsley," *Blackwood's Edinburgh Magazine*, June 1855, 627.
[6] "Mr. Kingsley's Literary Excesses," *The National Review*, January 1860, 19.

Kingsley and the Incarnation

For Charles Kingsley, Christian faith begins and ends with Jesus. Although scholars have frequently characterized Kingsley as a broad or liberal churchman, the two-fold emphasis in his sermons on personal faith in Jesus and the role of Jesus's atoning death and resurrection in salvation make him sound very much like an evangelical churchman. But, while he had a great deal of sympathy for evangelicalism, he found himself frequently at odds with evangelical leaders both in the Established Church and among dissenting groups, because, as he explains to his fiancée Fanny Grenfell in a letter, evangelicals failed "to combine both the dogmatic and the experimental. We must be catholic; we must hold the whole truth; we must have no partial or favourite views of Christianity, like the Dissenters and the Tractarians."[7] Furthermore, evangelicals' increasingly literalistic approaches to the Bible put Kingsley at odds with the mainstream of evangelical hermeneutics at midcentury.[8]

On the other hand, because of Kingsley's emphasis on catholicity, his deep admiration of thinkers like F. D. Maurice and Thomas Arnold, and his enthusiastic embrace of Darwin's *Origin of the Species*, he is often considered to be a "broad" churchman. In many ways, this description is fitting. Kingsley had a broad understanding of the range of acceptable beliefs within the church and he embraced the natural sciences, consequently reading parts of the Old Testament in genre-specific and nonliteral ways. But Kingsley was never a true theological "liberal" because of his commitment to the ancient creeds and his refusal to explain Jesus's divine sonship or resurrection as metaphors or myths. Moreover, because the terms "liberal" and "broad" are highly problematic as currently used in literary criticism (in part because of the changing ways in which such terms are used theologically in the twentieth and twenty-first centuries), one must parse these terms within their historical context before being able to determine where Kingsley's theological affinities lay.

---

[7] Charles Kingsley, *Letters and Memoirs*, 2 vols., *The Works of Charles Kingsley* (Philadelphia: J. F. Taylor & Co, 1899), 1.52. Regarding Kingsley's letters, although *The Works of Charles Kingsley* is treated as the definitive edition of his novels, it is inadequate as a definitive edition of his letters. The *Letters and Memoirs* section is an edited version of his wife's earlier, lengthier biography. Consequently, the single volume *Charles Kingsley: His Letters and Memories of His Life; Edited by His Wife* contains additional information. Furthermore, as Klaver points out, even more letters remain unpublished. Whenever possible, I have cited from the letters in the *Letters and Memoirs* section of *The Works of Charles Kingsley*.

[8] Ian C. Bradley, *The Call to Seriousness: The Evangelical Impact on the Victorians* (New York: Macillan, 1976), 194.

In the early and mid-nineteenth century, one was theologically liberal if he or she supported things like Catholic emancipation, the restructuring of the Irish church, and the funding of the Catholic seminary at Maynooth. This sort of political (or perhaps better said, ecclesiastical) liberalism was the sort of "liberalism" that people like John Keble and Henry Newman preached.[9] Beginning in the late 1840s, the definition of "liberal" began to change, shifting from questions about political policy and ecclesial structures to questions about theology and biblical interpretation. In this later use, "liberal" denoted those who questioned, revised, or reinterpreted traditional Christian doctrines such as the nature of the Bible, the divinity of Jesus, and the bodily resurrection. Thus, in the 1830s and 1840s a person was "liberal" if that person was in favor of full civil rights for Catholics. After the 1850s, a person was "liberal" if he or she believed the doctrines of the incarnation and bodily resurrection to be negotiable. Unlike "liberal," the term "broad" church was not actually used to describe the English church before 1850.[10] While there was frequent confusion over the term "broad" in the Victorian period (Maurice denied even knowing what it meant), it was generally used to describe the historical tendency of the Church of England to encompass a range of theological understandings and spiritual practices. So, although all liberals were broad churchmen, not all broad churchmen were liberals—or, at least, they were not the same type of liberals.

To complicate these terms even more, when the meaning of these terms was most in flux at midcentury, and the "broad church" was home to both political and theological liberals, the theological liberals were also a messy group. Among those with a "liberal" approach to the biblical text (i.e., those who did not read the entire Bible as a literal, historical document and who were open to developments in science and biblical criticism) there were two main groups of thinkers. The first group, following in the tradition of Coleridge and Maurice, were Platonists who "thought of God in personal terms," and were concerned with biblical principles. The second group, represented by thinkers like Thomas Arnold, Matthew Arnold, and Benjamin Jowett, were Aristotelian in their approach to theology and biblical criticism, emphasizing formal logic and thinking of God "as a first cause... rather than a Person."[11] Although Kingsley clearly fits within the Platonic liberal tradition, Kingsley's deep and traditional

---

[9] Norman V. Hope, "The Issue between Newman and Kingsley: A Reconsideration and a Rejoineder," *Theology Today* 6, no. 1 (1949): 80.
[10] In parsing these terms, I am indebted to the helpful overview in Winn, "*Tom Brown's Schooldays* and the Development of 'Muscular Christianity,'" 64–6.
[11] Winn, "*Tom Brown's Schooldays* and the Development of 'Muscular Christianity,'" 65.

orthodoxy (demonstrated by his enthusiastic membership in the Committee for the Defense of the Athanasian Creed) highlights the fact that the Platonic broad churchmen could be downright conservative in their Christology.

In the mid- and late nineteenth century, when Christology and biblical criticism were lively public debates, Kingsley's firmly orthodox Christology made it difficult for conservative churchmen to dismiss his progressive views on the Bible and science as insidious examples of German liberalism. As a result, he serves as an important voice in bringing science and faith together in British discourse.[12] That said, and although Kingsley's version of broad churchmanship was not completely unique in the Victorian church, it did place him in a precarious position. To Tractarians, some later high churchmen, and evangelicals his thinking was easily characterized as too progressive. To his progressive friends, ranging from Thomas Huxley to J. A. Froude, he was the conservative churchman committed to the creeds.[13]

What makes Kingsley's theology both hard to pin-down and unique are not his views regarding Jesus and the Bible but the priority he gives to particular theological commitments. Unlike evangelicals, dissenters, and many low-churchmen who shared Kingsley's dogmatic commitment to creedal Christianity, the center of Kingsley's faith was not the Bible. The core of Kingsley's faith was the incarnation. As he wrote to John Bullar on March 12, 1856, the incarnation of God in Jesus was "the one fact which is to me worth all, because it makes all others possible and rational, and without it I should go mad."[14] These sentiments did not merely express a passing phase in Kingsley's intellectual life. Upon Kingsley's death in 1875, the Reverend H. Percy Smith wrote to Kingsley's wife praising her husband's lifelong "reverent belief... that the great fact of the Incarnation is the source of all life and goodness, that is or ever shall be."[15]

---

[12] For Kingsley's relationship to Darwin's work, see Piers J. Hale, "Darwin's Other Bulldog: Charles Kingsley and the Popularisation of Evolution in Victorian England," *Science and Education* 21, no. 7 (2012).

[13] Kingsley's writings on social and economic issues placed him in an awkward position similar to his position between liberals and conservatives in the church. While he helped found the Christian socialists and lambasts the property-controlling practices of the wealthy and the middle-class dependence on cheaply produced goods, he simultaneously endorses a sort of paternalism from the church and state toward the working class, meaning that, while his thinking angered and scandalized the respectable middle and upper classes, it did not go far enough for many of the more radical Victorian thinkers.

[14] Kingsley, *Letters and Memoirs*, 2:10.

[15] For Kingsley, the incarnation of God in the person of Jesus was the foundation of and guide for all religious faith and all intellectual pursuits. See *Charles Kingsley: His Letters and Memoreis of His Life; Edited by His Wife* (London: Henry S. King & Co, 1877), 1:238.

For Kingsley this joining of divinity and humanity in the incarnation rendered Jesus the archetype for each human being. Kingsley, following second- and third-century patristic thinkers, believed that although the *imago dei* that each person bears was marred at the fall, it was not erased. In the incarnation, Jesus's full divinity and fully humanity serve as a reaffirmation of the image of God in the human person. Moreover, his life offers a pattern illustrating what it means for people to bear the divine image. Thus, for Kingsley, the incarnation is not a paradox in which the diametrically opposed identities of God and human are put into one body in Jesus. The incarnation is the reaffirmation of an essential alignment between God and humanity in which Jesus reveals each person's real identity as God's image-bearer in the created world.

Kingsley's deep commitment to the incarnation impacts his thinking in three discrete ways. First, God's willingness to be human affirms material existence and the entire material world as fundamentally good. Second, Jesus's humanity and his materiality offer a message of salvation to all people, regardless of their ability to be "spiritually" or "heavenly" minded. Third, the incarnation affirms that humans can have a relational knowledge of God through Jesus, and this knowledge is what ultimately "saves" people by revealing and renewing their true identity as human beings.

Considering each of these consequences in turn helps elucidate why Kingsley, especially in his Parson Lot days, insists on the socially revolutionary demands of Jesus's cosmic kingship—and why in his novels he repeatedly tries to structures the conclusion and resolution around Jesus. First, the doctrine of the incarnation shapes Kingsley's thought by affirming material existence as inherently good, and with it the human body. The teaching that God became a flesh-and-blood human in the historical person Jesus of Nazareth means that God was able to have a material existence in Jesus without compromising his divine perfection. Consequently, as Kingsley repeatedly argues in his letters, novels, and sermons, Christians must affirm that the material world and body are good and not fundamentally "sinful" or "depraved," materiality is to be enjoyed, appreciated, and embraced because God first created the material world and then, even after the fall, reaffirmed materiality by becoming incarnate in Jesus.

In a similar vein, because Jesus is the eternal word by whom all things were made and who reaffirms the goodness of the material world by taking on flesh, Kingsley's scientific works repeatedly argue that the truths science uncovers are God's truths. In his preface to *Town Geology*, Kingsley writes that as long as he and his readers believe that Jesus is truly God incarnate, then they "shall not fear to investigate Life; for we shall know, however strange or novel, beautiful or awful, the discoveries we may make may be, we are only following the Word whithersoever He may lead us; and... He can never lead us amiss."[16] Thus, according to Kingsley, science should never be perceived as a threat to Christian faith but, rather, should be undertaken by the Christian with both intellectual rigor and wonder at God's handiwork.

Not only did the incarnation's reaffirmation of materiality undergird Kingsley's lifelong study of biology and support for science, it also undergirds his attitude toward the human body and sex. As Kingsley puts it in a letter to his wife Fanny, "What is sensuality! Not the enjoyment of holy glorious matter, but blindness to its spiritual meaning."[17] For Kingsley, the body is "holy glorious matter" to be enjoyed because the human body is the very form God assumed when he became a material being. Kingsley's focus on the human body is a common theme in literary scholarship, particularly in terms of gender constructions and what Kingsley calls, "Christian manliness" (which scholars dub "Muscular Christianity").[18] For Kingsley, "Christian manliness" was not about masculinity but being fully human. However, regarding Kingsley's assertions that Christian manliness is nothing more than "a healthful and manly Christianity; one which does not exalt the feminine virtues to the exclusion of the masculine," Klaver comments, "one wishes for clarity's sake that Kingsley had added that the

---

[16] *Town Geology* (New York: D. Appleton and Company, 1873), lvi.

[17] J. M. I. Klaver, *The Apostle of the Flesh: A Critical Life of Charles Kingsley*, ed. A. J. Vanderjagt, Brill's Studies in Intellectual History (Boston: Brill, 2006), 79.

[18] Norman Vance's foundational work, *Sinews of the Spirit*, gives extended consideration of Kingsley's theology particularly in relationship to manliness and the human body. Consequently, it serves as the theological foundation for most later works. Although a very helpful study, Vance's focus on Christian Manliness means that he approaches Kingsley's theology through gender, instead of addressing Kingsley's theology as an epistemic base from which Kingsley's diverse thought develops. Moreover, Vance mentions the doctrine of incarnation only a few times and he never ties Kingsley's thinking on the body, creation, or the significance of human life to this major theological idea. Consequently, further work on Kingsley and constructions of gender in light of a theology of the incarnation is needed. See Norman Vance, *Sinews of the Spirit: The Ideal of Christian Manliness in Victorian Literature and Religious Thought* (Cambridge: Cambridge University Press, 1985). For treatments of manliness in *Alton Locke*, see David Alderson, "The Anatomy of the British Polity: *Alton Locke* and Christian Manliness," in *Victorian Identities: Social and Cultural Formations in Nineteenth-Century Literature* (New York: Macmillan, St. Martin's Press, 1996); Rosmarie Bodenheimer, *The Politics of Story in Victorian Social Fiction* (Ithaca: Cornell University Press, 1988); Joseph W. Childers, *Novel Possibilities: Fiction and the Formation of Early Victorian Culture* (Philadelphia: University of Penn Press, 1995); Justin Prystash, "Rhizomatic Subjects," *Nineteenth-Century Literature* 66, no. 2 (2011): 141–69; Alan Rauch, "The Tailor Transformed: Kingsley's *Alton Locke* and the Notion of Change," *Studies in the Novel* 25, no. 2 (1993): 196–213; Stanwood S. Walker, "'Backwards and Backwards Ever': Charles Kingsley's Racial-Historical Allegory and the Liberal Anglican Revisioning of Britain," *Nineteenth-Century Literature* 62, no. 3 (2007): 339–79; C. J. W.-L. Wee, "Christian Manliness and National Identity: The Problematic Construction of a Racially 'Pure' Nation," in *Muscular Christianity: Embodying the Victorian Age*, ed. Donald E. Hall (Cambridge: Cambridge University Press, 1994), 66–88. Also see Vance, *Sinews of the Spirit: The Ideal of Christian Manliness in Victorian Literature and Religious Thought*. For Kingsley's relationship to later Victorian masculinities, see James Eli Adams, *Dandies and Desert Saints: Styles of Victorian Masculinity* (Ithaca: Cornell University Press, 1995).

contrary also held true for him."[19] While such clarity may have helped Kingsley scholars better understand his own conceptions of "manliness" as descriptions of humanity rather than masculinity, the evidence that he was thinking more in terms of species than gender is particularly clear in his early writings.

Second, although often remembered for his "muscular Christians," Kingsley insists that the incarnation must be good news for those who are not masters of their environments. The gospel must be good news for the poor, the working man, and the prostitute, not just the middle class. This sentiment drives Mackaye's rejection of Emersonian philosophy in *Alton Locke* because, as he explains, in Mr. Windrush's system "every puir fellow as has no gret brains in his head will be left to his superstition, an' his ignorance to fulfil the lusts o' his flesh .... A pretty Gospel for the publicans an' harlots, to tell 'em that if their bairns are canny eneugh, they may possibly someday be allowed to believe that there is one God."[20] The same sentiment finally convinces Philammon that Hypatia's philosophy is insufficient. As Philammon puts it, Hypatia's philosophy "had no gospel... for the harlot! No word for the sinner, the degraded [who, according to Hypatia, must] follow her destiny, and be base, miserable, self-condemned."[21]

In Kingsley's thinking, Jesus does not simply welcome the poor, weak, and marginalized of society to offer them a heavenly afterlife. The incarnation functions to reconstitute humanity through Jesus as the cosmic king, making Jesus himself the "the bond of unity" in whom "we are all brothers."[22] This conviction works hand-in-hand with Kingsley's belief that the incarnation affirms material existence, undergirding his concern for the material conditions of the working class and fostering his well-known "Christian Socialism." As he extols his listeners in his "Second Sermon on Cholera":

> If you really believe that you are all brothers, equal in the sight of God and Christ, you will do all you can to save your brothers from sickness and the miseries which follow it. If you really believe that your children are God's children, that at baptism God declares your little ones to be His, you will be ready to take any care or trouble, however new or strange it may seem, to keep your children safe from all foul smells, foul food, foul water, and foul air, that they may grow up healthy, hearty, and cleanly.[23]

---

[19] Klaver, *The Apostle of the Flesh: A Critical Life of Charles Kingsley*, 447–8.
[20] Charles Kingsley, *Alton Locke, Tailor and Poet; an Autobiography* (New York: Oxford University Press, 1983), 231.
[21] *Hypatia*, 2 vols., The Works of Charles Kingsley (Philadelphia: J. F. Taylor and Co, 1899), 2.164.
[22] Kingsley, *Alton Locke*, 359.
[23] "Second Sermon on the Cholera," in *Sermons on National Subjects* (London: Macmillan, 1890), 152.

Yet, Kingsley's views on the incarnation go beyond affirming the goodness of the body and, thus, affirming the importance of caring for people's physical bodies and material circumstances. While such social work is certainly important, in itself it does not adequately represent Kingsley's understanding of the human brotherhood in Christ.

The incarnation, as Kingsley understands it, literally renews the image of God in each and every human being. While interpreting the incarnation as renewing the *imago dei* is not new—it is most strongly associated with the fourth-century Alexandrian theologian Athanasius—it is an interpretation that Protestant theology (with its emphasis on the atonement) frequently ignores, preferring instead to view the incarnation as the necessary condition for Jesus's death to satisfy divine wrath. While his sermons affirm that the death and resurrection of Jesus atone for the sins of humanity, Kingsley does not limit the significance of the incarnation to a precondition of the atonement. Rather, following Maurice, Kingsley understands the incarnation as reconstituting humanity in Jesus rather than Adam.[24] Insofar as British theology in the first half of the nineteenth century is shaped by evangelicalism, it typically identifies individuals with Adam due to sin. As a result, Maurice and Kingsley's recovery of Alexandrian Christology is a significant theological shift because it reorients human identity, insisting on the original narrative of the image of God in each person rather than the narrative of Adam and sin. This is not to say that Maurice and Kingsley deny the marring effects of sin upon human life or creation; both recognize the ongoing destruction of sin and argue that people must work to mitigate its consequences. In Maurice and Kingsley's understanding of the incarnation, Jesus's life is neither solely that of a prophet characterized by exemplary moral teaching that might help make the world a nicer place, nor is Jesus's life a prelude to a priestly atoning act that saves souls in preparation for an ethereal heaven. In Kingsley's Christology, Jesus's mere existence and entire life from conception to resurrection renew and save humanity by making humanity more truly and rightly human. As such, Jesus binds humanity

---

[24] For more on Maurice's Christology, see Paul Dafydd Jones, "Jesus Christ and the Transformation of English Society: The 'Subversive Conservatism' of Frederick Denison Maurice," *Harvard Theological Review* 96, no. 2 (2003): 205–28; Jeremy Morris, *F. D. Maurice and the Crisis of Christian Authority* (New York: Oxford University Press, 2005).

together, making each individual equal to every other person, be they a worker, a drunk, a harlot, or a parson.[25]

Kingsley represents this reconstituted and unified human identity mythically at the end of *Alton Locke*'s oft-discussed dream sequence, through the veiled prophetess. In the scene, a veiled woman appears to Alton and declares a vision of renewed human brotherhood, restored to Paradise. She concludes:

> Out of Paradise you came, from liberty, equality, and brotherhood, and unto them you shall return again. You went forth in unconscious infancy—you shall return in thoughtful manhood.—You went forth in ignorance and need—you shall return in science and wealth, philosophy and art. You went forth with the world a wilderness before you—you shall return when it is a garden behind you. You went forth selfish-savages—you shall return as the brothers of the Son of God.[26]

While Stanwood S. Walker declares the passage a "bald absurdity," it is a poetic statement of Maurice and Kingsley's shared theology.[27] And, when read carefully, the passage is dense with biblical allusions that make sense only in light of the prophetic language of Genesis, Psalms, Isaiah, and Revelation.[28] Each allusion bears a traditional link to Jesus as both the author and perfecter of human identity, be it in the *imago dei* of Genesis, the Psalmist's cry for messianic renewal both individually and corporately, Isaiah's promises of individual and communal salvation that are appropriated by the gospel narratives and liturgy surrounding

---

[25] Putting Kingsley and Maurice's thinking on Christian brotherhood into practice in mid-century England was not always easy: the Christian Socialists' attempts to reform society through conversations with the working class and Chartists were frequently highly paternalistic and resulted in little actual reform. For more on Kingsley's work with the Christian Socialists and the realities of working-class agency, see chapter 10 "Christian Socialism and Cooperative Association," in *Reform Acts: Chartism, Social Agency, and the Victorian Novel, 1832–1867*, ed. Chris R. Vanden Bossche (Baltimore: Johns Hopkins University Press, 2014).

[26] Kingsley, *Alton Locke*, 350.

[27] Walker, "'Backwards and Backwards Ever': Charles Kingsley's Racial-Historical Allegory and the Liberal Anglican Revisioning of Britain."

[28] See bracketed citations in the following quote for the biblical cross-references: Out of Paradise you went (Gn 3:23-24), and unto Paradise you shall return (Re 21:1-3); you shall become once more as little children (Mt 18:3), and renew your youth like the eagle's (Ps 103:5, Is 40:31). Feature by feature, and limb by limb, ye shall renew it (Ps 104:29-31); age after age, gradually and painfully, by hunger and pestilence, by superstitions and tyrannies, by need and blank despair, shall you be driven back to the All-Father's home, till you become as you were before you fell, and left the likeness of your father for the likeness of the beasts (Gn 1:26; 5:1). Out of Paradise you came, from liberty, equality, and brotherhood, and unto them you shall return again. You went forth in unconscious infancy—you shall return in thoughtful manhood.—You went forth in ignorance and need (Gn 3:17-21)—you shall return in science and wealth, philosophy and art (Rv 21:26). You went forth with the world a wilderness before you (Ex 13:18-20)—you shall return when it is a garden behind you (Rev 21:1-3). You went forth selfish-savages—you shall return as the brothers of the Son of God (Heb 2:9-12).

Jesus's birth, or the paradigm of creation and recreation (also frequently thought of in terms of death and rebirth) in the parallel passages of Genesis and Revelation. Moreover, the final vision pointing to the city of God in Revelation not only anticipates Jesus's awaited return to earth in Christian eschatology but also the ongoing work of renewal that the church is (supposedly) carrying on in his absence—the very work upon which Kingsley's Christian Socialism insisted. Throughout the passage the incarnation as a harbinger of Jesus's ultimate reign functions as the unnamed force in each allusion, giving coherence to Kingsley's vision of human renewal.

The third impact of the incarnation on Kingsley's thinking grows from his belief in the goodness of the material world and his sense that Jesus must offer something more than simply heavenly rest for those who cultivate a refined spirituality. Because of the incarnation, Kingsley insists that God is knowable in human, relational terms. For Kingsley, knowledge of God begins in empiricism (he was a good Lockean in his epistemology, if not in his ideas about human identity). People can only know what they experience through the material world. As *Yeast's* Lancelot Smith declares, when asked what he believes in, "In the earth I stand on, and the things I see walking and growing on it."[29] So, as Lancelot goes on to explain, empiricism requires that God make himself through the material world: "if He who made me intended me to think of spirit first, He would have let me see it first. But as He has given me material senses, and put me in a material world, I take it as a fair hint that I am meant to use those senses first, whatever may come after."[30] The incarnation is the obvious answer to this demand for a material revelation. Moving beyond human deduction about God's character from the natural world, the incarnation presents humanity with a God who can be known as a historical person. As Kingsley writes in August of 1842 to Fanny, "The Christian religion is all through anthropomorphic, or suited to the intellect and feelings of finite man, and proposing the worship of a God, not only manifested as similar to us in intellect and feelings, but even incarnate in a human body."[31] Through the incarnation, God becomes a character whom human beings can "relate to." Through Jesus, God becomes a person with whom others can sympathize, a person whom others can understand and come to know.

---

[29] Kingsley, *Yeast; Poems*, 159.
[30] Kingsley, *Yeast; Poems*, 159–60.
[31] *Letters & Memoirs*, 1.62.

Kingsley's insistence on the knowability of God in human terms continues throughout his writing. In October of 1842, Kingsley praises the Bible, not because of its propositional truths but because of its anthropomorphic nature:

> It... is all about earth, and men, and women, and marriage, and birth and death, food and raiment, trees and animals; and God, not as He is in Himself, but as He has shown Himself in relation to the earth, and its history, and the laws of humanity. And all attempts at arriving at the contemplation of God as He is in Himself,... have ended in forgetfulness of the Incarnation.[32]

In 1858 Kingsley again writes to John Bullar expressing the necessity of the incarnation to human understanding of God:

> The doctrine of Christ and His apostles is, that man is made in God's likeness, and that therefore man's goodness, justice, love, are patterns of God's, and mirrors in which he may see what his heavenly Father is like. The doctrine of Christ and His apostles is, that Christ's incarnation proves this. That Christ manifested the Father, and showed to men the exact likeness of God's character, not by being a good angel, or good anything else, save a good man. And, therefore, when you impute to God feelings or acts which would be inhuman in any and every sense in you or me, you deny the meaning of our Lord's incarnation.[33]

Kingsley's insistence in this passage on the agreement between divine and human ideals of goodness is foundational to his understanding of God's knowability. If God is fundamentally and always "other," then Jesus, as a human being, does not fully reveal God's character. Similarly, if Jesus fully reveals God but remains unknowable or unsympathetic to others, then Jesus is not fully human—he becomes a "good angel," akin to the sentimentalized, infantilized Jesus of Christmas celebrations and Sunday School lessons. Kingsley's understanding of the Christian tradition is that Jesus is fully human *and* fully reveals God. Consequently, he must be knowable just like any other human being is knowable—a historical character to whom people can relate and sympathize. And, because this same historical figure reveals the fullness of God, humanity can also know God. Jesus's full divinity is why Kingsley so vehemently dismisses— and even derides—the "Manichean" tendencies in any Christian tradition that insists upon God's ultimately mysterious character or any tradition that deems the material world a hinderance to knowing God. In Kingsley's view, anyone who denies the possibility of knowing and relating to God denies the incarnation, be they Roman Catholics, Tractarians, evangelicals, dissenters, or pagans.

---

[32] *Letters & Memoirs*, 1.90.
[33] *Letters & Memoirs*, 2.93.

Because true human identity is made known through Jesus, Kingsley's understanding of the incarnation has significant narrative consequences, too. In Kingsley's writing, a fictional character can only reach a narrative resolution involving a true realization of her or his identity through an encounter with Jesus, since he alone reveals true human identity. Granted, these endings reinforce the work of empire and involve anti-Semitic turns against Jewish characters, along with turns against political and economic elites. Such structural moves are tremendous problems in Kingsley's thinking, not least because of his view of the incarnation. Despite such reflections of the racist and paternalistic attitudes that justify empire, Kingsley's understanding of the incarnation still inevitably leads to his experimental, mysterious, and critically derided endings. In the 1851 book-edition of *Yeast*, the prophetic Barnakill's final lines direct Lancelot to "a living temple... Jesus Christ—THE MAN."[34] In *Alton Locke* the solution to Alton's yearnings for social equality and economic justice is found in "Jesus who died upon the cross."[35] Finally, in *Hypatia*, the fulfillment of Raphael Ben Ezra's philosophical inquiries and his national narrative are found in "the Galilean."[36] While such endings feel like a deviation or sloppiness in Kingsley's form, these narratives that conclude in conversion and theological mystery are better read as a form of narrative experimentation growing directly from Kingsley's understanding of the incarnation, an understanding that demands characters find their narrative resolution in the person of Jesus.

The Re-formed Conversion Narrative

Kingsley's insistence upon the centrality of the incarnation leads him to experiment with character resolution grounded in an encounter with Jesus. The problem is that this same insistence on the incarnation, combined with Kingsley's commitment to realism, means that Jesus is not just a sacrificial victim. He is the cosmic king who unites all people through himself; he is simultaneously a real, robust, historical human character. But, because Jesus had been marginalized in the eighteenth-century evangelical conversion narrative's structure, Kingsley had little narrative precedent for exactly what Jesus might look like as a novel character with narrative agency.

---

[34] Kingsley, *Yeast; Poems*, 333.
[35] Kingsley, *Alton Locke*, 359.
[36] *Hypatia*, 243, 90–1.

Unsurprisingly, within *Alton Locke*, the novel in which Jesus makes the most significant appearance, Kingsley's attempt to bring Jesus to life insists upon affirming the materiality of the incarnation and the knowability of Jesus. But materiality presents more of a challenge than one might realize, because materiality necessitates particularity. Since Jesus was a historical person in a real body, he cannot be represented in a text through a modern-day Christ figure or Jesus-like character because such a character would undermine the historical, material specificity of the incarnation as Kingsley understood it. Likewise, a purely imaginative encounter with the historical Jesus mediated through the Bible would undermine the embodied, relational aspects of the incarnation. This puts Kingsley in a bind. How can a novel affirm the bodily, material, relational elements of the incarnation, and affirm the historical particularity of Jesus as a first-century carpenter and preacher, and be set in the nineteenth century—all at the same time? Kingsley's restructured conversion narrative in *Alton Locke* is hardly ideal, but it is an important attempt to bring Jesus to life through the novel, while being true to orthodoxy, history, and human experience at the same time.

Alton Locke tells the story of a working-class boy's journey to manhood as he searches for an identity. He is a poet of the people, a Chartist, and a tailor; but none of these identities quite work. In the end, he finds his vocation as a writer through an encounter with Jesus and, upon writing his autobiography in light of his conversion, he dies. Given the intense scrutiny that the novel gives to the writing and publishing industry, working-class rights and economic hardship, and Alton's ongoing quest to gain Lillian and achieve poetic freedom, the work is often read as both a "condition of England" novel and a working-class *Bildungsroman*.[37] But reading the novel as essentially either of these forms leads

---

[37] Building on Catherine Gallagher's work on the individual and Rosemarie Bodenheimer's consideration of *Alton Locke*'s fragmentary form, scholarship has focused on Kingsley's representations of the working-class individual, Chartism, constructions of masculinity, and engagement with science. While not totally silent on religion, most scholars treat it as a socio-political force rather than an alternate epistemology and value system. See Alderson, "The Anatomy of the British Polity: *Alton Locke* and Christian Manliness," 43–61; Bodenheimer, *The Politics of Story in Victorian Social Fiction*; Catherine Gallagher, *The Industrial Reformation of English Fiction: Social Discourse and Narrative Form 1832–1867* (Chicago: University of Chicago Press, 1985); Anne Graziano, "The Death of the Working-Class Hero in *Mary Barton* and *Alton Locke*," *JNT: Journal of Narrative Theory* 29, no. 2 (1999): 135–57; Richard Menke, "Cultural Capital and the Scene of Rioting: Male Working-Class Authorship in *Alton Locke*," *Victorian Literature and Culture* 28, no. 1 (2000): 87–108; Prystash, "Rhizomatic Subjects," 141–69; Rauch, "The Tailor Transformed: Kingsley's *Alton Locke* and the Notion of Change," 196–213; *Useful Knowledge: The Victorians, Morality, and "the March of the Intellect"* (Durham, NC: Duke University Press, 2001); Richard Salmon, "'The Unaccredited Hero': *Alton Locke*, Thomas Carlyle, and the Formation of the Working-Class Intellectual," in *The Working-Class Intellectual in Eighteenth- and Nineteenth-Century Britain*, ed. Aruna Krishnamurthy (Surrey: Asgate, 2009), 167–94; Walker, "'Backwards and Backwards Ever': Charles Kingsley's Racial-Historical Allegory and the Liberal Anglican Revisioning of Britain," 339–79; Wee, "Christian Manliness and National Identity: The Problematic Construction of a Racially 'Pure' Nation," 66–88.

to frustration. In reality, *Alton Locke* is better understood, not as a *Bildungsroman* (a decidedly middle-class form), but as a working-class conversion narrative. As discussed in Chapter 1, both the *Bildungsroman* and conversion narratives share many similar features, but their end goal is different. The narrative work of the *Bildungsroman* is to integrate the protagonist into middle-class society, bringing about a middle-class identity and sense of agency in the process. Conversion narratives also work toward integration, but they find narrative resolution by integrating the protagonist into the community of believers without altering class identity, bringing about a new psycho-spiritual identity and (at least in content, suggest) a much more ambivalent sense of agency.

Read as a *Bildungsroman*, Kingsley's attempt to create an alternative characterization for a working-class protagonist angry about the state of British society is revolutionary. But such an attempt is also problematic. The "self" Kingsley fashions in *Alton Locke* is an inherently unstable self, a self without a clear voice or coherent personality whose defining characteristics are material poverty and personal desire. He lacks material possessions, he lacks a voice, he lacks a stable personality, and he lacks the power to change his psychological or material circumstances. Primarily, Alton is characterized by *lack* and by the desire that comes from such absence. His lack of a core personality functions as a marker of Alton's particular, class-defined subjectivity—it is also a significant deviation from the typical patterns of characterization in realist fiction.

The notion of a core self or central personality provides a foundation for virtually all considerations of characters within realist novels. An essentially Lockean notion, the core self is the agent who records experiences in memory, becoming an individuated character over time. Deidre Lynch describes "Locke's individual" as "the cumulative product of his private stockpile of sensations and reflections."[38] The problem, as Lynch notes, is that Locke's sense of the initial personality as a blank slate still involves a preexisting mind with both the agency and capacity to "inscribe" memories, a process that is always interpretive, particularly when it is performed by the character within a novel.[39] Thus, Locke's "model tracing the formation of the subject does not, from a modern vantage point, seem to offer satisfactory answers to the questions it raises about the relations between wholes and parts and between the self and its properties."[40]

---

[38] Lynch, *The Economy of Character: Novels, Market Culture, and the Business of Inner Meaning*, 85.
[39] Lynch, *The Economy of Character: Novels, Market Culture, and the Business of Inner Meaning*, 34.
[40] Lynch, *The Economy of Character: Novels, Market Culture, and the Business of Inner Meaning*, 85.

While this ambiguity remains, the Lockean self with its authoritative core shaped by experience remains the model of selfhood when discussing character within the novel.

Scholarly efforts to move away from the middle-class *Bildungsroman* have not managed to move away from Locke. In his examinations of working-class autobiographies, Richard Salmon does not challenge the basic assumption of a core self when he cites Thomas Carter's *Memoirs of a Working-Man* as an important formal source for *Alton Locke* and Kingsley's friend Thomas Cooper as a significant model for Alton himself.[41] For Salmon, while Alton's "self-imposed toil of intellectual improvement" reflects a "truncated development, of intellectual potential unrealized," it remains a *self-imposed* project. The "images of fractured or dismembered wholeness suggest the awareness... of the difficulties of adapting the Goethean ideal of *Bildung*—the development of a complex, multiform subjectivity towards a state of harmonious self-integration—to the material circumstances of working-class self-education."[42] Moreover, the very form of a "working-class" autobiography creates a complicated formal situation because "the 'rise' of [autobiography] during the early nineteenth century [was associated] with an emerging middle-class cultural hegemony," in that such autobiographies "raised the question 'of whether in embracing literature as a means of discovering itself the working class had sacrificed its cultural independence at the very outset.'"[43] Despite examining these difficulties of character, class, and form, Salmon does not challenge his own assumption of the normative Lockean self. Since Alton is never a "defined central character," reevaluating Lockean assumptions about the relationship between selfhood, agency, and coherence might prove helpful in understanding Alton's development.[44]

Regardless of whether or not it is an accurate representation of real working-class subjectivity, *Alton Locke* is revolutionary because it does not assume that the relatively stable, authoritative individual subjectivity of middle-class narratives

---

[41] Richard Salmon, *The Formation of the Victorian Literary Profession* (Cambridge: Cambridge University Press, 2013), 140.

[42] Salmon, "'The Unaccredited Hero': *Alton Locke*, Thomas Carlyle, and the Formation of the Working-Class Intellectual," 180.

[43] Salmon, "'The Unaccredited Hero': *Alton Locke*, Thomas Carlyle, and the Formation of the Working-Class Intellectual," 184.

[44] See Lynch, *The Economy of Character: Novels, Market Culture, and the Business of Inner Meaning*; Watt, *Rise*. Also see Salmon, "Unaccredited Hero," 167–94; *Formation of the Victorian Literary Profession*.

is normative. By construing Alton's sense of self in ways that go against narratives like *Jane Eyre* or *Great Expectations*, *Alton Locke* argues that the idea of the more-or-less coherent, self-authorizing individual is a middle-class construct and offers instead an alternative model of the self: a self characterized by lack, even the lack of a core personality.

The problem with *Alton Locke* as a *Bildungsroman*, then, is that the most obvious "solutions" to Alton's material and psychological needs will, in some way or other, fill these voids. However, by satisfying Alton's desires, such solutions simultaneously negate Alton's primary character. Making matters worse, Alton is committed to his class and bound by his class—it is a working-class identity that he cannot deny and does not wish to escape. To remain a working-class, communal self, Alton recognizes that he must find some form of structural, material, and relational transformation that does not inadvertently make him a middle-class self. Consequently, Alton seeks more than economic mobility. Alton repeatedly rejects material improvement as a sufficient answer for his aspirations because better living and working conditions still fail to bring about systemic change, leaving "the people"—his friends—without social and political authority. For much of the novel, Alton locates the answer to his desire in the realm of politics, treating "poetry, science, and democracy" as his religion.[45] In the end, these were only sufficient "to leave a mighty hunger in [his] heart," but he "knew not for what."[46] For a time, Alton imagines that his love for Lillian would satisfy the definitional lack at the center of his character; but at the novel's conclusion he realizes that this, too, is an illusion.

Rather than a hole that needs filling through material possessions, the right to vote, or romantic love, Alton's characteristic longing is grounded in his lack of authority, a problem that is represented in clearly Lockean terms by the manipulation of his authorship. If the core Lockean self is the memory-inscribing consciousness, then the efforts of Dean Winnstay to censor Alton's poems—preventing Alton from inscribing his Chartist politics and class frustration—represent the ultimate negation of Alton's character. The solution to Alton's neediness, both within the story and in terms of the novel's form, must be located in Alton's act of writing, of voicing his own life. But, to do this *sui generis*, out of his own agency, is impossible because to do so would be to mark

---

[45] Kingsley, *Alton Locke*, 2.77.
[46] Kingsley, *Alton Locke*, 2.77.

Alton as a fundamentally middle-class self, a self-sufficient consciousness who is no longer "of the people."

Alton does not need a patron like Dean Winnstay or even a mentor like Mackaye; both threaten to override Alton's inscription of his own voice. Only a dialogue that calls forth Alton's voice—empowering him by creating space for Alton's self-inscription—can both maintain Alton's definitional lack of agency *and* activate his character as a memory-inscribing self. The difficulty lies, however, in finding such a dialogue partner. And the search for a dialogue partner is where we return to the need for a material and historical characterization of Jesus. As a result of Kingsley's beliefs about the incarnation as the moment when God enters the material world, affirming both its valuable otherness and its simultaneous need for the divine self, the only dialogue that can authorize Alton's identity while affirming his definitional lack is a dialogue with Jesus. And, because of the incarnation's affirmation of the material world and the novel's nineteenth-century setting, this encounter must be mediated through the Christian community.[47]

To represent Alton's search and eventual discovery of this authorizing dialogue, Kingsley turns to a well-known narrative tradition, the evangelical conversion narrative. The evangelical conversion narratives of the eighteenth century offer a significant narrative tradition of selfhood—even working-class selfhood—that emphasizes a fundamentally unstable and undefined self that only finds coherence through an experience of divine dialogue. Furthermore, these widely read accounts also provide a formal tradition that helps explain the presence of Jesus in *Alton Locke*, particularly at the novel's beginning and end. Although the evangelical conversion narrative was dying out by the mid-nineteenth century as a discrete genre of life writing, its form was already deeply engrained in the culture.[48] When one had a conversion "experience," it was

---

[47] Kingsley's belief in the power of dialogue also shaped his politics and vision for class reconciliation, as Chris Vanden Bossche discusses in chapter 10 of *Reform Acts: Chartism, Social Agency, and the Victorian Novel, 1832–1867*.

[48] As Richard Salmon points out, in the early 1980s David Vincent suggested in *Bread, Knowledge, and Freedom: A Study of Working-Class Autobiography* that the conversion narrative is a formal influence on Alton Locke that was familiar to "vernacular culture." In the same analysis, Salmon also notes Kingsley's hostility to Goethe in his "objection on religious grounds to the autonomous cultivation of the self at the exclusion of acknowledging a dependence on God." Even Allan John Hartley points to the role of the conversion narrative as a structuring form for Kingsley's novels. Yet, despite the obvious link between conversion narratives and *Alton Locke*, the influence of the conversion narrative—and particularly the evangelical conversion narrative—on Kingsley's *characterization* has been entirely neglected. See Salmon, *Formation of the Victorian Literary Profession*, 160, 71. Also Allan John Hartley, *The Novels of Charles Kingsley: A Christian Socialist Interpretation* (Folkstone: The Hour-Glass Press, 1977), 19–20.

understood in terms of a dramatic spiritual crisis famously encoded by John Wesley's "strangely warmed" heart.[49] Given the predominance of evangelicalism, it is not a historical stretch to assume that, when Kingsley wrote a novel ending in conversion, it would reflect the common features of an evangelical conversion narrative. Looking to this autobiographical genre reveals that what scholars have perceived as a problematic character coming to a problematic resolution in *Alton Locke* is actually an alternate narrative tradition that understands the individual in profoundly different terms.

As discussed in Chapter 1, the evangelical conversion narrative is a particular subset of autobiographical conversion narratives growing out of the traditions of Puritan spirituality, flourishing, as the name suggests, through the evangelical movement of the eighteenth century and dying out in the nineteenth century. The original manuscripts for these evangelical conversion narratives, some of which reflect a very limited level of literacy, were often published as letters and magazine features for readers across broad cross-sections of society.[50] These narratives "appear in clusters" and make frequent use of popular hymns, pointing to the profoundly communal nature of the narratives.[51] Moreover, the shared language of hymnody upon which these narratives draw is particularly significant. In the eighteenth century, hymnody was a new mode of expressing first-person religious experience, but the works were intended for communal singing. As such, the interplay between the self, God, and the community represented by hymns is an apt model for the self depicted in these conversion narratives. Like hymns, evangelical conversion narratives record a unique charismatic religious experience that shaped the community, even as they were shaped by the pre-existing traditions of that community, thereby presenting a model of identity that "qualifies the notion of self-fashioning."[52]

---

[49] David Bebbington provides a helpful examination of the institutionalization of the "conversion experience" and its forms in the nineteenth century in *Evangelicalism in Modern Britain*, 5–10. The evangelical conversion narrative strongly influenced Victorian autobiography, even among the non-religious. For the influence of the conversion narrative in Victorian autobiography, see Richard Hughes Gibson and Timothy Larsen, "Nineteenth-Century Spiritual Autobiography: Carlyle, Mill, Newman," in *A History of English Autobiography*, ed. Adam Smyth (Cambridge: Cambridge University Press, 2015).

Although Kingsley was not an evangelical in terms of his church party affiliation, he was profoundly shaped by his evangelical mother and was conversant with the tradition. His complaint against evangelicalism was its tendency to be unthinking in terms of doctrine, science, and the arts. Nowhere does he express any argument with evangelicalism's emphasis on experiential conversion as typified in conversion narratives. For more, see the introduction in Klaver, *The Apostle of the Flesh: A Critical Life of Charles Kingsley*.

[50] Hindmarsh, *The Evangelical Conversion Narrative: Spiritual Autobiography in Early Modern England*, 71.

[51] Hindmarsh, *The Evangelical Conversion Narrative: Spiritual Autobiography in Early Modern England*, 62, 64.

[52] Hindmarsh, *The Evangelical Conversion Narrative: Spiritual Autobiography in Early Modern England*, 6.

Within these evangelical conversion narratives "the recovery of a right relationship with God" is "the great desideratum of human life."[53] These narratives often begin with the shaping influence of the home and "world" on the self, frequently highlighting the inadequacies of an individual's religious background and, at times, a longing for something transcendent. The narrative then moves through a wayward period in which the individual attempts to discover some sense of direction, purpose, or satisfaction in life, sometimes involving a preliminary conversion or a conversion to what is later perceived as a partial truth. Yet, even when one's business, social, and personal ventures are successful, the individual remains unsatisfied. Finally, the individual is presented with the gospel—usually in the form of a sermon or conversation with another evangelical—and experiences some sort of supernatural interaction with God. The subject will reflect briefly on the ways in which God has made him or her a "new" person and satisfied his or her deepest longings, summarizing their ongoing life as a Christian before concluding the narrative.[54]

Within these accounts the self is embedded in a complex world of material circumstances that is in part divinely ordained and in part "the will of the world and of the devil"—a tension frequently identified as the key source of ambivalence in *Alton Locke*.[55] Yet this tension is hardly a fatal inconsistency in the setting of the conversion narrative; to the contrary, this very tension characterizes the supernatural reality of a world ruled by God but occupied by the devil. Furthermore, most of the narrative focus is on the false attempts at selfhood, the life spent in "sin," which makes sense because such misadventures are typically full of narrative action, close-calls, and suspense. The individual can only be delivered from this narratively exciting life of sin through a definitive break with the past (figured frequently as the "death of the Old Man") and a subsequent rebirth. As a result, the post-conversion "self" narrating the conversion is always markedly different from the "self" depicted throughout the narrative, making

---

[53] Hindmarsh, *The Evangelical Conversion Narrative: Spiritual Autobiography in Early Modern England*, 8.
[54] Hindmarsh explains that, by the late eighteenth century, English Dissenters had individuals provide oral or written versions of their conversions as "part of a public profession of orthodox belief." Consequently, individuals "learned the grammar" of conversion before experiencing it for themselves (287, 296). In these conversion narratives, the individual treated their religious upbringing within the dissenting community as God's way of preparing them for salvation. Thus, the individual self is also part of a communal salvation narrative in which individual agency, divine providence, and the deterministic forces of sin are at work in each individual and in the community at large, leading to "identities [that are] bestowed supernaturally" on the individual through conversion (10). For more on the formalization of this particular conversion narrative, see Hindmarsh, chapter 9.
[55] Kingsley, *Alton Locke*, 2.

the evangelical conversion narrative "an authoritative act of retrospective self-interpretation."[56]

Somewhat ironically, these narrative practices are precisely what make Alton's characterization so markedly different from the typical novelistic practices for characterizing the Lockean self referenced in Alton's surname. Alton "does not gradually merge with the narrator," achieving literary atonement in typical novel fashion; "rather he becomes the narrator by gradually dissolving and being reborn."[57] Such rebirth certainly "mak[es]... normal characterization obsolete" but not because "it generates a narrative about the near impossibility of becoming a self."[58] Alton's dissolution and rebirth make normal characterization "obsolete" because it is grounded in a different understanding of human selfhood and human agency.

Alton's retrospective characterization of himself grows out of an understanding of human identity in which individual agency is activated and authorized by Jesus, the model of human perfection authorized by divine agency. On the most literal level in the narrative, this rebirth into a divinely authorized identity happens through Eleanor's commissioning of Alton's autobiography, which is presented as an unmanipulated act of self-inscription resulting in the text of *Alton Locke*. Yet, the interaction between Eleanor and Alton that leads to *Alton Locke*'s writing is really Alton's encounter with Jesus through Eleanor. As such, it is Jesus who authorizes Alton's act of self-inscription in *Alton Locke*. Within evangelical conversion narratives, an experience like Alton's—affirmed by the reading community's shared experience of rebirth into a divinely authorized identity—is made possible through a relationship with Jesus.

For *Alton Locke* the challenge is that, while the community within the text affirms Alton's identity, this textual community does not necessarily include the reader. Kingsley clearly wants readers to affirm Alton's new identity. But, in keeping with Kingsley's theology of the incarnation, Alton's conversion is predicated on a supernatural encounter with Jesus—and not with the biblical text, as is traditional in eighteenth-century evangelical conversion narratives. While this shift from an encounter with the Bible to an encounter with Jesus reflects Kingsley's emphasis on the primacy of the incarnation, it also means

---

[56] Hindmarsh, *The Evangelical Conversion Narrative: Spiritual Autobiography in Early Modern England*, 323.
[57] Gallagher, *The Industrial Reformation of English Fiction: Social Discourse and Narrative Form 1832–1867*, 96.
[58] Gallagher, *The Industrial Reformation of English Fiction: Social Discourse and Narrative Form 1832–1867*, 96.

that Kingsley has to bring Jesus to life within the imagination of the reader. Even if readers are sympathetic to Alton's experience of conversion as a general principle, if Alton's vision of Jesus is not compelling—if he is weak, distant, passive, or simply boring—Alton's assertion of self-discovery in Jesus becomes unbelievable and even farcical, undermining the novel's conclusion and, retrospectively, Alton's characterization throughout the novel. Essentially, *Alton Locke*'s narrative resolution and aesthetic coherence depend on Kingsley's ability to resurrect Jesus as a revolutionary, divine-and-human king within the novel.

Kingsley's characterization of Jesus begins early in *Alton Locke*. Jesus's name is everywhere, cropping up in missions to the working class, church societies, church parties, and the like. But in each instance, the name Jesus is a "watchword o' exclusiveness."[59] In fact, it seems as if the more frequently "Jesus's name is bandied about, the less influential he is in the scene. At the end of the book, when Jesus is most present in the narrative, his name is almost entirely absent, with Eleanor referring to him through capitalized pronouns and titles. This play between signifier and real presence highlights the importance of understanding Jesus as a bodily and narrative reality that must be respected in his own right, as opposed to a name that can be appropriated at will for a character's own purposes or presented as a token of culturally appropriate piety and social acceptance. To separate Jesus from sentimental domestic ideals, religious baggage, and scholarship, Kingsley develops competing characterizations of Jesus that represent common religious and cultural uses of his character, only to suggest all these representations are inadequate. In the end, *Alton Locke* creates a vision of Jesus as an older brother who is defined by his friendship with believers rather than his sacrificial death.

To understand Kingsley's final characterization of Jesus, we need to first understand the many competing characterizations the novel offers. Jesus's first appearance pits Alton's hope for a loving Jesus against the Calvinistic Jesus of his Particular Baptist mother.[60] In the opening chapter, Alton's mother views God as an all-powerful overlord who has predestined the fate of each individual soul. As such, she refuses even to pray for Alton's conversion because "her clear logical sense would yield to no such tender inconsistency."[61] Because she insists that Alton "had 'no part nor lot' [of Jesus] till [he] was 'converted,'" she does not even

---

[59] Kingsley, *Alton Locke*, 208.
[60] The Particular Baptists (sometimes called Strict and Particular Baptists) were a sect of Baptists that split from the Independent Baptists in the seventeenth century. They were a closed-communion sect who held a strict doctrine of election and insisted on adult baptism.
[61] Kingsley, *Alton Locke*, 8.

read him stories of Jesus, preferring instead Old Testament narratives. Alton identifies "fear" as the "only motive" in his religious education, represented by the "gods... [of] hell, the rod, the ten commandments, and public opinion."[62]

Despite his mother's religion, Alton "yearns" for Jesus, going so far as to write a hymn about Jesus's love for children.[63] While the hymn is indebted to Wesley's "Gentle Jesus, Meek and Mild"—borrowing its tone, meter, and even Wesley's first line—Alton's hymn emphasizes Jesus's love through its third person meditation on Jesus character.[64] Alton's second stanza in particular focuses on the story of Jesus blessing the children, drawing attention to the historical Jesus by embedding a short narrative from his life within the hymn. The hymn speaks of Jesus's love for "one and all," introducing the idea of Jesus as an inclusive figure, bringing people of all classes together.

But Alton's own youthful vision of Jesus is in stark contrast to that of Calvinistic Dissent. One of his mother's pastors, Mr. Wigginton, rebuffs the young Alton for his "bad doctrine," reminding the child that "Jesus does not love one and all.... Christ loves none but His Bride, the Church. His merits, my poor child, extend to none but the elect."[65] Wigginton's subsequent reflection on the privilege of those elected for divine salvation serves to introduce the first and repeated false characterization of Jesus: the exclusive Jesus who offers redemption "only to one human being out of a thousand," leaving " the other nine hundred and ninety-nine... lost and damned from their birth-hour to all eternity—not only by the absolute will and reprobation of God... but... by the mere fact of being born of Adam's race."[66]

While Alton's hymn opens up the possibility of an inclusive Jesus in opposition to the characterization offered by his mother and her pastor, the young Alton still felt his vision of Jesus was missing something. Alton's own emphasis on meekness troubled the young poet, who did "not see... very clearly what to do with [a meek and mild] spirit when [he] obtained" it.[67] Instead, he preferred "to fight material Apollyons with material swords of iron... or to go bear and lion hunting with David."[68] While the desires for material action and adventure are

---

[62] Kingsley, *Alton Locke*, 8.
[63] Kingsley, *Alton Locke*, 18.
[64] For an extensive look at the theology and revisions of Wesley's "Gentle Jesus, Meek and Mild," see Eric J. Sharpe, "'Gentle Jesus, Meek and Mild': Variations on a Nursery Theme, for Congregation and Critic," *Evangelical Quarterly* 53, no. 3 (1981).
[65] Kingsley, *Alton Locke*, 19.
[66] Kingsley, *Alton Locke*, 12.
[67] Kingsley, *Alton Locke*, 18.
[68] Kingsley, *Alton Locke*, 18.

quintessentially Kingsley, these desires further suggest the trajectory for how an authentic Jesus will be characterized. Jesus will be a man of love, but that love will not be passive, meek, or circumscribed by a sacrificial death. An authentic Jesus will demonstrate love through action. He will be a "reformer," "vindicator," and "champion."[69]

Competing characterizations of Jesus continue throughout the novel, and in each instance the novel affirms a vigorous and revolutionary characterization of Jesus. When Alton determines to leave home after coming across two different biblical portraits of Jesus as a son—one in which a passive Jesus submits to his parents as a boy and another in which Jesus the grown man denies his mother—the novel unsurprisingly endorses the active, adult Jesus over the passive child.[70] The emerging characterization of Jesus as a teacher demanding justice for the poor comes into sharp focus when Alton himself points to Jesus in order to contrast the standard of living embraced by the deans and bishops of the Church of England with that of the man they claim to follow. Acknowledging the revolutionary call in Jesus's teachings, Alton argues that although the deans and bishops have few luxuries in terms of their own class, they live extravagantly when their lives are compared to the suffering of the working class and the example of Jesus.[71] Eventually, the novel rejects inadequate characterizations of Jesus outright. Mackaye decries the exclusive Jesus who offers no gospel for the poor; and Alton expresses contempt for the jail chaplain's well-intentioned but utterly insufficient presentation of Jesus, which fails to address Alton's questions about Strauss's *Das Leben Jesu* and the inaction of the church on behalf of the working class.[72]

Throughout most of the novel, the representation of Jesus as a political radical challenges religious and sentimental constructions of Jesus, but throughout it he remains an idea rather than a character in the novel. While the idea of Jesus as a revolutionary leader highlights the politically and religiously subversive Jesus of the biblical text, it does not bring Jesus to life as novel character. As a person from the first century, Jesus cannot exist in the novel's nineteenth century without becoming a disembodied spirit or losing his historical particularity, both of which would undermine Kingsley's commitment to the incarnation. Thus, it is no surprise that, until the novel's conclusion, Jesus is separated from the other characters and closed off from the narrative action.

---

[69] Kingsley, *Alton Locke*, 361.
[70] Kingsley, *Alton Locke*, 53–5.
[71] Kingsley, *Alton Locke*, 158.
[72] Kingsley, *Alton Locke*, 208, 88–9.

In the novel's experimental conclusion, Kingsley uses the liminal space of illness as a narrative annex, making an embodied encounter with Jesus across space and time theoretically possible. This Jesus-centered scene particularly troubles critics, with Alan Hartley describing it as "grotesquely contrived" and "something outside [the story]" and Catherine Gallagher commenting that Alton's dreamworld signals a break with realism.[73] But these assessments are only partly true. Because fever-induced delusions precipitate the scene chronicling Alton's conversion, the entire episode forms, in Suzanne Keen's phrase, a "narrative annex."[74] Following Keen's definition, the conversion scene in *Alton Locke* is a surreal world attached to the real world of the narrative, entered into through the conditions of illness and bounded by Alton's sickroom. Such annexes are not really a break with realism, so much as an identifiable technique that realist novels use to address taboos or issues believed to be unfit for realism. Through these annexes, novelists "solve problems of plotting and characterization... [by] demarking zones in which Victorian novelists struggle to represent improbable, awkward, unsuitable, embarrassing, or downright threatening ideas, characters, actions, and social problems."[75] It is within this narrative annex that Alton is reborn as the narrator by being mystically united with Jesus, who emerges in the scene as both a historical personality and a present character, a revolutionary king who brings about Alton's conversion and acceptance of a divinely constituted identity.

While the narrative annex may be an identifiable textual feature, Jesus's presence in the sickroom scene is not without complications. Unlike the rest of the novel, in which Jesus is a historical figure appropriated, misused, and debated by various characters, Jesus becomes a present character in the final section. But even when he seems present, he is simultaneously a secondhand or reflected presence made manifest through Alton's conversation with Eleanor. To bring Jesus into the novel, Kingsley first merges Eleanor with the veiled prophetess of Alton's dream. Once imbued with semiprophetic, almost magical powers, Eleanor is able to project an image of Jesus through her descriptions of Jesus and his teachings. While this projected Jesus is not the same as an unmediated vision of Jesus, it should be taken seriously as an encounter with Jesus because Alton experiences and narrates it as such, minimizing Eleanor's presence by

---

[73] Hartley, *The Novels of Charles Kingsley: A Christian Socialist Interpretation*, 77; Gallagher, *The Industrial Reformation of English Fiction: Social Discourse and Narrative Form 1832–1867*, 89.
[74] Suzanne Keen, *Victorian Renovations of the Novel: Narrative Annexes and the Boundaries of Representation* (Cambridge: Cambridge University Press, 1998), 1–10, 41.
[75] Keen, *Victorian Renovations of the Novel: Narrative Annexes and the Boundaries of Representation*, 9.

representing her through the litany-like repetition of "she spoke of him as... ." Moreover, within evangelical tradition believers frequently report encountering Jesus through the spoken words of another person, most typically through sermons. Of course, nineteenth-century novels are full of after-the-fact reports of such experiences. What makes Kingsley's approach in *Alton Locke* unique is that, through Alton's narration, Kingsley recreates the actual moment during which the novel's character encounters Jesus, rather than simply reporting that such an encounter took place. As such, it is appropriate to treat Alton's dialogue with Eleanor about Jesus as an actual encounter with Jesus.

The characterization of Jesus that Eleanor gives within the passage is grounded in action and strength, in keeping with the novel's preferred Jesus to this point. Upon awaking from a feverish dream and seeing Raphael's "Miraculous Draught of Fishes," hanging at the foot of his bed, Alton muses on Jesus sitting "in his calm godlike beauty" with his "eye ranging over" the scene of the mountains and lake before him. Set amid the "glassy lake," with the "waters and mountains, receding into the dreamy infinite of the still summer sky," and the imagined "hum of eager multitudes" at its "distant shore," Jesus occupies a decidedly material world. His disciples add to the fleshy image, as the "averted and wily" face of Judas contrasts with "the self-abhorrent humility of Peter, as he shrank down into the bottom of the skiff, and with convulsive palms and bursting brow."[76] Using the painting as the site for the first visual impression of Jesus, Kingsley is able to reflect on the physicality of Jesus and his contemporaries while simultaneously maintaining his historical particularity. This material Jesus set among real men creates the imaginative space for Alton and Eleanor's sickbed conversation.

When Eleanor begins speaking of Jesus, her initial reflections focus on Jesus's strength. She makes use of traditional titles for his office of king, such as "vindicator," "champion," and "king over earth," along with "master," "king," and the one to whom "all power is given."[77] While such titles are standard identifiers of Jesus's royal role in the traditional threefold office, within the political context of novel, they assume a more revolutionary edge. Because these titles are embedded in paragraphs about social revolution, Chartism, and human rights, each title sounds a decidedly earthy and social inflection that reiterates Jesus's character as a man of strength and a leader among men. These titles combine with the emphasis on social revolution to make clear that Jesus is the revolutionary earthly king and not just the heavenly king of the afterlife.

---

[76] Kingsley, *Alton Locke*, 355.
[77] Kingsley, *Alton Locke*, 361.

Within this context, Kingsley turns to Jesus's youth and his temptation, and it is in this scene that Jesus's own presence as a character becomes most vivid. Alton describes the "dawn of [Jesus's] manhood... [when he] went up into the wilderness, as every youth... must" to prove himself.[78] In Alton's imagination, Jesus is not a stagnant, predetermined God ready to conquer Satan. Rather, Jesus has only a "dim consciousness" and "strange yearning presentments" about his power and destiny.[79] In the wilderness, isolated and "alone with the wild beasts, and the brute powers of nature," Jesus is cast as a promethean figure, the archetypal Romantic individual in a sublime, physical world.[80] It is only within this setting that Jesus comes to his own identity. He begins to understand humanity's—and his own—"kingship over earth, [and] His sonship under God."[81] In this growing self-awareness, Jesus's character actually *changes*. It is a small point but an important break from the stagnant Jesus who is always knowing, always loving, and always saving. Kingsley's Jesus is only dimly aware of his own identity as the temptation begins; this makes his yet-unexplored power all the more dangerous because it is not clear at first how he might use that power. As Jesus begins to grow in his self-understanding, he is tempted to use his "creative powers for selfish ends—to yield to the lust of display and singularity... to do one little act of evil" that would secure his own power.[82] But Jesus resists this temptation.

Unlike most engagements with the Jesus narrative, Kingsley grounds Jesus's suffering in his very resistance to temptation. Because he does not secure his own power, Jesus suffers "the agony of calumny, misconception, [and] misinterpretation" as he "fought with bigotry and stupidity."[83] In his Jesus story, Jesus's suffering and the brief narrative's conclusion do not come through the cross. Rather, the suffering that typically concludes Jesus's story comes in the weeping "in the bitterness of disappointed patriotism... when He had tried in vain to awaken within a nation of slavish and yet rebellious bigots the consciousness of their glorious calling."[84] Kingsley's decision to cut the Jesus narrative off at this point reorients Jesus's character away from the inevitability of Calvary and maintains instead the open-ended, indeterminate characterization created in the scene thus far. With this ending, the same Jesus

---

[78] Kingsley, *Alton Locke*, 356.
[79] Kingsley, *Alton Locke*, 356.
[80] Kingsley, *Alton Locke*, 356.
[81] Kingsley, *Alton Locke*, 356.
[82] Kingsley, *Alton Locke*, 356.
[83] Kingsley, *Alton Locke*, 356.
[84] Kingsley, *Alton Locke*, 356.

who learns and grows in the temptation and who experiences disappointment has the potential to keep learning, growing, and facing temptation. As such, he remains a dynamic character in Alton's imagination and, potentially, in the reader's imagination as well.

Kingsley's Jesus is a strong, dynamic, and open-ended character, but he is also a relational human being. The narrative marks his relational potential through a short but complicated allusion in which Alton describes Eleanor speaking like "Mary may have talked just risen from His feet."[85] The ambiguous nature of this reference to "Mary... just risen from his feet" alludes to the entire narrative tradition of women intimate with Jesus, including his mother, but most particularly Mary Magdalene and Mary, Martha's sister. What all the Mary-Jesus narratives have in common are a deep love and transgressive physicality between Mary and Jesus. Mary, Martha's sister, loved Jesus, bucking convention by ignoring her domestic duties to sit at his feet and learn. In anointing Jesus's head and feet at a dinner in Bethany, she publicly handled the body of a man who is not her husband, even though it provoked the ire of Jesus's disciples. She fell at Jesus feet in grief—seeking comfort while expressing her total confidence in his power—and asked him to heal her already dead brother Lazarus. This Mary's devotion to Jesus's body, intellectual engagement with his teaching, and need for his saving strength make her an excellent example of femininity within Kingsley's oft-discussed constructions of gender. That said, Mary Magdalene also adores Jesus. She offers the same bodily devotion as Mary, Martha's sister, but does so out of hopelessness and degradation. As mentioned above, for Kingsley the gospel was not "good news" unless it had something to offer the harlot as well as the philosopher. While Mary Magdalene is no longer recognized as a "fallen woman" by biblical scholars, the Victorian imagination still cast her in the role of forgiven prostitute. And, as the stories associated with Mary Magdalene make clear, she loved Jesus in proportion to the forgiveness she received from him: she is one of only three people to follow him all the way to the cross and to the tomb. She is also, according to the Gospel of John, the first person to see him after his resurrection, at which time she falls to his feet in worship. As such, she becomes the first person to announce the resurrection, carrying the news back to the (male) disciples. Mary Magdalene's devotion to Jesus and role as evangelist also fit well with the bedside description of Eleanor, as she tells Alton about Jesus. The allusive nature of the line "Mary... just risen from [Jesus's] feet"

---

[85] Kingsley, *Alton Locke*, 355.

thus underscores Alton's remark about the "personal" nature of Eleanor's words by raising this web of biblical stories. The Jesus Eleanor speaks about is, for her and for Alton through her, a real man with whom she interacts, a historical individual whom she knows, and a real person with whom she is in dialogue, as she listens and responds to his words of love with acts of love.

While Jesus is dynamic and relational, the novel also characterizes him as frustrated, both emotionally and in terms of his mission, creating distance between the novel's conception of Jesus and popular image of Jesus. When Jesus feels "the agony of calumny, misconception, [and] misinterpretation" and "[fights] with bigotry and stupidity," he is characterized as exasperated, even irritated.[86] Such frustration with the faults of others is not typically viewed as a virtuous trait, which makes Kingsley's Jesus both more human and potentially less perfect in terms of cultural values. But a frustrated Jesus also has solid biblical precedent, making these descriptions surprising but not unfounded.[87] Another humanizing element of this description lies in Jesus's apparent lack of power over the world as it is. He might fight against "bigotry and stupidity," but he does not conquer them. Instead, he weeps in disappointment at his failure to "awaken" the people to their "glorious calling."[88] In many Christian traditions, Jesus meekly accepts his rejection and sets his face toward Jerusalem and the cross, implying that Jesus was not really trying to overcome his rejection or avoid death. Not so in this passage. Kingsley characterizes Jesus's struggle against the brokenness of society and ultimate failure to overcome the status quo as a real and painful fight. And in this failure, Jesus becomes a character with whom Alton, the working-class protagonist characterized by lack, can sympathize.

Ultimately, Jesus's struggle against the status quo and active choice against his own singularity in the temptation scene undergird his characterization as a revolutionary. In fact, the novel asserts that, under Jesus leadership, all revolutionary ideas, "even the most frantic declamations of the French democrat, about the majesty of the people, the divinity of mankind, become rational, reverent, and literal."[89] With the French Revolution a living memory for some of Kingsley's readers and Chartism raising revolutionary fears in Britain,

---

[86] Kingsley, *Alton Locke*, 356.
[87] While a sentimental, meek Jesus was common in Victorian art and piety, the Jesus of the Gospels is not quite so friendly. For example, the first chapter of the Gospel of Mark presents Jesus as having "authority" (1:22), being "stern" (1:25), "indignant" (1:41), and giving "strong warnings[s]" (1:43). Although these words are not apparent in the KJV, as a scholar of Greek and Patristic thinkers, Kingsley would have recognized the harsher language of the original text.
[88] Kingsley, *Alton Locke*, 356.
[89] Kingsley, *Alton Locke*, 362.

such revolutionary claims mark Jesus, once again, as a potentially dangerous (albeit just) political king. That said, these characterizations also answer Alton's deepest longings for social reform, pointing to a society where the working class do not have to become middle class in order to be accorded human dignity. The passage suggests that Jesus's form of revolution redeems the revolutionary ideals that created political and social instability in France because it is Jesus who makes men "free," but also "equals" and "brothers," giving all people "the rights of sons of God," binding all people "in an everlasting covenant."[90] In Kingsley's characterization, Jesus's revolution ends not in bloodshed but in brotherhood.

The problem with Kingsley's attempt to narrate Alton's encounter with Jesus is that, right as the encounter is reaching its culmination, the narrative trails off, interrupted by Alton's (and later Crossthwaite's) weeping.[91] Although Jesus is discussed after this scene ends, the narrative never returns to him with the same storytelling clarity. He becomes a figure to follow whole-heartedly, but what it means to encounter or experience Jesus beyond following his teachings is never articulated or represented within the narrative. In fact, it appears that the only way to appropriately respond to Jesus is through shaping society in accordance with the ideals of human unity represented by Jesus's death for all, a death which makes everyone "children of God, members of Christ, of His body, of His flesh, and of His bones."[92]

While the novel characterizes Jesus in new and intriguing ways, it does not really explain how Alton experiences Jesus and, by extension, how he becomes unified with the narrator. There is some suggestion of a union between character and narrator grounded in Alton's experience of Jesus through the narrative's structure, but this structural union is complicated and problematic. Structurally, Alton's encounter with Jesus takes place through a refracted narration built upon multiple levels of reported conversation. Readers never see Jesus directly, nor does Alton, for that matter. Eleanor, serving in a Beatrice-like role as Alton's guide, describes Jesus as "near" and "watching" them, suggesting that he is an actual presence in the room who sees them. But the only way Jesus is ever "present" to the reader is through Alton's report of Eleanor's description of him. Granted, this description of Jesus is so vivid that Alton "turn[s]...half-startled...expect[ing] to see Him standing by her side."[93]

---

[90] Kingsley, *Alton Locke*, 361.
[91] Kingsley, *Alton Locke*, 357, 65.
[92] Kingsley, *Alton Locke*, 362.
[93] Kingsley, *Alton Locke*, 356.

Now, insofar as readers are "going along" with Alton, they too may experience Jesus as a present character within the scene, and even expect to see Jesus standing in the room next to Eleanor.[94] But if readers are not "going along" with Alton, then the whole scene—and Jesus with it—becomes the unsatisfactory ravings of an ill man.

What Kingsley does not explain in terms of content he attempts to embody in the form: an identity-producing dialogue that brings about a new sort of self, a self that is at once formed by and contingent upon human bodies and human community and, within this unity, still a differentiated consciousness. Significantly, there is no primary agent provoking Alton's conversion in this communally constructed experience of Jesus. Alton is shaped by Jesus through Eleanor, but he must allow himself to go along with Eleanor for his transformation to take place. The reader might see Jesus through Alton listening to Eleanor, but the reader must go along with Alton for this new vision of Jesus to be successful. While the reader or Alton could refuse to participate, neither Alton nor the reader can affect their own transformative vision of Jesus. Likewise, while the agency lies with Jesus through Eleanor, neither Jesus nor Eleanor can effect change in Alton or the reader without consent. Thus, in keeping with Alton's communal vision and Kingsley's commitment to the material world affirmed in the incarnation, nothing in this scene—no vision of Jesus, no understanding of his character, and no new identity—can exist without the participation of multiple, embodied characters.

Assuming that Kingsley wanted Jesus to be a real presence to his readers, his narrative strategy is a calculated risk because Jesus will only be a present and compelling character if readers are sympathetic to Alton. The advantage of Kingsley's form of refracted narration is particularly evident in the list of titles and characteristics with which Alton first introduces Jesus. The characteristics are prefaced by "she spoke of him as…, " reminding the reader that whatever title or characteristic follows is merely a summary of what was actually said. This allows the reader to supply their own mental image of what it means to be a "great Reformer," "inspirer of all new truths," or "champion of the poor," who "had passed victorious through [his] vilest temptations" and "sympathized

---

[94] Alton's experience of listening to Eleanor mirrors the reader's experience of sympathizing with Alton. As Rae Greiner explains, "Sympathetic realism mobilizes the imagination in encouraging readers to 'go along with' the virtual perspectives of others situated in time and space. The historicizing impulse meets the sympathetic in nineteenth-century realism, which depends for both on the power to imagine what it's like to be somebody else, somewhere else entirely." See Greiner, *Sympathetic Realism in Nineteenth-Century British Fiction*, 16–17.

with [his] every struggle."⁹⁵ The effectiveness of such narration is particularly evident in the "vilest temptations" Jesus experiences. Using this indeterminate descriptor forces the reader to supply his or her own most secret and perverse thoughts, whatever they may be. Ascribing such temptations to Jesus makes him disturbingly human, distancing him from sentimentalized characterizations while simultaneously aligning the reader and Jesus in temptation. This both frees the narrative from the burden of articulating what "vilest temptations" look like and increases the likelihood that the reader experiences Jesus and his temptations as "real," since those temptations and relevant emotional connotations are supplied by the reader.

The narrative risk in this structure is that readers will not be convinced enough by Kingsley's portrayal of Alton to sympathize with him in his conversion. If readers do not find themselves sympathetic to Alton, then Alton's description of Jesus will be read as feverish delusions, or (as critics read it) a poorly crafted scene in a poorly crafted novel. Moreover, if readers find Alton unconvincing, overwrought, or otherwise annoying, they may not be willing to perform the readerly work of imaginative participation, negating the work that the relationally contingent structure of the scene is attempting to perform. Such breakdowns in sympathetic identification render Alton's conversion and his rebirth as the narrator ineffective and even unintelligible. In the judgment of most critics, the scene fails to impress because Kingsley is unable to quell his inner preacher, resulting in a lengthy and overly determined sermon. Whether the scene ultimately succeeds or fails in the mind of the reader, Kingsley's desire for readers to understand Jesus as a real, present individual leads to significant formal experimentation: it generates an innovative, multilayered form of narration that attempts to bring Jesus into a single, contemporary scene as a real human character.

Regardless of its success in brining Jesus to life through the novel, *Alton Locke* is instructive because it highlights the extent to which thinking about Jesus as a living character is not simply a theological or cultural problem. While it may be challenging to imagine Jesus as more than a crucified savior, the difficulties in creating the narrative framework to make a present-day encounter with

---

⁹⁵ Kingsley, *Alton Locke*, 356. Caroline Levine's book *The Serious Pleasures of Suspense: Victorian Realism and Narrative Doubt* makes the argument that mid-nineteenth-century realism used suspense to encourage readerly speculation in ways that challenge the status quo. While Kingsley's description of Jesus is not "suspense," his use of veiling allows for the same sort of readerly participation—a participation in which readers must supply their additional knowledge to what is given in the text and speculate, not about the plot, but about the character of Jesus. See Caroline Levine, *The Serious Pleasures of Suspense* (Charlottesvillle: University of Virginia Press, 2003), 8.

Jesus plausible inevitably draw attention to the same questions in real life. How, exactly, is it that people experience Jesus or know Jesus? How is Jesus, in the words of many nineteenth-century hymns, a "friend"? The structural difficulty of representing a contemporary encounter with Jesus raises the vexing question: if an experience is not narratable, is it also not believable?

On one level, the structural problems Kingsley faces are obvious—encounters with divine beings are typically key markers of myth, not narrative realism. But in a culture where intelligent, mentally stable, highly capable people routinely report such an experience, the demands of realism require exactly this sort of formal ingenuity if a writer is going to be able to craft contemporary characters with religious commitments. Moreover, insofar as the realist author is a part of a believing community, as Kingsley was, the charge to make such a narrative project successful becomes all the more urgent for that community's intellectual credibility.

While Kingsley's refracted characterization of Jesus is not without complications, he does manage to make the incarnation, rather than the atonement, the central theological focus in the explicitly Protestant idiom of the conversion narrative. In doing so, Kingsley further underscores the move in English Protestantism and specifically evangelicalism away from thinking about the atonement as the heart of Christianity. Instead, he puts Jesus the cosmic king incarnate at the center of narrative thinking about Christian faith while highlighting the real political, social, and economic implications of Jesus's role as king. And, regardless of Kingsley's literary merit or success, his popularity incites other writers to engage his characterization of Jesus and wrestle for themselves with strategies for making this God-Man present and new to the readerly imagination.

4

Jesus the Reconciling High Priest

Charles Kingsley reimagined Jesus's office as the cosmic king, fleshing out the revolutionary implications of Jesus's kingship and moving the incarnation to the narrative center of the believer's narrative in the process. But despite, or perhaps because of, the increasing attention to Jesus's bodily life, Jesus's traditional office of high priest was both more central to characterizations of Jesus and more troubling for many Victorian Protestants. As high priest for all humanity, Jesus in historical Christian creeds and traditional theologies officiates over the offering of the ultimate sacrifice to God the Father. What is more, the sacrifice is Jesus himself. While such a cultic understanding of Jesus as priest fits nicely with Victorian typological readings of the Hebrew Bible, in which Israelite priests and priestly offerings were interpreted as a type or forerunner for Jesus, Victorians also grew increasingly uncomfortable with this understanding of Jesus as it highlights the teaching that divine wrath demands the blood of the Son. As Andrew Miller points out, "The thought that Jesus suffered for what he had not done came to repulse thoughtful Christians," particularly when this theology characterized God the Father as a tyrant in need of blood and Jesus as the passive victim of divine wrath, ready and willing to save the individual believer.[1] In fact, the more Victorians focused on the incarnation and thus upon Jesus's "real" humanity, the more reasons they found for discomfort with, if not outright revulsion toward, traditional views of Jesus's high priesthood for all humanity. Not only was Jesus also the sacrifice, and the

---

A previous version of this chapter was published as "Not an Average Man? Jesus and the Commonplace Heroic of Adam Bede" in *Victorians Institute Journal*, Vol. 43, 2015, pages 189–216 by Jessica Ann Hughes, ©Copyright 2015, The Pennsylvania State University. This article is used by permission of The Pennsylvania State University Press.

[1] *The Burdens of Perfection: On Ethics and Reading in Nineteenth-Century British Literature* (Ithaca: Cornell University Press, 2008), 21.

more fleshed-out the emphasis on his incarnation, the more sympathetically human he became, making unavoidable the human sacrifice at the center of the Christian teaching of atonement. Moreover, the more sympathetically incarnate Jesus's character became in Victorian imagination, the more Jesus's role as high priest cast doubts on God's justice. A wrathful God who demanded blood and accepted—even required—Jesus as the victim because of his innocence undermined the very notion of justice, as Miller points out. How then was the traditional office of Jesus the high priest to be understood in a way that might bring about justice and reconciliation? Could his be a bloodless priesthood? Might he bring about reconciliation between God and humans, and bring outspoken, brave justice with pity and even love to fraught situations, making peace between parties?[2]

George Eliot takes on exactly this sort of imaginative recasting of Jesus the reconciling high priest, as she wrestles with his identity early in her literary career. Like Charles Kingsley, George Eliot spent much of her early life thinking about the identity of Jesus. Whereas Kingsley's deep commitment to the incarnation makes it nearly impossible for him to represent Jesus within the novel, Eliot's love for the story of Jesus is not hemmed in by doctrine or complicated by a commitment to a particular theology or dogma. Also in contrast to Kingsley's commitment to patristic thinkers, Eliot's thinking about Jesus was firmly rooted in German biblical scholarship with its emphasis on Jesus's humanity and the church's subsequent mythologizing of his character. Despite these dogmatic differences, Eliot and Kingsley shared the same struggle to bring Jesus—and the experience of Jesus—to life through the novel. Nowhere is this project more obvious than in her first full-length novel, *Adam Bede*.

Despite Eliot's philosophical humanism, to treat her as a voice of secularism is to miss her real love for the character and story of Jesus. Influenced by evangelicalism in her youth, Eliot's early letters reflect a deeply earnest love for Jesus. By the time she translated *Das Leben Jesu*, the evangelical faith of her childhood was very much at an end, and yet viewing her figure of Thorvaldsen's *Risen Christ* helped her "endure" her "Strauss-sick[ness]" in the winter of 1845–6.[3] Ten years later, translating Feuerbach, Jesus disappears entirely from her letters, only to appear again, very briefly, just after the publication of *Adam Bede*. And yet, even as Jesus appears to fade from Eliot's personal writings, within

---

[2] Victorians wrestled with multiple ways of understanding and reimagining sacrifice beyond penal substitution, see Schramm, *Atonement and Self-Sacrifice in Nineteenth-Century Narrative*.
[3] George Eliot, *The George Eliot Letters, 1836–1851*, 9 vols. (New Haven: Yale University Press, 1954), 1:206.

Adam Bede Jesus exists as both a religious vision and as a character brought to life through Adam.[4]

Through Adam, Eliot crafts an answer to her own concern that German higher criticism, particularly in the works of thinkers like David Friedrich Strauss, has lost sight of the "beautiful story" of Jesus.[5] This is not to say that she fundamentally disagrees with Strauss or Feuerbach. In fact, she thinks that, while Strauss is "in many cases... wrong," his theory is "an idea which has general truth."[6] And it is from Feuerbach, with whom Eliot "everywhere agree[s]," that she draws her reworking of Jesus's priesthood in moral and interpersonal terms.[7] For Feuerbach, even though individuals may be "defective, imperfect, weak, [and] needy" through friendship individuals "atone for the failings of the other. Friend justifies friend before God" because valuing the virtues of one's friend, while condemning the evil within oneself, serves as an acknowledgment that one does indeed value and commend the good.[8] Thus, when individuals are "called to account for any sins, weaknesses, and faults" they may "interpose as advocates, as mediators, the virtues of [the] friend" to receive pardon.[9] Feuerbach's construal of the friend as mediator transforms the virtuous friend into the divine image because, as he insists earlier, "the real God of any religion is the so-called Mediator."[10] Thus, our real, moral mediators—our

---

[4] U. C. Knoepflmacher's readings of Eliot's early novels in the mid-1960s suggest a connection between Adam and Jesus, and critics including J. Hillis Miller continue to repeat Knoepflmacher's observation that Feuerbach influenced Eliot's works. But the implications of Knoepflmacher's early scholarship on Eliot—that Adam is somehow equivalent to Jesus—have remained unexplored. While Knoepflmacher sees Adam eventually becoming or converting to Feuerbach's "man of sorrows," he seems uncomfortable with Adam as a consistent manifestation of Jesus in the text. He rushes past one of the many images of Adam depicted as Jesus, saying that "it seems hardly necessary to elaborate the symbolic parallel of... the bearded son of a carpenter.... In an era in which we teach our students to hunt for 'Christ-figures' in the works of Hemingway or Faulkner, such a parallel is all-too evident." While the parallel may be all too evident, the fact that Eliot consistently marks Adam as a version of Jesus in recent history and not as a suffering Christ figure deserves consideration, particularly considering the insignificance of the historical Jesus to Feuerbach's philosophy. Adam's Jesus-consciousness suggests that Eliot is doing more than simply repeating Feuerbach in a novel. See U. C. Knoepflmacher, *George Eliot's Early Novels* (Berkeley and Los Angeles: University of California Press, 1968), 39. For Miller's argument, see J. Hillis Miller, *Reading for Our Time: Adam Bede and Middlemarch Revisited* (Edinburgh: Edinburgh University Press, 2012).
[5] Eliot's frustrations are shared by Mrs. Charles Bray to Sara Sophia Hennell in a letter dated February 14, 1846. Eliot, *Letters*, 1:206.
[6] Eliot expresses her views on Strauss in an 1845 letter to Sara Sophia Hennel. *Letters*, 1:203.
[7] Eliot approves of Feuerbach in an 1854 letter to Sara Sophia Hennel, *The George Eliot Letters, 1852–1858*, 9 vols. (New Haven: Yale University Press, 1954), 2:153.
[8] Ludwig Feuerbach, *The Essence of Christianity*, trans. Marian Evans (London: Trübner & Co., 1881), 156–7.
[9] Feuerbach, *The Essence of Christianity*, 157.
[10] Feuerbach, *The Essence of Christianity*, 74.

upright friends—are those who reconcile us to our ideals of God, justice, and goodness.

The language that Eliot uses in her translation of Feuerbach fuses his emphasis on human mediation with the language of mediator, advocate, and reconciler who characterize Jesus as high priest in both the King James Version of Hebrews and the Book of Common Prayer.[11] Consequently, when the virtuous Adam strives to mediate for and reconcile those around him with their own moral ideals and himself, Eliot joins her Adam to this highly allegorized idea of Jesus as priest. But, through her anthropological insistence on particularity, Eliot goes beyond Feuerbach's anthropotheism and joins his work with the historicizing tendencies in Strauss, to give us a particularized, historicized (but not historical) Jesus.

To better understand Eliot's construction of Jesus's character and how it both parallels and differs from more traditional construals of Jesus, it is helpful to compare her understanding with that of Kingsley. For Kingsley, Jesus is the revelation and renewal of the image of God in humanity. Insofar as Eliot agrees with Feuerbach, her interest lies in virtuous humanity *as* God. For Kingsley, each person has innate value because God became human, hallowing the ordinary and the human. For Eliot, following Feuerbach, each person *is* God, which likewise hallows the ordinary and the human. Thus, although both Kingsley and Eliot emphasize the practice of seeing the material world as in some way divine, the theological stakes that differentiate their beliefs are particularly high, especially with regard to the unique identity of Jesus. While for Kingsley Jesus must be a unique incarnation of God, for Eliot Adam can offer a more or less equivalent incarnation of God, bearing traditional markers of Jesus but freed from the burden of pious preconceptions for Eliot.

With these shared aesthetics but different theological constructions in mind, *Adam Bede* looks quite a bit like (as Peter Brooks argues all narratives are) "a form of understanding and explanation," a way of asking and answering questions about the identity of Jesus.[12] Eliot is not interested in this as a traditional question nor in orthodox answers. Rather, *Adam Bede* explores what a reconciling Jesus would be like in the modern world, apart from miracles and myths. The brilliance of her answer lies as much in its form as in its philosophical content: by addressing the question of Jesus through a story, Eliot teaches her readers

---

[11] See Heb 8-12 and the BCP, particularly the closing address of "only mediator and advocate" in multiple collects, including those for morning and evening, along with the juxtaposition of priestly language in the General Confession and Comfortable Words.

[12] Peter Brooks, *Reading for the Plot* (New York: Alfred Knopf, 1984), 10.

to see a fully relational, demythologized Jesus—the fully human being—in the character of Adam and, by extension, in those like him.

In *Adam Bede* Eliot reimagines Jesus as high priest, maintaining the altruism of self-sacrifice embedded within Jesus's character in traditional constructions of the atonement, while removing its problematic passivity and embarrassingly barbaric construction of God as a wrath-filled deity in need of blood, through Adam's ongoing, active work to defend and redeem others. She does this in part by separating the divine, suffering Jesus of religious piety from the human carpenter and teacher, moving beyond Kingsley's understanding of the incarnation that leads to his characterization of Jesus as a political revolutionary. More significantly, in joining Feuerbach's anthropological theology to the historical emphasis of Strauss, Eliot to reworks Jesus's characterization as high priest and the atonement theology it suggests. In the end, Eliot's Jesus exists within a commonplace heroic that celebrates ordinary family life and renders Jesus a real, relational human being in the process.

The Jesus of Faith and the Jesus of History

Imagining Jesus as a member of a family is central to the gospel narratives of his life but also imaginatively complicated within many traditional Christian orthodoxies. While the infant Jesus is Mary's son, and a twelve-year-old Jesus can be found teaching in the temple in the canonical Gospel of Luke, imagining Jesus as a four-year-old with a skinned knee and a snotty nose belongs to the age-old realm of apocryphal speculation and heterodox fantasy. Beginning with the early "infancy gospels" retelling Jesus childhood, writers imagined Jesus cursing bullies (who promptly died) and fashioning clay birds that he would then bring to life.[13] For theological reasons, stories that imagine Jesus as a man with desires for a wife and family of his own—and thus a sexual being—have been treated as heretical within much of Christian tradition. While serious literary attempts to imagine Jesus as a grown man with brothers, with a mother, with a trade, with friends, and with a sense of mission are less common in the Christian traditions that antecede Victorian England, they are typical of the Jesus novel or the Lives of Jesus in the nineteenth century.

---

[13] The infancy gospels are a group of noncanonical writings retelling the childhood of Jesus, including the Gospel of Pseudo-Matthew, the Infancy Gospel of Thomas, and the Gospel of James, among others. Some date from as early as the second century.

Despite the orthodox rejection of stories related to imagining Jesus as a frustrated teenager (or a generous husband), in order to craft Adam Bede as a version of Jesus living in the recent past, Eliot needs to place Adam firmly within the messiness of real family life. Thus, she gives him a meddling mother, a kind younger brother, and a drunken carpenter for a father. This less-than-ideal family imparts a gritty realism to Adam, if only by association. But by itself such a family would at best suggest a vague parallel between Adam's and Jesus's history, grounded almost entirely in Adam's work as a carpenter. To mark Adam as an historical, wholly human version of Jesus, Eliot relies upon literalizing the metaphor of marrying Jesus by structurally aligning Adam and Jesus as potential life-partners for Dinah. Through Adam's role in this unconventional love triangle, Eliot communicates the experience of being in a love-based relationship with Jesus and imagines Jesus in relationship to others, which gives readers multiple perspectives for sympathizing with Jesus.

The obvious attraction and potential romance between Adam and Dinah become the focal point of the novel after the tragic events surrounding Hetty and Arthur come to a conclusion in Book V.[14] While Dinah has attempted throughout the novel to maintain what Knoepflmacher describes as her "almost nunlike... devotion to Jesus," her response to Adam's proposal brings the theological stakes of both the marriage plot and Adam's character into sharp relief.[15] After confessing that she is "drawn" to Adam, she states, "It seems to me as if you were stretching out your arms to me, and beckoning me to come and take my ease and live for my own delight, and Jesus, the Man of Sorrows, was standing looking towards me, and pointing to the sinful, and suffering, and afflicted."[16]

The vision Dinah describes is reminiscent of a cartoon: Dinah stands with a weeping Jesus on one shoulder and the broad-shouldered Adam on the other, debating which course of action to choose. By setting Jesus and Adam in contrast to each other like this, the novel equates them, connecting them structurally as two versions of the same thing. Jesus and Adam are both

---

[14] While the romance of Adam and Dinah was not part of Eliot's original conception, George Henry Lewes suggested that the novel should conclude with their marriage, which Eliot then had in mind from the third chapter onward. The attraction between the two characters was evident to Eliot's publisher from the start; John Blackwood commented after reading what would comprise the first quarter of the novel, "I should not wonder if Dinah fell in love with the manly fellow." See Eliot, *Letters*, 446, 503.

This conversation between Eliot, Lewes, and Blackwood is recounted in Eliot's letters. See Eliot, *Letters*, 446, 503.

[15] Knoepflmacher, *George Eliot's Early Novels*, 107.
[16] Eliot, *A.B.*, 455.

potential life-partners for Dinah, one offering her pleasure and the other self-denial.[17] It would be easy to read this passage as Dinah choosing between all the great literary binaries: evil and good, man and God, self and others, body and spirit. But such a reading is not in keeping with either Adam's or Dinah's characters nor with the historical circumstances in which Eliot has set the novel. Adam, himself a staunch churchman, in no way expects or requires Dinah to "give up" Jesus or her Methodist version of the Christian faith. He insists, "I'd never think o' putting myself between you and God, and saying you oughtn't to do this, and you oughtn't to do that. You'd follow your conscience as much as you do now."[18] Moreover, in no way does Adam's proposal keep Dinah from continuing to minister to the "sinful, and suffering, and afflicted."[19] As Hetty so clearly illustrated, sin, suffering, and affliction are very much alive in the country and Dinah knows this. As far as Dinah's personal sense of her own preaching ministry, while she expresses to Adam a particular concern for the factory town of Snowfield, she also saw Hayslope as a mission field at the novel's opening, when she gave her Sermon on the Green.[20] Clearly Adam does not intend to separate Dinah from Jesus. Dinah, on the other hand, views her own singleness as a marker of her devotion to Christ and of her vocation as a preacher, forcing this standoff.

Reading Dinah's preaching and celibacy as an invalidation of her public voice renders Dinah's narrative a choice between Adam and Jesus essentially a choice

---

[17] Early Methodism did, in fact, see a revival of celibacy among believers, particularly itinerate preachers who often struggled to support themselves. John Wesley himself, with varying degrees of vehemence throughout his life, supported celibacy as a way to eliminate the distractions and demands that take time and energy away from the individual believer's spiritual life and union with Jesus. That said, attempting to distinguish his views from Catholic teaching, he also insisted that marriage was, in no way, an inherently inferior state than celibacy for believers. In early Methodist thinking, while the spiritual life may be hampered by marriage, the two were never set in exclusive opposition to each other. More importantly for considering *Adam Bede*, while Wesley encouraged celibacy, both male and female Methodists preachers did marry and Elizabeth Evan, Eliot's aunt, on whom Dinah was loosely based and from whom Eliot first heard the basic infanticide story, was a married woman while also a preacher. For a detailed examination of celibacy within Methodism, see Anna M. Lawrence, *One Family under God: Love, Belonging, and Authority in Early Transatlantic Methodism* (Philadelphia: University Penn Press, 2011).

[18] Eliot, *A.B.*, 454.

[19] Eliot, *A.B.*, 455.

[20] Setting Adam and Jesus against each other as mutually exclusive options for Dinah's future is a significant structural move on Eliot's part. As a slight but significant exaggeration of Methodist teaching on celibacy, some read the novel's alignment of celibacy and spirituality as part of Eliot's efforts to invalidate Dinah's preaching. According to Christine Krueger, not only is Eliot "acceding to the historical forces which silence the woman preacher" when Dinah marries Adam and gives up preaching; but Eliot is subtly suggesting that such preaching is unacceptable by linking women preachers with the perceived deviant celibacy represented by resurgent religious sisterhoods. See Christine L. Krueger, *The Reader's Repentance: Women Preachers, Women Writers, and Nineteenth-Century Social Discourse* (Chicago: University of Chicago Press, 1992), 263.

between private and public. The problem with this reading is that Dinah does not construe her decision to marry in terms of losing her public voice and, as Adam insists, she would be free to follow her own conscience if she accepts his proposal. What Dinah construes as an exclusive choice is the choice between Adam and Jesus as characters. It is not simply that Dinah will potentially be distracted from Jesus and preaching by her love for Adam; in her vision they are on opposite sides beckoning her in opposite directions. This is reinforced by the novel's conclusion. Once Dinah chooses Adam, all reference to Jesus disappears. In Dinah's words, she and Adam are united, not by Jesus, but by "the Divine Will."[21]

Although the choice between Adam and Jesus does not mean Dinah must deny her faith or give up her ministry, setting Adam and Jesus against each other does mark Adam as equivalent to Jesus. She could commit her life and her heart to either of the men she envisions as beckoning her. Either could be her husband. But this is not the only way the novel marks Adam as another version of Jesus. Through the novel's descriptions of Jesus and Adam, both are presented as traditional—but often opposite—representations of the man from Nazareth.

When Dinah speaks of Jesus, she consistently depicts him in a state of sorrowful suffering, as spiritualized, or both. Toward the end of the Sermon on the Green, Dinah has a vision of Jesus present, weeping and bearing the marks of the crucifixion in his body. She calls out, "See where our blessed Lord stands and weeps and stretches out his arms towards you …. See the print of the nails on his dear hands and feet …. Ah! How pale and worn he looks!"[22] She goes on to describe the crucifixion that has left him so marked, describing his "great agony" and "exceeding sorrow" as he was "buffeted," "scourged," "mocked," "bruised," "nailed," and "parched with thirst," before being "shut out from God."[23] The description, a litany of traditional devotional images of Jesus's passion, seems to invoke an intense sense of Jesus as a physical being, a physical presence among the crowd. But, the narrator precludes that possibility, explaining that, as Dinah "sees" Jesus, her eyes are fixed "on a point" a little above the crowd.[24] By placing Dinah's vision in midair, and making it invisible to everyone else, the narrator subverts any suggestion of Jesus's real physical presence, rendering him a sad, brooding spirit passively offering mercy to those who seek him.

---

[21] Eliot, *A.B.*, 475.
[22] Eliot, *A.B.*, 27–8.
[23] Eliot, *A.B.*, 28.
[24] Eliot, *A.B.*, 27.

Dinah's depiction of Jesus is very much in keeping with the broader Puritan and evangelical vision of Jesus that held sway in English theology from the late seventeenth century until the early nineteenth century. While he has suffered much, he is also "risen from the dead,... [and] praying for [sinners] at the right hand of God."[25] As Dinah makes clear, Jesus's life and death were for the sole purpose of "toiling" for her listeners: his primary function is saving sinners.[26] Consequently, while Dinah speaks extensively about Jesus in her sermon, the point is not for the crowd to have a better sense of Jesus as a complicated, robust human being to whom they must somehow relate. The purpose of her sermon is to persuade her listeners to avail themselves of Jesus's help in order to secure eternal salvation.

Adam, on the other hand, is a direct challenge to the suffering, even ethereal, construction of Jesus that Dinah envisions. From the beginning of the novel, Adam is marked typologically as a representation of Jesus through his name, occupation, and habits. That said, Eliot eschews the bloody palms and cruciform shadows that frequently mark characters as self-sacrificing Christs in favor of typological markers that emphasize Jesus as a historical human being. The name "Adam Bede" draws on the standard representation of Jesus in Christian art and literature as a "new Adam" who reverses the narrative of the fall, making it a narrative of redemption. As such, this typological representation is particularly focused on Jesus's human nature and the actions in his life that echo the first Adam's, such as naming, building, tending, and resisting temptation. In the hands of almost any other author a carpenter named Adam would be disastrously transparent in its symbolic resonance, but Eliot employs this obvious signifier to connect Adam and Jesus. Joining Adam to "Bede" contextualizes this Jesus figure firmly within the specific, familiar, and historic material culture of England. Somewhat counterintuitively, this English context emphasizes the historical embeddedness of Jesus. Rather than trying to recreate the materiality of Judea, which would inevitably be a romanticized, exotic construct at the far end of the British Empire in readers' minds, Eliot places her Jesus figure in a very prosaic England so that he can be firmly embedded in mundane materiality. Within the context of Adam as a new, alternate representation of Jesus, Adam's hymn-singing becomes particularly evocative. As Alisa Clapp-Itnyre points out, Eliot places only the most secular verses from Methodists hymns in Adam's mouth

---

[25] Eliot, *A.B.*, 28.
[26] Eliot, *A.B.*, 28.

and she never lets him finish any of these hymns.[27] Eliot's secular selections from these sacred songs point to the intersection of the secular and sacred in the character of Adam. His character is part of the sacred tradition but a historical and human manifestation of those ideals. The open-endedness of his hymn-singing reinforces this intersection of sacred and secular, of revealed religious history and progressive anthropological history. Like the hymns he sings, Adam is an open-ended, undetermined Jesus, one who is not constrained by a previously concluded set of dogmatic statements but a human being revealing the divine. In this way, Adam is a representation of Strauss's historical Jesus in recent British history, a representation that maintains Strauss's "general truth" about Jesus, while recapturing the "beautiful story" through Adam's narrative.

Given these typological markers, Dinah's choice between Adam and Jesus is really the choice between the Jesus of Methodist piety and the Jesus of history. Once we see this, it is easy to recognize that the confrontation has been set up throughout the novel. Beginning with her opening sermon, Dinah repeatedly says things like, "Ah, wouldn't you love such a man [as Jesus] if you saw him—if he were here in this village? What a kind heart he must have! What a friend he would be to go to in trouble!"[28] Within days, Dinah goes on to reflect on Adam's gentleness, kindness, and strength in conversations with Hetty and others.[29] Ultimately the novel has set up Adam's marriage proposal such that Dinah is not choosing between Adam and Jesus. She is choosing between a spiritual, disembodied Jesus and a material, bodily Jesus.[30]

But crafting an embodied Jesus for Dinah to marry creates a unique set of imaginative challenges. First, the language of loving Jesus, being saved by Jesus, and being wed to Jesus creates uncomfortable subject positions for both male and female believers if taken seriously. A focus on Jesus as a man, having "broad shoulders" and "skillful hands," as Adam is described, who is also the believer's spouse, collapses the sexual and spiritual. This collapse not only threatens Victorian constructions of femininity by making the spiritual (potentially) sexual, but also implies a potentially homoerotic spirituality among men. Because of the erotic implications underlying any emphasis on Christ as the believer's

---

[27] Alisa Clapp-Itnyre, "Dinah and the Secularization of Methodist Hymnody in Eliot's *Adam Bede*," *Victorians Institute Journal* 26 (1998).

[28] Eliot, *A.B.*, 24.

[29] Eliot, *A.B.*, 106–7, 128–9.

[30] Rachel Ablow argues that Dinah's choice between Adam and Jesus "eradicates selfishness while maintaining the self-consciousness necessary for ethical relationships," thus rendering the marriage between Adam and Dinah a humanized version of salvation. See Rachel Ablow, *The Marriage of Minds: Reading Sympathy in the Victorian Marriage Plot* (Stanford: Stanford University Press, 2007), 71.

spouse, it is no wonder that Christian tradition frequently de-emphasizes Jesus as a physical being. Thus, when the eighteenth-century evangelical George Whitefield preaches on "Jesus, the Believer's Husband," he talks about union with Christ, the ascended Lord, and not union with a baritone-voiced carpenter.

For this reason, Victorian novels almost always present Jesus as a temporally distanced figure when he interacts with both male and female characters. Like Dante's Beatrice or Eleanor in *Alton Locke*, female characters can be vehicles for the male encounter with Jesus, which distances male characters from the homoerotics implied by the language of religious romance and underscored by narratives in which the believing man is passively rescued from his own weakness and sinfulness by Jesus. Similarly, women's narratives do not experience, meditate upon, or otherwise engage Jesus as a human man. For example, in Cardinal Wiseman's *Fabiola*, a widely popular Catholic response to Kingsley's works, the female characters of Miriam and Fabiola never talk about Jesus as a historical, bodily person but about his teachings and his role in securing salvation for believers. Agnes and Cecelia, early nuns, do speak of Jesus. But while they repeatedly talk about Jesus in the language of marriage, the novel repeatedly emphasizes their child-like physiques and innocent natures, and their visions of Jesus are clearly ethereal manifestations for mystics. The sense of a physical, male Jesus is undercut by the youthful nature of the girls, which renders talk of Jesus as one's "spouse" highly imaginative. Moreover, the content of their mystical visions echoes a long tradition in Catholic art of aestheticizing the imagery of Jesus's physical suffering and stripping it of its historical and material referents. In this, Wiseman's subversion of the female vision of Jesus is very much in the same spirit as Eliot's subversion of Dinah's vision of Jesus while preaching: neither Wiseman nor Eliot is comfortable to let such visions stand as "real" events involving a real, physically present *man*. Correspondently, the evangelical novel *Against the Stream* by Elizabeth Rundle Charles depicts conversions of a brother and sister. In this work, the brother explains his conversion in terms of Jesus's biography, whereas the sister's conversion is articulated through understanding God's maternal love as a replacement for her dead mother. In a similar vein, Charlotte Elizabeth Tonna's *Helen Fleetwood* spends pages detailing the female believer's relationship to God through the Bible but almost no time on Jesus as an actual person: he is the crucified and exalted God ready to save believers from their sins, not a brawny carpenter from Galilee.

Rather than distance Jesus or embrace a feminized Jesus as did other writers and artists (discussed in Chapter 1), Eliot engages these gender dynamics to redefine masculinity through Adam as both physically robust and morally uncompromised. Of course, such a redefinition of masculinity was also necessary because Victorian gender discourse viewed men as morally compromised because of their participation in the public sphere. Thus, Eliot must imagine a masculinity that is somehow uncompromised. Ironically enough, by focusing on Adam's body and physical prowess, Eliot is able to sidestep the squeamishness of thinking about Jesus as a masculine body and create a morally upright construction of masculinity.

The focus on Adam's body begins with the novel itself. The opening lines describe Adam as the tallest of the workmen, with a rich baritone voice, "jet-black hair," "keen... dark eyes," a "well-poised head," "broad chest," and arms "likely to win the prize for feats of strength" that end in "long supple hand[s]... ready for works of skill." As to his general air, the narrator tells us that, "when he drew himself up to take a more distant survey of his work, he had the air of a soldier standing at ease." While Eliot makes use of the trope of the sexually irresponsible soldier through Arthur later in the work, this initial portrait of Adam with its military reference serves to mark Adam as sexually desirable, as it does Arthur.[31] Adam's desirability is underscored in his subsequent comparison to Seth, whom critics characterize as "effeminate" or even the "castrated male."[32] Seth's "benign" demeanor and "thin" hair only reinforce the sense of Adam as a model of virility and, by extension, a desirable mate.[33]

To see Jesus in such a light is at once startling and sensible, particularly in light of the works of Charles Kingsley, which Eliot read and declared herself "in love with [Kingsley's] genius, and... 'riled' by his faults."[34] While Eliot was particularly annoyed by Kingsley's tendency to moralize, "never trust[ing] the impression that the scene itself will make," she appropriated much of his muscular Christianity in *Adam Bede*, even alluding to T. C. Sanders's review of Kingsley's *Two Years Ago* in which he coined the phrase. As Sanders wrote, Kingsley's "muscular Christian" is a man who "fears God and can walk a thousand miles in a thousand hours—[he] breathes God's free air on God's rich earth, and at the same time can hit a woodcock, doctor a horse, and twist a poker around his

---

[31] For an examination of the soldier trope in *Adam Bede*, see John R. Reed, "Soldier Boy: Forming Masculinity in *Adam Bede*," *Studies in the Novel* 33, no. 3 (2001).

[32] Reed, "Soldier Boy: Forming Masculinity in *Adam Bede*," 274.

[33] Jennifer Panek argues that Darwinian ideas regarding the survival of the fittest participated in forming the standards of male attractiveness in strong brother / weak brother pairings in a number of Victorian novels including *Adam Bede*. See Jennifer Panek, "Constructions of Masculinity in Adam Bede and Wives and Daughters," *Victorian Review: The Journal of the Victorian Studies Association of Western Canada and the Victorian Studies Association of Ontario* 22, no. 2 (1996).

[34] Eliot, *Letters*, 86.

fingers."[35] When Eliot describes Adam as a man who "can walk forty mile a-day, an' lift a matter o' sixty stone," one of the "strong, skilful men [who] are often the gentlest to the women and children," she points to the exact characteristics of physical strength, gentleness, and practical knowledge that Sanders identifies in Kingsley's construction of Christian manliness. Kingsley's project of rehabilitating activities and lifestyles deemed "coarse" is not far removed from Eliot's own celebration of Dutch painting, with "monotonous homely existence" that so many "lofty-minded people despise."[36] Since both Eliot and Kingsley share a theologically inflected aesthetic that values the commonplace and the material, Eliot's appropriation of Kingsley's Jesus—and his other "muscular Christians"— through Adam is a natural extension of their shared attitude toward the ordinary. Moreover, the emphases on Adam's ordinary humanity—his physical strength and attractiveness—become important markers of the mundane, human Jesus that Eliot recovers through Adam.[37]

While Eliot clearly genders her historical Jesus figure as markedly masculine through Adam, such a construction is not necessary in terms of thinking about Jesus as a historical person. After all, Jesus could just as easily have been a less virile man and still been both fully divine and fully human. Consequently, her presentation of Adam, particularly in contrast to Seth, raises questions as to what sort of work she is attempting in regard to Jesus's characterization as a real, historical man. As Kingsley's reconstruction of Jesus highlights, whoever Jesus was in history, he was not a passive, tame character. Rather, he was a man of passion, anger, action, and justice. The issue is that the pursuit of justice that characterizes Kingsley's Jesus frequently sits at odds with the constructions of mercy that characterize Jesus within much of Christian tradition. Eliot, influenced by Strauss and Feuerbach, knows well that the Jesus of the biblical text embodies both angry justice and tender mercy, and that these characteristics underlay the notion of the atonement. Thus, in order to recreate Jesus and reimagine the

---

[35] T. C. Sanders, "Reviews: Two Years Ago," *The Saturday Review* 1857, 176. Sanders's review, though treated as a denigration of Kingsley's work in recent criticism, explicitly commends Kingsley's writing for presenting the possibility that "coarseness" and "sport" do not have to be synonymous. see Norman Vance, "Kingsley's Christian Manliness," *Theology* 78, no. 30 (1975).

[36] Eliot, A.B., 161. As Norman Vance has argued, Kingsley was particularly concerned because of his pastoral work and work in London's slums that Christian models of masculinity did not exclude the "wild" working-class Esaus, in favor of the "smooth" Jacobs of middle and upper classes. Thus, Vance contends that "Christian manliness" (the term Kingsley preferred for his vision of Christin life) was, at least in part, about overcoming the class divides created by versions of Christianity that required high levels of literacy and intellectual reflectiveness, while eschewing the physical activity that frequently characterized the work and leisure activities of those of the working class.

[37] Eliot, *A. B.*, 15, 129.

atonement in human terms, Eliot appropriates Kingsley's muscular Christianity to create a masculinity in which a morally appropriate anger can exist.

Justice, Mercy, and Reconciliation

In most of Christian tradition and literary scholarship, thinkers tend to separate justice and mercy, as if the two cannot co-exist. Unsurprisingly then, in reading *Adam Bede*, scholars do not argue that Adam needs to learn sympathy but rather assume it, often making the remark in passing as a self-evident fact of the text.[38] Readings of *Adam Bede* that assume Adam needs to be more sympathetic base their readings on Adam's anger toward both his drunken father and Arthur. The understanding of sympathy in such scholarship is relatively consistent, following the general shape of Samuel Johnson's 1755 definition, in which sympathy is "fellow-feeling; mutual sensibility; the quality of being affected by the affections of another." As George Landow and Rae Greiner have argued, Adam Smith and other moral philosophers including Dugald Stewart and Thomas Reid developed a more nuanced definition, emphasizing the imagination and placing oneself imaginatively in the place of the other.[39] As Greiner argues, this sense of "going along with" the other is essential to the process of sympathetic identification between reader and character. It is also essential to the moral philosophy of human sympathy that Eliot is famous for illustrating in her novels.

Assumed within this construction of sympathy is the idea of mercy. When literary scholars discuss Adam's need for sympathy, they imply that he must "go along with others," experiencing the "affections" and "sensibilities" of characters like his father or Arthur. But this is not all. Most scholarship then assumes that if Adam learned to share the perspective of Arthur, he would not then condemn Arthur for his actions. In other words, sympathy should produce a form of mercy that eliminates judgment entirely. Ironically, this ends up being counter

---

[38] The trend appears to begin with Knoepflmacher and continues through Hillis Miller's recent rereading of *Adam Bede*. For other examples of this assumption, see Mary Ellen Doyle, *The Sympathetic Response: George Eliot's Fictional Rhetoric* (Teaneck, NJ: Fairleigh Dickinson University Press, 1981); Susan Morgan, *Sisters in Time: Imagining Gender in Nineteenth-Century British Fiction* (Oxford: Oxford University Press, 1989); R. E. Sopher, "Gender and Sympathy in *Adam Bede*: The Case of Seth Bede," *George Eliot—George Henry Lewes Studies* 62/63 (2012).

[39] For more on the school that Landow dubs "emotionalist moral philosophy," see George P. Landow, *Images of Crisis: Literary Iconology, 1750 to the Present* 2nd ed. (New York: Routledge, 2014), 22–8. Also see Greiner, chapter 1.

to Adam Smith's idea of sympathy as a moral system and to the very idea of selfhood that sympathy was meant to produce. Smith's conception of sympathy as a moral system is based on the idea of a person "imagin[ing] in what manner he would be affected if he was only one of the spectators of his own situation" in order to "abate the violence" of his passion, "especially when in their presence and acting under their observation." Ultimately, learning to be in sympathy with one's observers produces a balanced, less passionate and more reasonable individual. While Smith also discusses the role of the spectator in imagining the suffering of the individual in question, the purpose of Smith's system is not to foster endless mercy and understanding for human weakness, suffering, and passion. Rather, sympathy functions to mitigate the passion of the sufferer, ensuring "the equal and happy temper that is so necessary for self-satisfaction and enjoyment."[40] Moreover, while sympathy is essential in creating a shared understanding of virtue and moral behavior, Smith does not use sympathy as grounds for breaking "the general rules of morality" or overlooking such offenses. Rather sympathy is as an empirical ground for determining the immorality of a given action such as murder and promiscuousness and as a vehicle for self-reflection.[41] Smith does on occasion link pity and compassion to sympathy but he denies that such feelings override justice. Thus he writes, "When an inhuman murderer is brought to the scaffold, though we have some compassion for his misery, we can have no sort of fellow-feeling with his resentment."[42] Smith recognizes that people might be "disposed to pardon and forgive [a murder], and to save him from that punishment which in all their cool hours they had considered as the retribution due to such crimes" because of the suffering he or she faces in execution, such pity should not override the concerns of justice. Rather, such pity must be "counterbalance[d]" by "reflect[ing] that mercy to the guilty is cruelty to the innocent."[43]

While critics may separate justice and mercy, Eliot's letters point to an understanding of sympathy much more in keeping with Smith, an understanding in which justice is mixed with mercy. As she explains to her publisher, Blackwood, in a letter from February 18, 1857, "My artistic bent is directed not at all to the presentation of eminently irreproachable characters, but to the presentation of mixed human beings in such a way as to call forth tolerant judgment, pity, and

[40] Adam Smith, *Theory of Moral Sentiments; to Which Is Added a Dissertation on the Origin of Languages* (London: T. Cadell in the Strand, 1767), 29.
[41] Smith, *Theory of Moral Sentiments; to Which Is Added a Dissertation on the Origin of Languages*, 397–8.
[42] Smith, *Theory of Moral Sentiments; to Which Is Added a Dissertation on the Origin of Languages*, 121.
[43] See Smith, *Theory of Moral Sentiments; to Which Is Added a Dissertation on the Origin of Languages*, 152.

sympathy."[44] Eliot's thinking here reflects Adam Smith's philosophy but implies a lessened sense of justice and a greater sense of pity for the wrongdoer. Whereas Smith's sympathy for wrongdoers is grounded in bodily suffering at execution, Eliot's sympathy for her wayward characters is grounded in the tragedy of human folly and circumstance. Eliot recognizes the social structures that lead her characters into wrongdoing and, because of the force of those structures, is able to feel and evoke pity for the wrongdoer. Thus, the same judgment that considers murder abhorrent also considers the circumstances that produce human brokenness and consequent crimes abhorrent. Only a full or complete *judgment* on both the individual wrongdoer and the systems in which individuals are enmeshed can foster the sympathy that leads both to mercy for the wrongdoer and to mercy—and justice—for the victim.

In *Adam Bede* individual and systemic judgment reveals that almost everyone is both a wrongdoer and a victim, except perhaps Adam. And, as Eliot's treatise on realism in the middle of the novel highlights, such holistic judgment can only come through a deep relational knowledge of the individuals and systems in question. Abstract ideas about what is right and wrong will never provide a sufficiently comprehensive understanding to facilitate right judgment and, ultimately, sympathy. Keeping this in mind, we see that Adam's judgments actually allow the novel to enact justice on behalf of abused or oppressed characters and to affirm a commonly held morality (including prohibitions against drunkenness, licentiousness, and murder), while also fostering sympathy for wrongdoers, a sympathy that Adam also manifests consistently through the novel but only after judgment is spoken.

The theological stakes of Adam's mercy-seeking justice are hard to miss. Just as literary critics set justice and sympathy at odds in Adam's character, theologians have often portrayed divine justice and mercy as warring drives within God that are appeased through Jesus's death on the cross. Thus, in substitutionary atonement, justice is served by the death of Jesus on behalf of wrongdoers and, because of that sacrificial payment, God can then extend mercy and be reconciled to sinners. Eliot reframes this old theological tension through the character of Adam. Rather than divine drives to be satisfied, human anger and sympathy are an emotional dynamic that become equivalent to divine justice and mercy. By grounding this matrix of judgment and sympathy in the character of Adam and consistently coupling Adam's anger with a sympathy that leads to

---

[44] Eliot, *Letters*, 299.

reconciliation, Eliot begins to imagine a Jesus figure in which anger is actually good and in which atonement does not require blood.

Within this paradigm of judgment that leads to sympathy, Adam's moments of apparent harshness take on new valences. Although critics typically deem Adam hard or harsh, the novel repeatedly presents a set of mixed emotions. In each instance where Adam demonstrates anger, he also demonstrates sympathy for the weak, frequently manifesting this in his efforts to defend or rescue others from some form of misuse. At the same time, Adam also expresses mercy for the wrongdoer, stating the need for sympathy and reconciling with him. Importantly, this pattern of righteous anger and uncompromised justice that ends in mercy is established in the novel's opening scene. Thus, Adam does not learn sympathy or mercy. He is, from the beginning, a representation of a complicated emotional being whose interactions with others consistently end in sympathy.

Adam's fistfight with Arthur is the most helpful passage for understanding the theological significance of Adam's righteous—even violent—anger. Frequently read as Adam's least sympathetic moment, the fight is really a moment when appropriate anger is expressed toward a powerful individual using his power in a sexually predatory way. Arthur has known for weeks that "no gentleman, out of a ballad, could marry a farmer's niece," yet he continues his illicit affair with the vain and gullible Hetty, who truly believes Arthur will marry her.[45] Adam recognizes that "things don't lie level" between Arthur and Hetty and intervenes to stop Arthur from continuing to exploit a young, poor woman.[46] Even so, Adam is also determined not to fight until Arthur makes light of his treatment of Hetty, at which point Adam uses physical force to break Arthur's irresponsible and damaging perspective.[47] In the end, the only reason Adam feels that his actions were harsh is because they are too late to alter the inevitable wreckage.[48] What Adam intuits—and what the novel will bear out—is that he has failed to stop Arthur's wrongdoing before consequences have taken hold.

It is difficult to read the fight between Adam and Arthur and not be reminded of Jesus cleansing the temple. Both Jesus and Adam are marked by an anger that disrupts space and human bodies as they intervene physically to stop those in power from abusing the poor. Yet in both instances, violence is used to call the wrongdoers to repentance rather than meted out as a form of punishment.

---

[45] Eliot, *A.B.*, 126.
[46] Eliot, *A.B.*, 278.
[47] Eliot, *A.B.*, 269–70.
[48] Eliot, *A.B.*, 272.

Through these parallels, Eliot gives us the Jesus Strauss was attempting to uncover in *Das Leben Jesu*. It is telling that Strauss, in working methodically through each gospel story to determine which aspects were historical and which were myth, consistently upheld Jesus's moments of anger and frustration as real history. And as he argues regarding the cleansing of the temple, there is no mythological or evangelical reason to craft a false story that depicts Jesus in such a violent light.[49] Yet, despite this violence and Strauss's reflections on the obvious forethought and "unseemliness" of Jesus twisting a scourge, he does not challenge the justness of Jesus's views. Essentially, Strauss's historical Jesus looks quite a lot like Adam Bede, particularly in his anger and his willingness to act decisively—and even forcefully—for the sake of justice.

In light of the dynamics of Adam and Arthur's fistfight, Adam's final interaction with Arthur does not suggest that Adam has become more sympathetic. Rather, he is willing to disavowal harshness "toward them as have done wrong and repent."[50] It is only *after* Arthur makes it abundantly clear that he understands the wrong he has done and he demonstrates true repentance that Adam accepts Arthur's hand.[51] Even Adam's musings on his own harshness in this scene suggest the Jesus of the Gospels. As Adam considers those toward whom he was most sympathetic, a distinct pattern emerges—Adam's sympathy always goes with the weaker individual, be it Seth, his mother, or Hetty. His final observations on sympathy are not those of compromising niceties that will bear a general goodwill toward all regardless of their actions. Rather, his disavowal of harshness comes in the face of Arthur's hard-won repentance and only after the damaging effects of sin have been fully faced by all. In the end, Adam's moral fortitude and uprightness join his gentleness toward the weak with sympathy for the broken.

Given Adam's ultimate forgiveness of Arthur, many scholars have argued that he learns sympathy, but a careful look at the novel's earliest events demonstrates that Adam is consistently just and merciful in his dealings with other. When Adam confronts Ben in the carpenter's shop, we see that he is not a hot-headed man or a man who quickly rushes to judgment. Neither does Adam uphold some abstract sense of mercy and kindness in all situations. Rather, his response to the situation is grounded in his specific, relational knowledge of the individuals involved and the situation. Largely patient, he only intervenes to defend his

---

[49] Strauss, *The Life of Jesus, Critically Examined*, 402.
[50] Eliot, *A.B.*, 420.
[51] Eliot, *A.B.*, 421.

brother's faith or to save his (unfinished) carpentry work, which is not surprising given the high value Adam places on doing one's work well. Moreover, Adam's refusal to join the initial laugher and his condemnation of teasing reveal that, while he is willing to speak the truth regarding Seth's oversight in finishing the door or Ben's drinking, he takes no delight in the failings of others or from judging others for their failures. He is a "preacher" to be sure, but he is also accurate in his observations and just in what he says about the men who stop working for the day leaving "a screw half-driven in" and drop their hammers "while in the act of lifting [them]."[52]

Keeping this first scene in mind is particularly important when examining Adam's response to Thias's negligent drinking. Intermingled with Adam's midnight reflections is an account of Thias Bede's descent into alcoholism.[53] Readers are told that, as a child, Adam felt a great deal of pride in his father but, when Adam was a teenager, Thias began to drink. By the time Adam is an adult, Thias is drinking regularly, sometimes spending the entire night away from his wife and family and failing to complete his carpentry contracts. Consequently, Adam has become the family's provider, not just supporting his mother, father, and brother financially but also completing the work his father fails to do so that others will not suffer. While there is no indication that Thias is an abusive drunk, we are told that he is "wild and foolish" when drinking and that Lisbeth's eyes are, at this stage in her life, "dim... —perhaps from too much crying."[54] As readers soon find out, Thias's drinking is so severe that it leads to his death. Clearly, Thias's drinking has hurt Adam, Lisbeth, and Seth in a variety of ways. Consequently, Adam's anger at his father is understandable, particularly as it is tied up in "shame" at his father's actions; love for his father, mother, and brother; and a recognition of his own responsibility to "bear... the sore cross" of his father.[55]

Setting aside the assumption that anger is inherently bad for a moment, Adam's reaction to his father is neither harsh nor inappropriate. Adam provides an honest assessment of the situation, while reflecting the frustration and deep disappointment that only the vulnerability of real love can produce. Adam has been deeply hurt by his father, yet he maintains a strong desire to protect his father from public shame and to provide for the material needs of others, which

---

[52] Eliot, *A.B.*, 11.
[53] Eliot, *A.B.*, 36–45.
[54] Eliot, *A.B.*, 36, 44.
[55] Eliot, *A.B.*, 44–5.

leads to the practical action of finishing the coffin for Tholer. Adam also feels a deep "pity" for his father, which was suggested almost immediately after his initial burst of anger, when he admits that he "thinks too much on [what a good father Thias was before he took to the drink] everyday."[56] Finally, Adam's tender thoughts toward his father upon learning of his death reveal the extent to which he did not delight in his anger.[57]

Adam's matrix of anger, pity, love, and disappointment is somewhat flattened by the closing observation that "when death, the great Reconciler, has come, it is never our tenderness that we repent of, but our severity."[58] Severity is literally the final word of the chapter, casting Adam's emotional state through the entire scene as severe, though it is not. This final comment comes on the heels of a chapter replete with free indirect discourse and immediately after a sentence in which readers are given a glimpse into Adam's mind as it "rush[es] back over the past in a flood of relenting and pity."[59] This renders the final observation of the chapter as much Adam's own reflection as the narrator's, marking the comment as Adam's decision to favor pity and love in both the particular case of his father and as a guiding principle for human relationships. That said, Adam never repents of his actual judgment that his father was an irresponsible alcoholic, just as he never repents of his judgment regarding Ben and the other workers, nor of his judgment regarding Hetty and Arthur. What the novel presents in Adam, then, is a character who mixes just judgment and pity, who expresses appropriate anger at mockery and abuse but who does not enjoy the failings of others in any way. In short, we see a man who embodies the justice and mercy traditionally ascribed to the divine from the beginning to the end of the narrative.

Adam's alignment with Jesus through the novel's structure and through his typological markings directs readers to consider his embodiment of justice and mercy as a means of imagining what Jesus was like in the real world. If he was morally upright and concerned with the treatment of women and the poor, then none of Adam's actions are out of keeping with Jesus. Additionally, the physical nature of Adam's anger underscores both his bodily existence and his masculinity, but by insisting on the uncompromising nature of Adam's judgments, Eliot hedges against the primary foible of Victorian masculinity—moral compromise. Moreover, Adam's anger and physicality are essential to

---

[56] Eliot, A.B., 38.
[57] Eliot, A.B., 49.
[58] Eliot, A.B., 49.
[59] Eliot, A.B., 49.

Eliot's creation of a "historical" Jesus who disturbs the safe and sedate Jesus of tradition, the one who merely comforts and befriends. Rather, Eliot's historical, embodied, man of action draws attention to the more difficult, disruptive ways in which God incarnate might actually behave.

While Adam often judges the actions of those around him, like Jesus he is also depicted as a kind man and helpful friend in times of trouble. Looking at the novel's structure, Adam's first actions in the novel, apart from singing a hymn celebrating earthly work and measuring a board, are to defend his brother from overly harsh teasing and promptly finish the work his father neglected. Moreover, Adam's own, very orthodox, interpretation of Christian faith emphasizes Jesus's teachings on the primacy of practical expressions of love. As Adam explains, the man who "builds a oven for 's wife to save her from going to the bakehouse [is] just as near to God, as if he was running after some preacher and a-praying and a-groaning."[60] While the point of Adam's observation echoes the parable of the Good Samaritan—that true spirituality is not found in wordy, emotional expressions of religiosity or great religious learning but in practical work, be it binding or building, on behalf of the other—it is no small point that Adam places his observation within the structures of marriage. By grounding his notion of spirituality in marriage, Adam makes true spirituality dependent upon relational knowledge of the other, a knowledge that is open to the other and responsive to the needs of the other. Moreover, in reiterating the longstanding metaphor of marriage as a model for the believer's relationship to Jesus, Adam's observation strips this metaphor of its sexual connotations. Adam, as both a man and Dinah's eventual husband, naturally aligns with the husband who builds the oven. But Adam is also marked as Jesus, not in the least through their shared occupation of carpentry, a building occupation that further aligns Adam and Adam-as-Jesus with the husband. Given the positioning of Adam as a human Jesus within the marriage plot and the repetition of the common Christian metaphor of marriage for expressing the union between Christ and the believer, the statement works to redefine the relationship between Jesus and the believer not in terms of erotic mysticism but in terms of practical acts of service and familial love.

While Adam's views on practical spirituality are in keeping with those of Jesus, he never talks about Jesus or quotes Jesus as Dinah does. In fact, he admits that he "like[s] to read about Moses best."[61] For this reason, some critics, such as Clifford Marks, have read *Adam Bede* through a sort of Marcionite hermeneutic,

---

[60] Eliot, *A.B.*, 9.
[61] Eliot, *A.B.*, 433.

in which Adam is a representation of Old Testament practicality or the Law and Dinah is a representation of Jesus's love and New Testament grace.[62] Indeed, such law-versus-grace (mis)interpretations of Paul enjoy a long and profoundly influential history in many Christian traditions, despite officially rejecting some extreme forms such as Marcion's. However, what critics such as Marks miss about the harshness of Adam's emotions and actions is that Adam-as-Jesus is not interested in the evangelical grace of conversion narratives, nor are his judgments those of an angry deity in need of appeasement. Rather, Eliot's Adam restores the character of Jesus from the spiritualization of an evangelicalism like Dinah's, and even dogmatic orthodoxies like Kingsley's, to a "real" human character whose love and concern for justice are characterized in concrete, human actions and interior emotions which have the Jesus of the gospels (more than of Paul's preaching about Jesusm or subsequent typological theologies) as their model. Moreover, by quoting the Old Testament rather than the New, Adam functions in the role of interpreter of the authoritative text much like the Jesus of the synoptic tradition, again showing Eliot's characterization of Adam *as* Jesus in his world, rather than a character who relates to Jesus or illustrates theological abstractions about Jesus. Marks's division of the novel between an Old Testament law figured in Adam's character and a New Testament grace in Dinah's interposes upon Eliot the very theological baggage that a Straussian view of a historical, human Jesus would (attempt to) eschew. Not only that, but the particular theological binary of Old Testament law and New Testament grace reiterates the dichotomization of justice and mercy that the novel transcends through its emphasis on a robust vision of sympathy grounded in relational knowledge.

The ongoing interplay of Adam's honesty, righteous anger, and practical love, which are grounded in his uncompromising moral sensibilities, serves as an important basis for what emerges as a particularly active, hence in Victorian context a particularly *masculine*, vision of sympathy. Dinah and Adam's moral sensibilities are very much in parallel throughout the novel: both insist upon speaking and acting honestly, treating others with love, doing one's duty, and living out one's convictions without compromise. But Dinah's sympathy is gendered in particularly feminine terms and Adam's in male terms. Consequently, while Dinah's moral sensibility is just as uncompromising as Adam's, she never throws anyone against a wall; she never punches anyone.

---

[62] Marcionism is a Christian heresy originating in the second century that views the God of the Old Testament and the God of the New Testament as different deities, with the God of Israel a harsh and judgmental figure and the God of the New Testament (represented by Jesus) a being of love and mercy.

Her presence while preaching or when in the Bede and Poyser homes is one of gentleness, comfort, and diligence that have the potential to influence those around her. It is not that her influence is passive, but it is construed particularly in terms of the verbal. She preaches, she chats with Hetty in her bedroom, and she comforts Hetty while in prison largely through speech. In fact, during her midnight conversation with Hetty and in the jail cell, Dinah is just as uncompromising with Hetty about the need to confront her own vanity and wrongdoing as Adam is with Arthur. That said, Dinah's reforming words and comforting presence do very little actual reforming. Her sermon brings about a change in Chad's Bess for a time, but it is not a lasting change. More significantly, despite living in the same home together, Dinah is unable to influence Hetty for good or intervene effectively when she senses trouble. In the end, Dinah does bring Hetty comfort and leads her to repentance, but it is too late to save Hetty or the baby she kills.

Whereas Dinah's sympathy is characterized as feminine through its reliance upon the verbal, Adam's sympathy is gendered in masculine terms through physical, practical action. Thus, Adam carries a heavy basket or child, finishes work for his father, or offers a reconciling handshake to Arthur. More importantly, his more active sympathy does bring about some reform. While Arthur is the most obvious example of a person changed through his relationship with Adam, the other workmen, Bartle Massey, and even Dinah are also somewhat changed by Adam. In light of the overall ineffectiveness of Dinah's sympathy, Adam's masculine sense of moral righteousness, honesty, and pity suggests that the novel's real concern is not reforming Adam's character but reforming the notion of sympathy.

What we have in Adam, then, is a dynamic representation of sympathy as it demands justice and ultimately extends mercy to all. Adam's harshness and his "peppery" personality ensure that significant injury does not go unrecognized.[63] If Adam only felt pity for his father and Arthur, then the wrongs suffered by his mother, brother, Hetty, and her child would be silenced, moved into the margins of the text—and Adam's sympathy would lack justice. Yet justice is only part of the picture. Adam's final judgments regarding the moral failings of others consistently favor pity; he consistently extends mercy. When pity and judgment join to foster reconciliation, we have Eliot's robust vision of sympathy. But such sympathy cannot be grounded in abstract notions. By offering a narrative

---

[63] Eliot, A.B., 15.

representation of sympathy that inseparably joins justice and pity, *Adam Bede* highlights the fact that the full workings of sympathy are best understood through narrative because only the novel's realism can create the experience of relational knowledge. Only the novel can represent multiple, shifting, and conflicting attitudes—the heteroglossia of people, ideas, and experiences—that form human relationships, joining these competing ideas together and constructing a whole that is truly greater than its parts. In this way, *Adam Bede*'s insistence on the embodied and relational nature of justice and pity echoes Kingsley's insistence on the incarnation. Whoever Jesus was, he was a specific person in a specific time and place. We can only understand his character and make sense of his ideals if we understand him in his physical and relational particularity.

By marking Adam as Jesus, Eliot's realism provides the perfect form to recover the anger, disappointment, and harsh condemnations that characterize the Jesus of the Gospels, even though these characteristics go uncelebrated in hymns and unrecognized in popular piety. The interiority that is such a defining habit of the realist novel allows Eliot to create a complicated portrayal of Jesus's interiority—a mixture of justice, mercy, harshness, and pity—which she draws from Christian tradition without being constrained by dogma. Unlike some Victorians, who in thinking about the Jesus of history focus on infant Jesus meek and mild, Eliot gives us an adult man, unidealized and un-sentimentalized. She gives us a Jesus who is not defined by a single act of sacrifice, but a Jesus known through his relationships to others and to a particular community.

In opposition to the traditional Jesus narrative, Adam is not marked by a heroic act of self-sacrifice to save his friends. But as his attitudes toward Hetty and Arthur, Seth and the workers, and even toward his father demonstrate, he is always actively using his agency and power to defend those around him, and to bring those around him back into right relationships with each other and himself. In this way, Eliot brings the theologies of justice and mercy together demonstrating the deep narrative coherence of these apparently opposite attitudes. Since justice and mercy are the two forces theologians grapple with when thinking about theories of the atonement, we begin to see that in *Adam Bede* Eliot is reworking the idea of atonement. Through Adam, the idea of atonement shifts from a single cosmic sacrifice to ongoing actions through which the divine simultaneously punishes injustice and restores the broken. In the material world of the novel, such atonement depends upon Adam as a man of action. It depends upon a bodily masculinity capable of taking physical action, while both upright and sympathetic. And it depends on creating a mundane, ordinary understanding of heroism in which routine faithfulness replaces superhuman self-sacrifice.

To speak of the heroic in *Adam Bede* seems, initially, a sort of anathema. After all, Eliot explicitly directs readers away from "cloud-borne angels, from prophets, sibyls, and heroic warriors," in favor of "common, coarse people who have no picaresque sentimental wretchedness."[64] She repeatedly chastises those who "pant after the ideal," arguing instead for the value of the commonplace: simple everyday people "with their work-worn hands... rounded backs and stupid weather-beaten faces."[65]

Despite Eliot's chastisement of her readers, Victorians liked heroes. Samuel Smiles's *Self-Help* (1859) celebrates a particular type of heroic repeatedly, one that is uniquely apparent in the life of the Duke of Wellington. Yet, it is not Wellington's prowess in battle that Smiles memorializes. For Smiles, the hero is an individual characterized by "self-reliance amidst trials and difficulties," "courage," "self-denial and manly tenderness."[66] Smiles is not alone in his view of the heroic. For Carlyle, the hero or "Great Man" is defined first and foremost by a penetrating "sincerity" that "cannot get out of the awful presence of this Reality."[67] In fact, the heroic is so important to Carlyle that to discount the possibility of the heroic is "literally [to] despair of human things" and to "despair of the world

---

[64] Eliot, *A.B.*, 161.

[65] Eliot, *A.B.*, 166–7, 162. If Eliot's own denouncement of sublime beauty and ideals was not enough, Alexander Welsh's seminal work on the Waverley novels reinforces the idea that heroics have no place in the historical and high realism of the nineteenth century. Welsh contends historical realism requires that the "serious anxieties" and "emotions" of the "hero" be represented and explored, resulting in "the hero of civilization and refinement... a passive hero of 'quiet and retiring' character" whose actions are directed by the "accepted morality of his public" (18–24). Moreover, beginning with Lukács' seminal work *The Historical Novel*, historical realism from Scott onward has been celebrated for its ability to allow readers to "re-experience the social and human motives which led men to think, feel and act just as they did in historical reality" (42). The historical novel is, as is oft rehearsed, about the man-in-history and not about the transcendent exploits of the timeless, heroic individual. While George Levine argues for an active heroism in Victorian realism, it is entirely psychological and self-focused, grounded in working through "the complexity of [the hero's] relationships to their own past and to society" (128). Such heroes "must all in their own ways make their peace with the practical world," resulting in a literary form that is, in essence, about the "quest for truth, for the fact, as opposed to the dream" (128). Thus, for literary scholars the realist heroic is, to a large extent about abandoning the claims to transcendence—the dream—in favor of historical particularity, in favor (one could say) of the commonplace. Given such analysis, traditional heroics involving action and even rescue would seem to be dead in nineteenth-century literature.

For the complete arguments, see Levine, *The Realistic Imagination: English Fiction from Frankenstein to Lady Chatterley*; György Lukács, *The Historical Novel*, trans. Hannah Mitchell and Stanley Mitchell (Lincoln: University of Nebraska Press, 1983); Alexander Welsh, *The Hero of the Waverley Novels, with New Essays on Scott* (Princeton: Princeton University Press, 2014).

[66] Samuel Smiles, *Self-Help, with Illustrations of Character, Conduct, and Perseverance* (Oxford: Oxford University Press, 2002), 89, 331.

[67] Thomas Carlyle, *On Heroes, Hero-Worship, & the Heroic in History* (London: James Fraser, 1841), 72–3.

altogether."⁶⁸ While Carlyle's construction of the hero has some issues in terms of reconciling the time-bound hero and transcendent authority, heroic qualities like sincerity, courage, self-reliance, self-denial, and tenderness—justice and mercy, even—are not out of place in a realist novel.⁶⁹ In fact, they sound very much like just the sort of qualities Eliot celebrates in lieu of an ideal heroic and uses to characterize her robust vision of sympathy. Consequently, to read chapter 17 of *Adam Bede* as a denunciation of any and all heroics misses the heart of the chapter and the novel as a whole.

Throughout *Adam Bede* Eliot develops a commonplace heroic very much in keeping with her aesthetic theory and with the wider nineteenth-century discourse on true heroism. In her discourse on aesthetics in chapter 17, "In which the Story Pauses a Little," Eliot is not arguing against heroism per se, but against ideals and idealization, against the "pomp," "absolute indigence,... tragic suffering or... world-stirring actions" of "heroic warriors."⁷⁰ Instead of these "extremes," she advocates a love of the commonplace and of common people.⁷¹ Such love requires a strength and fortitude that can well be called a commonplace heroism, the courage and constancy to "tolerate, pity, and love" people while clearly seeing their faults. Eliot knows that such love is no mean feat. People can very easily be "indifferent" to the "real breathing men and women" around them.⁷² Or, well aware of human weakness, some turn to cynicism, arguing that to "maintain the slightest belief in human heroism, you must never make a pilgrimage to see the hero."⁷³ Faced with such cynicism, Eliot admits that she has "meanly shrunk from confessing... [her] experience" that "people more or less commonplace and vulgar" are capable of "deep pathos" and "sublime mysteries."⁷⁴ Of course, not all that is commonplace and vulgar is heroic. But, if the heroic is bravery and sincerity, tenderness and self-denial, then the commonplace offers abundant examples of heroism. And, lest one think that heroism on the farm is less demanding than heroism in battle, the mundane materiality and vulgar people of realism invite us to ponder which is more difficult: actively loving the

---

[68] Carlyle, *Heroes*, 137, 200.
[69] Carlyle's vision of the heroic is not entirely satisfactory in terms of high realism. As Chris Vanden Bossche argues, Carlyle's heroic individuals embody the tension between historical particularity and the ideal in a way that "amounts to a contradiction rather than a resolution of the tension between historical and transcendental authority." See Chris Vanden Bossche, *Carlyle and the Search for Authority* (Columbus: Ohio State University Press, 1991), 98.
[70] Eliot, *A.B.*, 161.
[71] Eliot, *A.B.*, 162.
[72] Eliot, *A.B.*, 160.
[73] Eliot, *A.B.*, 166.
[74] Eliot, *A.B.*, 166.

same man or woman for fifty years with "fellow-feeling" and "forbearance" or cutting down fifty of one's enemies in an adrenaline-fueled battle frenzy?[75] Eliot's denouncement of extremes and recognition that her readers must be taught to love the commonplace suggests that the turn away from the heroic extreme is the more difficult and, thus, the more worthy of praise. For this precise reason, Eliot turns from "creat[ing] a world so much better than this" and attempts to develop an art that models and teaches sympathy, that teaches people to live lives of "outspoken, brave justice."[76]

One cannot speak of "outspoken, brave justice" as the culmination of fellow-feeling and forbearance in *Adam Bede* without thinking of Adam himself: he is the embodiment of such attributes. In fact, he so strongly embodies a heroic sympathy that Eliot is forced to admit, a mere two chapters after her discourse on the commonplace, that Adam "was not an average Man" nor an "ordinary character among workmen."[77] Despite this admission, Eliot continues to insist that "Adam... was by no means a marvellous man, nor, properly speaking, a genius," but she does caution readers against concluding that "the next... man you may happen to see with a basket of tools over his shoulder and a paper cap on his head has the strong conscience and the strong sense, the blended susceptibility and self-command, of our friend Adam."[78] In these apparent contradictions, Adam embodies the juxtaposition between the extraordinary and the ordinary that Susan Colón identifies as driving the Victorian use of parables to imagine new possibilities.[79] Thus, while Adam is commonplace, he is not common; his conscience, sense, and "blended susceptibility and self-command" are simply another reformulation of the commonplace heroic of chapter 17. In his strength and openness to others, his sense of right and wrong, his intelligence in evaluating situations, and his self-control in action, Adam is an exemplary (but not totally exceptional) man. To borrow from Colón's description of Victorian parables, Adam "respond[s] to an ordinary situation in an extraordinary way, a way that is fully on the plane of human action but which

---

[75] This question is a paraphrase of Wendell Berry, who makes the same point as Eliot regarding the truly heroic nature of the commonplace in his essay "The Gift of Good Land," in the collection, *The Art of the Commonplace*. He, however, sees the Judeo-Christian tradition as valorizing the deeds of great men, rather than endorsing everyday faithfulness. See Wendell Berry, "The Gift of Good Land," in *The Art of the Commonplace: The Agricultural Essays of Wendell Berry*, ed. Norman Wirzba (Washington, DC: Counterpoint, 2002), 293–304.

[76] Eliot, *A.B.*, 160.
[77] Eliot, *A. B.*, 192.
[78] Eliot, *A. B.*, 192.
[79] Colón, *Victorian Parables*, 13.

challenges ordinary ideas about, for example, how many times one can forgive another, or about whether people can change for the better."[80]

Adam, characterized as an uncommon and exemplary man, fits nicely with a demythologized, Feuerbachean model of Jesus. Adam, like Jesus, is a human whose exemplary behavior offers a vision of divine ideals. As such, he is positioned within the narrative to rework the priestly work of reconciliation embodied in the theology of the atonement along the lines of a commonplace heroic. In this reconstruction of the atonement, in which justice and mercy are brought together through narrative reasoning to restore relationships between characters, Adam serves as the primary actor seeking always to redeem those around him.

This redeeming impulse within Adam helps explain one of the narrative peculiarities of *Adam Bede*. In most novels named for individuals, the narrative action centers on that character's development as a person. Exceptionally, Adam does not develop or change, as every scholar writing on *Adam Bede* points out. Re-orientating the plot around Adam's work to redeem other characters is particularly significant in terms of Raymond Williams's argument that *Adam Bede* is a *Bildungsroman* in which the protagonist stays within the community. While Adam develops professionally, he does not undergo the same sort of psychic or social transformation typical of other protagonists in novels of development. In fact, he remains largely static not only in terms of his own person but, as Williams points out, in terms of his community.[81] Orienting the dynamic tensions of the plot around Adam's drive to rescue others allows Eliot to explore Adam's character and his relationships without challenging his ties to geography, family, or history. Such groundedness not only reinforces the commonplace heroic that Eliot fashions in *Adam Bede*, it helps explain why Eliot aligns Adam and Jesus in the first place. Jesus provides a perfect historical and ideological model for a vision of human life that is dynamic and significant, but that also remains rooted in a particular socioeconomic group. When scholars do identify "growth" in Adam, it is along the lines of learning sympathy, but a careful reading of the text demonstrates that Adam is sympathetic from beginning to end and he never repents of his attempts to enact justice on behalf of the weak. Unlike characters in many realist novels, Adam's action in the face of suffering is not driven by a desire to ameliorate his own psychic discomfort. Rather, his action is always centered around saving others. Adam's attempts to

---

[80] Colón, *Victorian Parables*, 37.
[81] See Raymond Williams, *The Country and the City* (New York: Oxford University Press, 1973), 165–81.

rescue Hetty are obvious throughout the novel, but he also attempts to rescue Seth from teasing, to save Thias from the shame of failing to complete a job, and to save Arthur from his own folly. Even in accepting the role as steward, he is working to save the wood from "ill management."[82] Adam even seeks out Dinah, integrating her into the community through marriage. Thus, throughout the novel, Adam's action is characterized, not by self-denial per se, but by a concern for the good of others that grounds Eliot's view of sympathy. After all, if we "tolerate, pity, and love" others, we will be bravely outspoken in the pursuit of justice on their behalf.

Of course, Adam's work to save his friends from themselves and others does cause Adam to suffer, but in this suffering Eliot challenges the passivity attributed to Jesus in the crucifixion narrative. Thus, while Adam suffers greatly because of Hetty and Arthur, he is never a passive "man of sorrows" in any real sense (*pace* Knoepflmacher). Nowhere is this more obvious than as he awaits Hetty's trial. Passing the night with Bartle Massey, he paces the floor, lamenting he must "sit still... and do nothing."[83] Adam's pacing and agitation coupled with his frustration over the evil done to Hetty and the impossibility of bringing back her child suggest a caged animal keen to act, not a man passively suffering or anxious about the right course of action. His suffering is real, but it does not characterize or contain him. Even the epilogue, which describes his deep emotion after hearing of Hetty's recent death, does not give sorrow the final word. Adam's sorrow is contained within the larger Edenic setting of pastoral domesticity, complete with the assurance of new life represented by Adam and Dinah's son and daughter. Unlike Dinah's description of Jesus as eternally scarred, suffering, and waiting, Adam is active as he returns home from seeing Arthur, kissing his daughter, and picking up his son. Dinah notices his "agitation" after meeting Arthur, but his emotions are at odds with the scene of happy domesticity, casting them as a transient and not a characteristic state. And in this concluding scene, as in the entire novel, Adam's suffering in the novel is never passive. When faced with sorrow or injustice, Adam is always active, be it building Thias's coffin, seeking out Hetty after she runs away, or embracing his children after saying goodbye to Arthur.

By orienting Adam's story around his active attempts to save others, Eliot suggests an alternative to Scott's passive, anxiety-ridden hero. Instead, Eliot offers a commonplace heroic that feeds into the redefinitions of masculinity

---

[82] Eliot, *A.B.*, 219.
[83] Eliot, *A.B.*, 410–11.

within nineteenth-century gender discourse and changing definitions of the gentleman, represented by Smiles's and Carlyle's visions of the heroic gentleman. Through her reorientation of the plot around redemption, Eliot reaffirms Adam as a representation of Jesus, particularly in his office as a reconciling high priest.

At mid-century, much of British Christianity was wrestling with Jesus's identity as a real, flesh-and-blood, historical man. And, increasingly, British Christians were troubled by characterizations of the Christian God as an angry deity in need of a blood sacrifice to appease his wrath. As Eliot's work suggests, the atonement needs to be reworked if Strauss and Feuerbach are right. If Jesus is not the eternal God incarnate, then his death achieves no cosmic ends, and the atonement becomes nothing more than a meaningless passivity in the face of evil. Within this fraught conversation *Adam Bede* plays an important role in creating an imaginative space in which the atonement can be reworked in light of a historical Jesus. Through Adam's courage and constancy, his physicality, and his dynamic, deep sympathy with both the guilty and those hurt by the guilty, Eliot gives us a human picture of Jesus, a peacemaker who reconciles people to each other and to himself. This image is set up in contrast to Dinah's ethereal Jesus from beginning to end, tying together both Eliot's respect for Strauss's emphasis on a real, historical Jesus stripped of Christian myth and Feuerbach's insistence on the reality of God existing only and through human beings. Ultimately, Eliot is able to reimagine the atonement as a commonplace heroic grounded in restorative justice through Adam's embodiment of Jesus's priestly office.

And yet, Eliot's Jesus-shaped Adam also opens up new questions, particularly about Jesus's real significance for humanity. If Jesus is not necessary to save the world from sin in the way his priestly role traditionally construes his work, then his most important contribution to human history (beyond serving as a useful narrative archetype of self-sacrifice) would appear to be as a philosopher and teacher. But how useful, in that case, are his moral teachings in the real world? This is exactly the question that later novelists will begin to address, as they further work to bring the Jesus of history to life through the Victorian novel.

5

Jesus the Moral Prophet

Whereas Charles Kingsley's Jesus draws upon the tradition of Jesus as the cosmic king, and George Eliot's Jesus reimagines Jesus's priestly role in terms of human reconciliation, other writers in the late nineteenth century reworked the traditional threefold characterizations of Jesus by emphasizing and even reinterpreting his role as the ultimate moral prophet. In Christian tradition, the role of the prophet—and by extension Jesus's office as prophet—is not only that of a soothsayer or fortuneteller predicting the future. Hebrew prophets traditionally called Israel back to the covenant obligations of worshiping only the God of Israel and seeking justice for the poor and oppressed; Jesus as the great moral teacher who calls for love and justice offers another potential way to reimagine Jesus within a world where miracles are intellectually suspect. But given the biblical background of prophets as socially disruptive and uncomfortable characters, it is not entirely surprising that when Victorian novelists approach Jesus as a moral prophet, their characterizations result in an impossibly idealistic dreamer who disrupts people's expectations even as he develops a cult-like following.

Much more directly than either Kingsley's or Eliot's work, the novels of Mary Augusta Ward and Eliza Lynn Linton directly challenged popular and pious characterizations of Jesus through their representations of Jesus as a prophet. While Jesus the revolutionary king may disrupt the status quo, in Kingsley's representation Jesus the man is still very much God incarnate and very much in keeping with centuries of Christian theology. Eliot's historically human Jesus turns away from traditional understandings of Christ's divinity, demythologizing his reconciliatory work of justice and mercy as a commonplace but uncommon human exemplar of sympathy and fellow humanity. Although Eliot's representation of Jesus through Adam downplays his divinity, it never directly controverts the Christian creeds.

Such is not the case in Mary Augusta Ward's *Robert Elsmere*. In *Robert Elsmere* Ward imagines an intellectually acceptable Jesus, one who is explicitly and solely a human teacher misunderstood and misrepresented over the centuries, whose teachings demand progressive social reform. Despite her human Jesus, Ward shapes her protagonist around Charles Kingsley's vision of reform, narrating Robert's life as he strives to live out Jesus's teachings in the London slums. But the end result of Robert's imitation of Jesus appears to foster little systemic change. In the end, while Ward upholds the spirit of Jesus's teachings, the novel itself ultimately supersedes Jesus's ideas by presenting the family and domestic affection as the true sources of individual redemption and interpersonal reconciliation. Within this vision, Jesus is a great moral teacher akin to Aristotle, worthy of study and in some respects imitation, but not worship.

While Ward moves beyond Jesus, Eliza Lynn Linton's *The True History of Joshua Davidson: Christian and Communist* takes Jesus at his word, reimagining Jesus's life literally repeated within Victorian England and the Paris Commune. The results are disastrous for Linton's modern-day Jesus. Joshua is killed and his followers are scattered. In the end, the novel's narrator and Joshua's best friend suggests that, given the consequences of Joshua's teachings, Joshua's—and by extension Jesus's—moral vision is ultimately misguided and not worth pursuing.

Given the profound ways in which these novels ultimately discredit Jesus, it is not surprising that both *Robert Elsmere* and *Joshua Davidson* created sensations in Victorian Britain. In particular, *Robert Elsmere*, published in 1888, spoke directly to a zeitgeist anxious about biblical scholarship, struggling with religious doubt, and filled with spiritual longing. Robert's journey, from a generally orthodox faith including a belief in the divinity of Jesus, to a "demythologized" faith in which he "believes no longer in an Incarnation and Resurrection" was a frighteningly familiar journey for many Victorians.[1] And the conclusion that Christianity might exist simply as the belief that "Christ is risen in our hearts, in the Christian life of charity" and the corollary that "Miracle is a natural product of human feeling and imagination; and God was in Jesus—pre-eminently, as He is in all great souls, but not otherwise," left some Victorian believers with a more traditional Christology deeply troubled. While this demythologized Christology maintains the narrative shape of Jesus's life, it also renders him unnecessary in any real sense. For Robert, Jesus is an example, an inspirational template like any other noble character. But, like all such useful characters, his usefulness proves exhaustible.

While initial reviews of *Robert Elsmere* were slow to appear, and Walter Pater's early review was mixed, the novel made "extraordinary headway among library subscribers," and so provoked a second wave of reviews largely denouncing it.[2]

---

[1] Ward, *Elsmere*, 276.
[2] John Sutherland, *Mrs. Humphry Ward: Eminent Victorian, Pre-Eminent Edwardian* (Oxford: Clarendon Press, 1990), 125.

These attacks culminated in a lengthy review from William Gladstone, "Robert Elsmere and the Battle of Belief," in which he praises the novel's emotional portrayal of Robert but faults the book for its many "dismal gaps" in intellectual argument.[3] There truly is no bad publicity, especially when one's detractor is the once and future prime minister. *Elsmere*'s sales continued to increase, and pirate publishers in America made the work so widely available that it became one of the most read novels in English during the whole of the nineteenth century.[4]

Despite this runaway success, the novel is little known today outside scholarship on literature and church history. The scholarly consensus holds that it is aesthetically problematic, lacking especially in structure and characterization—criticisms that originated with Gladstone and Pater, respectively.[5] Although it is a high realist novel in the vein of Eliot's works, *Robert Elsmere* is seldom discussed in terms of literary form but serves instead to illustrate the doubt, contested scholarship, and secularization that challenged much of British Christianity toward the end of the century. While the novel represents both the state of Victorian Christianity in the 1880s along with the real trauma that religious doubt can bring to a marriage, it is more than a window into the zeitgeist.

As Caroline Levine argues, for many Victorians like John Ruskin, realism functioned as a form of experimentation, teaching readers to suspend their judgments regarding characters and events, testing their initial reactions and thoughts through the course of the realist novel.[6] Thus, for Ruskin realism "is not about putting our faith in representation. It is about putting mimesis to the test."[7] For Ruskin—and for Levine through Ruskin—the purpose of realism is to test all the possible options and outcomes of a situation, producing "humble

---

[3] William Gladstone, "Robert Elsmere and the Battle of Belief," *The Nineteenth Century* 23 (1888): 770.
[4] For a detailed publication history, including American pirate editions, see chapter 11 in Sutherland, *Mrs. Humphry Ward: Eminent Victorian, Pre-Eminent Edwardian.*
[5] Virtually every scholar who has written on *Robert Elsmere* concedes that it is not a great aesthetic accomplishment, although no one bothers to consider why this might be. For examples, see Rosemary Ashton, "Doubting Clerics: From James Anthony Froude to Robert Elsmere Via George Eliot," in *The Critical Spirit and the Will to Believe: Essays in Nineteenth-Century Literature and Religion*, ed. David Jasper and T. R. Wright (New York: St. Martin's Press, 1989); Mildred L. Culp, "Literary Dimensions of Robert Elsmere: Idea, Character, and Form," *The International Fiction Review* 9, no. 1 (1982); Mark M Freed, "The Moral Irrelevance of Dogma: Mary Ward and Critical Theology in England," in *Women's Theology in Nineteenth-Century Britain: Transfiguring the Faith of Their Fathers*, ed. Julie Melnyk (London: Garland Publishing, 1998); Lynne Hapgood, "'The Reconceiving of Christianity': Secularisation, Realism, and the Religious Novel," *Literature & Theology: An International Journal of Religion, Theory, and Culture* 10, no. 4 (1996); Jonathan Loesberg, "Deconstruction, Historicism, and Overdetermination: Dislocations of the Marriage Plots in Robert Elsmere and Dombey and Son," *Victorian Studies* 33, no. 3 (1990); Perkin, *Theology and the Victorian Novel.*
[6] Levine, *The Serious Pleasures of Suspense*, 12.
[7] Levine, *The Serious Pleasures of Suspense*, 12.

skepticism," rather than slavishly and arrogantly imitate the real in a trompe l'oeil that "leads us to enjoy our command of representation and the world."[8] Applying this understanding of realism to *Robert Elsmere* helps clarify the relationship between theological content and literary form in Ward's novel. On the level of content, *Robert Elsmere* is an imaginative experiment to determine the most viable interpretation of Jesus for the modern world. To do this, the novel must recreate the world as carefully as possible in order to test all the understandings of Jesus and applications of his teachings across the lives of two particular characters, the scholarly Robert and his pious wife, Catherine. To run this literary experiment the novel characterizes Jesus as a historical figure who, through centuries of Christian tradition and mythmaking, was transformed by the church into a symbol of all things divine and perfect. Following this argument, since Jesus's divinity and perfection were not original to his character, the book emphasizes the teachings that cohere around a Jesus stripped of any metaphysical truth claims grounded in Jesus's identity. In other words, Jesus is a moral prophet whose teachings offer a profound vision of what human life might be, but nothing more.

Growing from this vision of Jesus, *Robert Elsmere* tests the possibility of patterning the self after Jesus through Robert, imagining the self in union with Jesus's mission, to see if such a life will serve as a healing, reconciling, and even redemptive force within society. Additionally, through the character of Catherine, the novel asks if this demythologized characterization of Jesus can ever become acceptable to orthodox Christians. The experiment apparently concludes that a historical, demythologized Jesus is a vibrant force of moral inspiration for Robert. Moreover, Catherine eventually comes to appreciate Robert's work, even if she cannot fully embrace his understanding of Jesus, suggesting that orthodox Christians may learn to live and work together amicably with followers of demythologized Jesus. Yet these findings are undermined by formal aspects of the narrative, particularly the increasing silence in Robert's primary relationships, his ineffectual death, and the novel's emphasis on marital romance. Moreover, in Ward's sequel, *Richard Meynell*, religion moves beyond Robert's vision of Jesus, further subverting the apparent success of Robert's Jesus. In the end, the same challenges of "authoritative and established representations" of Jesus that undermine literary realism also undermine Robert's imitation of Jesus.[9] Like an overdetermined plot, Robert's imitation of Jesus's ideals proves unimaginative

---

[8] Levine, *The Serious Pleasures of Suspense*, 14.
[9] Levine, *The Serious Pleasures of Suspense*, 14.

and, as such, impossible to bring to life. Where the novel's "realist experiment," as Levine dubs it, is most compelling is in its exploration of marriage—including marital love, strife, and sympathy—which proves to be the foundation for both character reconciliation and readerly sympathy.

Ward's *Elsmere* is not the only novel of doubt in the latter part of the nineteenth century to test the validity of Jesus's life and work for the modern world. Sixteen years before *Elsmere*, the best seller *The True History of Joshua Davidson: Communist and Christian* (1872) by Eliza Lynn Linton demonstrated the same narrative characteristics and theological emphases as *Robert Elsmere*, despite being far more akin to Samuel Johnson's *Rasselas* than to *Middlemarch*.[10] While the novel is traditionally viewed as a recasting of Jesus's life in the nineteenth century, that conclusion is not quite an accurate description of Linton's structure. *Joshua Davidson* tells the story of Joshua, a poor Cornish boy who is appalled by the hypocrisy of Christians around him. He first becomes disillusioned with established Christianity when, at the age of fourteen, he challenges the local rector about why Christians do not give their money to the poor as Jesus commanded. After the rector gives some dismissive answers, Joshua determines to live the gospel out as literally as possible. He eventually moves to London with his friend, the novel's anonymous narrator, where he works as a carpenter. After befriending and reforming a drunken thief (Joe) and a prostitute (Mary), the four begin living together in a sort of religious commune. Joshua continues emphasizing the literal enactment of Jesus's teachings, even as he tries to identify with Anglicanism and Unitarianism, both of which reject him as a heretic. Eventually, he comes to believe that the historical, demythologized Jesus would have been a socialist had he lived in the nineteenth century, so Joshua moves to France to be part of the Paris Commune. When he returns to London as an avowed Communist, he is stoned to death by an angry mob. Much more obviously than *Robert Elsmere*, *Joshua Davidson* appears to test whether or not Jesus's teachings can be viably enacted in the nineteenth century. Thus, although not strictly a realist novel, it attempts to perform the same epistemological work of realism, using some features of the so-called oriental tale with its explicit social questioning to more directly address the issue of Jesus's character

---

[10] Although little known today, *Joshua Davidson* went through three editions in the first three months after its publication. For more on its publication history, see Nancy Fix Anderson, "Eliza Lynn Linton: The Rebel of the Family (1880) and Other Novels," in *The New Nineteenth Century: Feminist Readings of Underread Victorian Fiction*, ed. Barbara Leah Harman and Susan Meyer (New York: Garland, 1996). Also J. M. Rignall, "Between Chartism and the 1880s: J. W. Overton and E. Lynn Linton," in *The Socialist Novel in Britain: Towards the Recovery of a Tradition*, ed. H. Gustav Klaus (New York: St. Martin's Press).

and his claim on modern life.[11] While *Robert Elsmere* tries to bring the ideals of Jesus's teachings to life through a unique plot, *Joshua Davidson* imitates a highly predetermined representation of Jesus by explicitly following the plot of his life. In the end, the failure of Joshua's mission and the challenges related to characterization and sympathy within the novel's form highlight the extent to which literal imitative representations, particularly those that become mimicry, are prone to fail, especially if the person being imitated is Jesus.

Imitating Jesus

In both *Robert Elsmere* and *Joshua Davidson*, the relationship between each protagonist and Jesus is entirely imitative. Robert and Joshua consciously follow Jesus's behaviors and teachings, but they do not see him as an present character with whom they are in dialogue (as the evangelical Alton and Dinah do), nor do the novels present their protagonists as new versions of Jesus living out the spirit of Jesus's teachings in situations that are sometimes parallel and sometimes disparate from the first-century contexts depicted in the Gospels. The protagonists' conscious imitation of Jesus means that neither Joshua nor Robert ever replaces Jesus or becomes Jesus in the way that Adam Bede does. The difference here is the difference between *being* someone and trying to *be like* someone, parallel to the enacting work of realism and the imitative illusion of trompe l'oeil. Robert and Joshua are never modern-day versions of Jesus in the same way Adam is because, in trying to be someone else, Robert and Joshua never have the same sort of primary consciousness, namely Jesus's, that a character like Adam Bede possesses: an authentic, open-ended consciousness that is characteristically fundamental to realist experimentation and, by extension, realist representation. Thus, when characters are in relationships to Robert and Joshua or readers imaginatively identify with them, they are not in sympathy with Jesus but in sympathy with passionate interpreters of Jesus.

This second-hand Jesus is almost inevitable when considering Jesus's traditional office of prophet. After all, a prophet's teachings ostensibly come from God, and the point of a prophetic message is for the audience to follow it. The focus, at least for the prophet, is on the teaching and the divine spirit behind

---

[11] For the origin and influence of the oriental tale, see James Watt, "The Origin and Development of the Oriental Tale," in *Orientalism and Literature*, ed. Geoffrey P. Nash (Cambridge: Cambridge University Press, 2019).

the teaching, not the prophet as a character. Given the intellectual pressure on much of Victorian Protestantism stemming from biblical criticism, the natural sciences, anthropology, and psychology, Jesus as a moral prophet presents an appealing path for reimagining Jesus's character and preserving the structures of Christian faith. Yet *Robert Elsmere* and *Joshua Davidson* make clear that the office of moral prophet can actually render Jesus himself dispensable. Stripped of the miraculous incarnation and resurrection, no longer a cosmic king, and not even a priestly reconciler, Jesus the moral prophet is only as valuable as his teachings prove to be because those teachings have lost any metaphysical grounding in divine authority. Consequently, as *Robert Elsmere* and *Joshua Davidson* conclude in their own ways, if Jesus's teachings prove impractical or disruptive to culturally valuable institutions like the family, economy, or nation, then the morally responsible thing to do is abandon Jesus altogether.

To fully appreciate the unique intellectual culture that frames *Robert Elsmere* and *Joshua Davidson*, it is helpful to remember the rapid changes taking place in British theology during the mid- to late nineteenth century. The religious doubt and soul-searching that characterize both *Robert Elsmere* and *Joshua Davidson* became a particularly public issue with the 1860 publication of *Essays and Reviews* which, as Owen Chadwick explains, publicly exposed the "gap between Christian doctrine and the real beliefs of educated men."[12] Of course, the issue was not simply that educated Victorians found it difficult to believe that Jonah had survived for three days in the belly of a whale. The real issue for traditional orthodoxies was the rejection of the miraculous altogether, which, while not a new development in British thinking, began to have widespread theological effects in the middle of the nineteenth century.

The origin and purpose of miracles have been points of contention as far back as the Gospels themselves. Even Jesus's disciple Thomas found the resurrection a bit too much to believe without seeing Jesus for himself. In European thought, Spinoza's late seventeenth-century works brought new and more widespread attention to the problem of the miraculous. Spinoza's pantheistic identification of God with creation meant that "any event happening in nature which contravened nature's universal laws would necessarily contravene the Divine decree, nature, and understanding."[13] In other words, any apparent miracle either had a naturalistic (although unknown) cause or was a "pseudo-miracle

---

[12] Chadwick, *The Victorian Church, Part 2, 1860–1901*, 76.
[13] Spinoza's thought and the effect it had on European understandings of Jesus are thoroughly explored in Colin Brown, "Jesus in the History of the Debates on Miracles," in *Cambridge Companion to Miracles*, ed. Graham H. Twelftree (Cambridge: Cambridge University Press, 2011), 277.

performed by a false prophet."[14] While eighteenth-century deism generally followed Spinoza's arguments, it was David Hume's "Of Miracles" (1748) that established the philosophical framework for disbelief in the nineteenth century. Hume's argument was routinely summarized as "miracles do not happen," a gloss that proved highly influential in Victorian thinking, haunting epistemology throughout the nineteenth century.

Strauss's *Das Leben Jesu* builds on such empiricism, ultimately arguing that the Jesus story developed as a myth among his (ignorant, primitive) followers who were quick to look for miraculous, rather than natural, explanations of their religious experiences. Ludwig Feuerbach carried Strauss's conclusions to their logical end, contending in *Das Wesen des Christentums* (1841, translated by George Eliot in 1854) that the idea of God in Jesus is a projection of the highest human ideals and virtues combined with religious mythmaking—but incompatible with modern standards of reason. While these thinkers scandalized many Victorian Christians, their suggestions that the stories around Jesus are historically unreliable because they developed over time reinforced Hume's thesis that one is never justified in believing reports about miracles. Such historical and contextual arguments about textual development enjoyed wide influence because, as Charles Taylor suggests, nineteenth-century historiography (particularly as represented in *Robert Elsmere*) understands history as "a clear master narrative, in which science emerges out of earlier ignorance and irrationality."[15] Quite reasonably, then, Robert and one of his intellectual mentors, Squire Wendover, believe they "have nothing to learn from first-century Palestinian fishermen."[16] According to this understanding of the natural world and past civilizations, the benighted disciples could not have seen an actually resurrected Jesus but must have fallen prey to their own hopes and superstitions.

If the solution to the problem of miracles was to be found in thinkers like Strauss, whose mythographical readings of the Gospel texts offered a thoroughly naturalized explanation of not only how but why miracle stories developed, then core tenets of the Christian faith—particularly the resurrection and the incarnation—were fabrications of later pious fancy. In this manner, German criticism brought the operative philosophical and historical frameworks together against traditional Christian belief, while pointing to a new way of

---

[14] Brown, "Jesus in the History of the Debates on Miracles," 277.
[15] Charles Taylor, *A Secular Age* (Cambridge: The Belknap Press of Harvard University Press, 2007), 386.
[16] Taylor, *A Secular Age*, 386.

understanding Christianity that freed it from "myth" and from miracle. This challenge to the resurrection and incarnation came at a particularly significant time in the history of British religious thought. As the second chapter argued above, Jesus had emerged as a key historical figure long before the "quest for the historical Jesus" fixated British theology. The renewal of the liturgical year, the emphasis on Christmas, the fictionalized biographies of Jesus in realist novels of conversion, the numerous gospel harmonies, and the "lives of Jesus" all worked together in the period from 1825 to 1860 to make the narrative of Jesus's life a primary focus for much of Victorian Protestantism. As argued in the first chapter, this attention to the human life of Jesus stood in narrative contrast to an earlier set of theological emphases (and complications) generated by the evangelical stress on the atonement conceived largely as a transaction between God and humans. Focusing on the life and teachings of Jesus, along with his death and resurrection, meant wrestling with Jesus as a human and frequently emphasized his character as an active, loving, and suffering God-man. Although this approach to Jesus's character left room for ideas about atonement, especially the repair of human relationships between individuals and within society, much less attention was paid to the mechanism by which atonement is achieved. Rather, as I argued regarding Eliot's *Adam Bede*, atonement becomes the work of a just peacemaker's agency rather than a victim's bloody sacrifice.

But focusing on the incarnation created a new set of questions. While the incarnation offered Victorians a way to think about Jesus as the cosmic king and even to reframe the atonement along less cultic lines, arguments against the intellectual validity of the bodily resurrection and incarnation weighed heavily on the late Victorian mind. For many, most notably in the literary circles of Matthew Arnold and his niece, Mary Augusta Ward, the answer was found in spiritualized interpretations of both Christian doctrine and the Bible itself. Although their particular methods of transforming Christian tradition varied, both Ward and Arnold understood the resurrection as a subjective event in which the life of Jesus continued to be lived out through Christian civilization. This approach frequently came to be described as "incarnational" because it stresses the ongoing presence of Jesus in the contemporary world through his followers. Yet, it is markedly different from the dogma of the incarnation, in which Jesus is a unique, particular, and historical revelation of God the Son. In this transition from a dogmatic understanding of incarnation to a more literary one, Matthew Arnold was quite blunt in stating the irrelevance of the dogma for late Victorian Protestantism. Writing in the 1883 preface to the popular edition of *Literature and Dogma*, he admonishes his readers:

> The *Guardian* proclaims "the miracle of the Incarnation" to be "the fundamental truth" for Christians. How strange that on me should devolve the office of instructing the *Guardian* that the fundamental thing for Christians is not the incarnation but the imitation of Christ! In insisting on "the miracle of the Incarnation," the *Guardian* insists on just that side of Christianity which is perishing. Christianity is immortal; it has eternal truth, inexhaustible value, a boundless future. But our popular religion at present conceives the birth, ministry, and death of Christ, as altogether steeped in prodigy, brimful of miracle;—and miracles do not happen.[17]

Because of what Arnold regarded as the problematic supernaturalism of the gospel, he concludes that one must focus instead on Christianity's eternal truth, which he believes consists of the imitation of Christ. Not only is Arnold arguing here specifically against giving any significance to the doctrine of the incarnation, in the traditional sense; he is arguing for a shift away from a "fundamental *truth*" to the "fundamental *thing*," which happens to be moral action. In other words, Arnold is shifting the focus of Christianity from theological and Christological ideas to its moral content. While such reasoning is frequently characterized as a form of secularization, it is clear from Arnold's declaration of Christianity's "inexhaustible value" and "boundless future" that he did not want to move away from Jesus or Christianity. Instead, he is offering a path for reconstructing Christian faith in light of contemporary scholarship, cultural assumptions, and the shared experiences of the modern world.

Like her uncle Matthew Arnold, Mary Augusta Ward believed that the only way forward for Christianity was through re-envisioning it as a sublime moral system rather than a set of doctrinal claims. In fact, she follows Arnold's basic argument against the incarnation so completely that, in Robert's moment of conversion (or "de-conversion" as some scholars call it), he actually quotes *Literature and Dogma*, concluding his catechism on the non-divinity of Jesus with "miracles do not happen!"[18]

For all their similarities, however, Arnold and Ward treat the Bible in very different ways. As Mark Freed points out, in *Literature and Dogma* Arnold insists on conserving the Bible because, even for considering biblical stories

---

[17] Matthew Arnold, "Literature and Dogma," in *Dissent and Dogma*, ed. R. H. Super, (Ann Arbor: University of Michigan Press, 1968), 146. In this declaration, Arnold's argument reflects Hume's thinking as well as Hume's language regarding the Bible in his reference to "prodigies and miracles." See David Hume, *Philosophical Esays Concerning Human Understanding*, 2nd ed. (London: M. Cooper, 1751), 174, 81–3.

[18] Ward, *Elsmere*, 259.

metaphorically, their literary form is necessary to preserve the fullness of their meaning. Ward, however, takes a different approach, insisting that what matters is the ideological content of Christian teaching rather than the narratives through which that content is transmitted. As Ward explains in *The New Reformation*, published the year after *Elsmere* and expanding on its themes, "The particular system of dogmas put forward by any religion is the *Vorstellung* or presentation, the *Begriff* or Idea is the underlying spiritual reality common to it and presumably other systems besides."[19] In fact, Ward goes on to insist that the formal features of the biblical narrative actually conceal the meaning of Christianity, dismissing the *Vorstellung* as "the imaginative mythical elements which hide from us the Idea, or *Begriff*."[20] Not only is it highly ironic that a novelist would argue against the significance of literary and narrative form. This also marks a telling departure from Eliot's approach to Jesus in *Adam Bede*, which not only imagined Jesus within a particular historical context and a particular set of human relationships but insisted on the narratives of commonplace heroism as context in which an authentic Jesus-consciousness is enacted. But Ward's departure from Eliot's realism in her emphasis on the *Begriff* helps explain why Oscar Wilde quips that *Robert Elsmere* is "simply Arnold's *Literature and Dogma* with the literature left out."[21] By grounding Robert's imitation of Jesus in the idea, the *Begriff*, of Christianity, Ward implies that the specificities of mundane life in which the teachings come have no real bearing on religion. Rather, as Arnold and Ward make clear in their works, "the imitation of Christ" is the "fundamental thing"[22] (146). This remark is particularly important because it highlights a shift in the dominant narrative within English theology—a shift away from a historically grounded and historically shaped narrative of Jesus's life back to an appropriation of the Jesus narrative by the believer. This appropriation, at work in the last part of *Robert Elsmere*, is made particularly literal in *Joshua Davidson*. In both works, Jesus only matters if his life provides a useful model for the modern human to imitate. But, as both works suggest, imitation is difficult because of the complicated relationship between imitation and abstraction.

---

[19] "The New Reformation: A Dialogue," *The Nineteenth Century* 25 (1889): 470.
[20] "New Reformation: A Dialogue," 470.
[21] Wilde's Cyril makes this comment to Vivian in *The Decay of Lying* (1889), specifically regarding the novel *Robert Elsmere*. While always quoted in discussions of the novel, the quip is frequently downplayed and dismissed as a funny but somewhat unfair observation. Given Ward's attitude toward idea and form, however, it proves to be a far more insightful comment than is often recognized.
[22] Arnold, "Literature and Dogma," 146.

In order to imitate Jesus, both works treat Jesus as an ideological unit that can be removed from one historical and relational context and dumped directly into another. *Robert Elsmere* takes Jesus's ideas and sets them down in Britain. In *Joshua Davidson*, the plot is taken and recreated in Victorian Britain. It is as if Ward choses to paraphrase Jesus's life in *Elsmere* to the extent that the original becomes only a few ideas, whereas Linton opts for a highly literal translation that, while accommodating some realities of the nineteenth century like the existence of communism, loses the idea of the original in its very literalness. Despite this literalness, Linton's use of the oriental tale also results in a radical abstraction of Jesus's teachings. Since Joshua seems almost to hover just above the plane of normal human relationships, he is never profoundly shaped by a time, place, or people. Alternately, while Ward keeps Robert fully grounded in the particularities of his marriage, his imitation of Jesus is entirely grounded in the ideals of love, equality, and service he sees in the New Testament, rather than specific teachings of Jesus. What these narratives of imitating Jesus reveal is that understanding Jesus as the great moral prophet easily slides into mimicry or idealism, an overly literal recreation or an insufficiently specific universal ideal. In either case the prophet from whom the message came becomes not only unnecessary but an inconvenience or, worse, intolerable.

In testing the validity of Jesus's moral teachings for modern life, *Robert Elsmere* and *Joshua Davidson* present remarkably similar representations of the Nazarene for each man to imitate. For both Robert and Joshua, Jesus is an inspirational historical individual, a moral prophet who represents the best philosophy for how humans ought to live and treat each other. In terms of Jesus's metaphysical identity, both Joshua and Robert come to understand Jesus as misguided in his own time and later misrepresented by the church regarding his claims to divinity. However, both Robert and Joshua insist upon the purity and goodness of his character, although no reason for this insistence is given. Both men summarize the core of Jesus's teachings as love, forgiveness, and caring for the poor, and point to these teachings as the reasons he is exemplary. Moreover, both Robert and Joshua recognize that Jesus's ideals obviously challenge the economic and class systems that structure their own societies, and neither struggles with this as a radical or new interpretation of Jesus. The question for both *Robert Elsmere* and *Joshua Davidson*, then, is what do Jesus's moral ideals look like when enacted in the modern world?

Both novels are remarkably similar in their assumption that Jesus's life and teachings would look much like they did in first-century Judea. Jesus's teachings call for a reworking of the socioeconomic system such that class barriers are removed, outcasts are restored to society, and each person has the material and social needs to live a life of dignity. While an economically and socially transformative Jesus was still difficult for many Victorians to accept, this characterization had made significant inroads into British thinking during the mid-nineteenth century. When Kingsley first popularized Maurice's idea of a profound human brotherhood grounded in Jesus and uniting classes, the idea was treated as revolutionary and perhaps heretical. The common interpretation of Jesus's social teachings during the first half of the century is concretely represented in the English attitude toward church pews: Jesus loved and welcomed everyone, so long as they stayed in their proper place.[23] Maurice and Kingsley's idea that class structures might be overturned by Jesus's identity as God incarnate—all the more so than by his teachings—was too revolutionary for early and mid-nineteenth-century social novelists like Charlotte Elizabeth Tonna who used Jesus's teachings to call for factory reform but not for a literal brotherhood or abolition of class. By the late nineteenth century characterizations of Jesus emphasizing the economic and social implications of his actions were increasingly common, even in highly orthodox circles.[24]

That said, the highly progressive human unity that Robert and Joshua imagine remained somewhat suspect, particularly because Linton, in order to capture the revolutionary energy associated with Jesus, concretizes his teachings in terms of communism, thereby aligning his social teachings with the revolutionary fears of the period. As Linton's use of communism suggests, each novel imagines achieving the lofty goals embodied in Jesus's teachings differently. Joshua attempts to build a communistic community in which shared housing and resources provide the structural support to get prostitutes and drunkards off

---

[23] Although Christopher Hill's *Society and Puritanism in Pre-Revolutionary England* has made the argument that Protestantism inevitably led to egalitarianism and equality, as Patrick Collinson argues, "It was 'orthodox' Calvinists who filled their churches with seating... which placed the parishioners 'in order, in their degrees and callings'... convert[ing] church interiors into visible representations of the social order" (118). While not all dissenters followed this habit of church organization, it is telling that, even in mid-century representations of dissent, such as Margaret Oliphant's *Salem Chapel*, social standing and one's role in the church were strongly linked. Moreover, dissenting congregations and denominations themselves were strongly tied to one's socioeconomic class, as Owen Chadwick explains (412-13). See Owen Chadwick, *The Victorian Church, Part 1, 1829–1859*, 2 vols. (London: Oxford University Press, 1966); Patrick Collinson, *The Religion of Protestants: The Church in English Society, 1559–1625* (Oxford: Oxford University Press, 1982); Christopher Hill, *Society and Puritanism in Pre-Revolutionary England* (New York: Schocken Books, 1964). Also Oliphant, *Salem Chapel*.

[24] Socially minded Christianities were increasingly common in the late Victorian period across all denominations, even evangelicals; the doctrinally conservative Spurgeon was deeply concerned with the poor and the implications of Jesus's teachings for social systems. For more on Spurgeon's socially progressive views, see Tomas J. Nettles, *Living by Revealed Truth: The Life and Pastoral Theology of Charles Haddon Spurgeon* (Fearn, Scotland: Mentor, 2013).

the street. Yet, despite the change in Mary's and Joe's lives, they are not able to be reintegrated into society. Mary is turned out from her job at Mr. C's house because of her past, and Joe's drinking leads to imprisonment for Joshua and the narrator, making them unemployable. Robert's enactment of Jesus's teachings is less revolutionary, more paternalistic, and more intellectually lofty. Robert sees education, particularly theological education, as a way to better the lives of the working class. His emphasis on lectures, readings, story-telling, and communal worship suggests that enacting Jesus's teachings means improving the minds of others, equipping them to better their own lives. While he is aware of systemic problems such as the need for sewers and safe housing, these concerns do not get the same narrative attention as his theological musings and efforts as an educator. While Joshua's and Robert's individual imitations of Jesus's moral ideals differ in their execution, both point to socioeconomic reform as a necessary aspect of social redemption and both see themselves as the true representation of Jesus's teachings amid false, superstitious, even hypocritical versions of Christianity.

In order to fully appreciate the philosophical conditions that lead Robert and Joshua to understand themselves as the true representation of Jesus's teachings within the world of false, hypocritical, and intellectually untenable Christian communities, it is helpful to look at Robert's self-catechesis and the relationship of his Christology to other popular forms of Victorian Protestantism to understand the points of intersection and divergence. Robert's conversion to his own understanding of Jesus takes place over a long period, but there are key moments that serve as signposts in that journey. The night after discussing Squire Wendover's book project, Robert awakes from a dream in which he beholds "the image of a purely human Christ—a purely human, explicable, yet always wonderful Christianity." Although the dream "[breaks] his heart,... the spell of it was like some dream-country wherein we see all the familiar objects of life in new relations and perspectives."[25] This image precipitates the intellectual crisis in which Robert's internal dialogue serves as a self-catechesis. Robert asks:

Do I believe in God? Surely, surely! "Though He slay me yet will I trust in Him!"
Do I believe in Christ? Yes,—in the teacher, the martyr, the symbol to us Westerns of all things heavenly and abiding, the image and pledge of the invisible life of the spirit—with all my soul and all my mind!

But in the Man-God, the Word from Eternity,—in a wonder-working Christ, in a risen and ascended Jesus, in the living Intercessor and Mediator for the lives of His doomed brethren?

---

[25] Ward, *Elsmere*, 245.

He waited, conscious that it was the crisis of his history, and there rose in him, as though articulated one by one by an audible voice, words of irrevocable meaning.

Every human soul in which the voice of God makes itself felt, enjoys, equally with Jesus of Nazareth, the divine sonship, and *"miracles do not happen!"*

It was done.[26]

In this self-catechism Robert explicitly rejects metaphysical claims about Jesus and the exclusive alignment of Jesus with the role of the Christ, or the "chosen one." In this Robert is simultaneously rejecting Jesus as both king and priest, claiming that only his work as the moral prophet is worth redeeming from Christian tradition. Robert's stated concern, fostered by Squire Wendover, regards the reliability of testimony. However, it is not so much the historical reliability of any testimony, but the reliability of testimony affirming Jesus's bodily resurrection and other miracles that troubles Robert. As he writes after his conversion, Christianity's "grounds are not philosophical but literary and historical. It rests not upon all fact, but upon a special group of facts. It is, and will always remain, a great literary and historical problem, a question of *documents and testimony.*"[27] The "special group of facts" are, first and foremost, the historicity of the bodily resurrection and, growing from that, the historicity of other miracles and ontological claims about Jesus's identity. In essence, he is concerned about the reliability of testimony that points to Jesus being God. Robert follows the Squire's narrative of progress, including the inevitable "evolution" of testimony, which has "like every other human product... *developed.*"[28] The Squire explains to Robert in one of their lengthy conversations that "Man's power of apprehending and recording what he sees and hears has grown from less to more,... just as the reasoning powers of the cave-dweller have developed into the reasoning powers of Kant."[29] This view of history inevitably challenges any testimony that is exceptional, particularly claims to miracles. Through the Squire's narrative about the nature of history, coupled with an assumption that miracles are impossible, Robert concludes that Jesus cannot actually be God. He is, rather, a great teacher, a moral prophet, from whom humanity has learned much, but whom the church gradually characterized as divine.

---

[26] Ward, *Elsmere*, 259.
[27] Ward, *Elsmere*, 308, italics original.
[28] Ward, *Elsmere*, 240, 42. (emphasis original)
[29] Ward, *Elsmere*, 242.

Although this self-catechesis appears to have settled the matter intellectually, Robert remains tortured by his changing ideas. Living in an intermittent state between two belief systems, Robert's spiritual journey re-enacts the evangelical conversion narrative, in which believers come to an intellectual understanding of Jesus but have yet to experience some sort of transformative personal encounter with Jesus. In fact, Robert's mental anguish continues until, after a conversation with Grey, he experiences a mystical vision. He sees "Christ" and only at that moment becomes able to let "the chafing pent-up current of love flow into the new channels" that his intellectual conversion had prepared.[30] As the vision continues, Jesus addresses Robert, assuring Robert that they shared the same struggles, doubts, dreams, delusions, weaknesses, and suffering. The vision concludes with Jesus affirming Robert's new knowledge "*shall not take [faith] from you; and love, instead of weakening or forgetting, if it be but faithful, shall find ever fresh power of realising and renewing itself.*"[31] Only after this vision is Robert able to embrace emotionally what his intellect had already concluded: Jesus was a great teacher, but only a man. Robert's need for a vision to solidify his thinking points to the ongoing tension between material artifacts, historical testimony, and spiritual experience within the novel. Despite the narrative insistence upon rational thought and material evidence that drives Robert's self-catechesis, Robert's demythologized faith is ultimately authorized by his own mystical encounter with Jesus.

As Robert's vision makes clear, his rejection of traditional dogmas does not exactly negate Jesus's role as "Christ." Rather, Jesus can be seen as the first of many "Christs," since his subsequent followers become Christs to each other through following Jesus's ethical ideals. This division between Jesus and the role of Christ is evident in Robert's initial catechism when he distinguishes the definition of Christ as "the teacher, the martyr, the symbol to us Westerns of all things heavenly and abiding, the image and pledge of the invisible life of the spirit" from the identity of the "God-man."[32] The use of terms such as "symbol" and "image" is important in this passage because they indicate an office or role, signifying function but not the thing signified itself. Robert believes in "Christ" because Christ signifies the heavenly role anyone might play. Thus Jesus is a prophet of heavenly ideals, not a manifestation of God himself. Furthermore, while Christ is the ultimate symbol of divine teaching, this role of the moral

---

[30] Ward, *Elsmere*, 273.
[31] Ward, *Elsmere*, 273. (italics original)
[32] Ward, *Elsmere*, 273.

prophet is not limited to Jesus. As Robert goes on to affirm, "Every human soul in which the voice of God makes itself felt, enjoys, equally with Jesus of Nazareth, the divine sonship."[33] Consequently, each individual can play the Christ role; each individual can be a symbol of the heavenly. What Robert rejects is "the Man-God, the Word from Eternity... a wonder-working Christ, in a risen and ascended Jesus, in the living Intercessor and Mediator for the lives of His doomed brethren."[34]

Much of what Robert says sounds like Charles Kingsley. In fact, Ward loosely pattered Robert on the young Kingsley. But, as with any theological issue, the devil is in the details. While Robert and Kingsley share a belief in the divine sonship of every human being, Kingsley understands this as originating in Jesus who is God incarnate, whereas Robert sees this as represented by Jesus who is one of many potential patterns of a human living out a divine message. The theological stakes of this difference are staggering, for him and for Victorian readers, but the narrative stakes are also significant. Because Jesus is the source or origin of divine sonship for Kingsley, Jesus's unique identity matters. For Robert, however, Jesus is a pattern; he has no unique identity. In terms of characterization, Kingsley's theology leads to narrative practices that treat Jesus as either a character to be developed or a character who, although not part of the scene, exists offstage. Robert's theology does not lead to narrative practices that treat Jesus as a unique character. As a prophet and martyr, Jesus is simply one of many prophets, martyrs, and potential Christs. His life matters only as a pattern to follow. In fact, trying to develop a robust understanding of Jesus's psychology—like Eliot's suggestion of his peppery personality or Renan's portrayal of a man carried away by his own fame—runs the risk of lessening Jesus's worthiness as a teacher. Such a psychology downplays Jesus as a form or pattern by drawing attention to his human particularity. For Robert faith in Jesus means accepting him as a moral teacher and viewing his teaching and Christian practices as a set of cultural fables; they carry a message of right action but no other truth claims. Consequently, Jesus can exist in *Robert Elsmere* without being developed as a discrete character. In fact, developing him as a discrete character would be counter to the ways in which Robert comes to value Jesus.

Robert's statement that Jesus is not "the living Intercessor and Mediator for the lives of His doomed brethren," ideologically moves Jesus's characterization solidly away from any priestly or kingly function, while amplifying the different

---

[33] Ward, *Elsmere*, 273.
[34] Ward, *Elsmere*, 273.

narrative practices surrounding Jesus's characterization in Ward's two novels.[35] Robert's Jesus is neither a living, active person, nor is he a person doing something on behalf of the rest of humanity, including Robert. As such, he is removed from the sphere of action and he is removed from his relational standing vis-à-vis Robert and everyone else, reinforcing that the only part of Jesus's life that matters is the body of his teaching and not his personality in history. Kingsley and Eliot both take a different approach. Kingsley asserts that it is "Not [a] self-chosen preference for [Jesus'] precepts" that matters—a statement in direct opposition to Robert's confession of faith—"but the overwhelming faith in [Jesus'] presence" that forms the foundation for the community.[36] Similarly, Dinah's ultimate choice of Adam over her disembodied understanding of a mystical Jesus underscores the real, interactive presence of Jesus as the foundation for Christian experience, even when understood historically. Because the emphasis is on Jesus's presence, both Eliot's and Kingsley's Jesus characters require narrative attention that creates a sense of his existence within the text. Thus, when Eleanor speaks to Alton about Jesus, both Eleanor and Alton largely disappear from the discourse. Eleanor's voice is obscured through Alton's report of her words, and Alton's voice is obscured through his litany-like phrase, "she spoke of him as..."[37] The result of this refracted speech is that the voices of both Eleanor and Alton become diffused within the passage, leaving Jesus the primary personality within the scene. Similarly, Adam obviously and undeniably exists in relationship with other characters and as a real character within *Adam Bede*. When Robert speaks of Jesus in *Robert Elsmere*, his speech is similar to Dinah's sermon on the Green: the narrative emphasis is on Robert's abilities as a speaker, with the novel reproducing the text of the lectures and his very clear narrative voice. Jesus is the subject and the ideal, but he is not a present personality in these passages.

To further understand the way Robert's theology shapes the novel's characterization of Jesus, it is helpful to also contrast Robert's and Adam's stances toward Jesus. While Robert attempts to imitate Jesus's life by practicing his teachings, he is never equated with Jesus or marked as Jesus through the text's images or structures. Adam, on the other hand, is marked as Jesus throughout the novel, even to the extent of being set in equal opposition to Jesus to the extent that Dinah's preference for Adam over the spiritual ideal of her devotion is not presented as a denial of her devotion to Jesus but a more fully realized expression.

---

[35] Ward, *Elsmere*, 273.
[36] Kingsley, *Alton Locke*, 359.
[37] Kingsley, *Alton Locke*, 356.

Furthermore, Robert's theological preoccupation with Jesus is, in large part, what works to differentiate him from Jesus. Because Robert is consumed with the question of Jesus's claim on modern life, the novel never allows for any slippage or collapse between Robert and Jesus. Conversely, it matters little to Eliot's novel whether or not Jesus is God, or whether or not he is an ongoing, active presence in the life of the believer. By taking Jesus out of the first century and not addressing doctrine directly, Eliot is able to set metaphysics and dogma aside, freeing her to retell the "beautiful story" of Jesus through Adam. The story of Robert's Jesus, however, is largely obscured by Robert's theological projects.

Robert's ethically focused Christianity is not a new or unique idea. From its roots in patristic writings and articulation in the eleventh century by Peter Abelard to more recent branches of mainline Protestantism, the Catholic worker movement, and certain parachurch organizations, many Christians have placed Jesus's ethical teachings at the center of their faith. Moreover, Robert's ethically focused Christianity was particularly common in nineteenth-century Britain. Contemporary reviewers of *Robert Elsmere*, including Gladstone and Pater, along with more recent critics like J. Russell Perkin, question how Robert's faith differs from Unitarianism specifically, since Robert rejects "Unitarianism of the old sort" as "the most illogical creed that exists" and one "that has never been the creed of the poor."[38] Despite the critical confusion, Robert's comment regarding Unitarianism and the poor is particularly helpful in sorting out exactly how Ward's thinking was unique among other understandings of Jesus as a moral prophet. When Robert specifically distances himself from the "old sort" of Unitarianism, it is not merely a figure of speech. Nineteenth-century Unitarianism was deeply divided between the "old" and "new" parties, with the "old" insisting on the sort of rational biblical literalism first modeled by Joseph Priestley.[39] Robert's comment distancing himself from "old" Unitarianism should be read in terms of the changes taking place within Unitarianism itself. Despite the familiarity of new Unitarianism in literary circles (thanks in no small part to people like the Martineaus), this "old" style of Unitarianism was actually the prominent form of Unitarianism until the 1880s.[40] The "old" Unitarianism, represented by writers

---

[38] Ward, *Elsmere*, 314.
[39] For more on the divide within Unitarianism, see Larsen, *A People of One Book: The Bible and the Victorians*, chapter 6; R. K. Webb, "The Limits of Religious Liberty: Theology and Criticism in Nineteenth-Century England," in *Freedom and Religion in the Nineteenth Century*, ed. Richard J. Helmstadter (Stanford: Stanford University Press, 1997); "The Unitarian Background," in *Truth, Liberty, Religion: Essays Celebrating Two Hundred Years of Manchester College* (Oxford: Manchester College, 1986).
[40] Webb, "The Limits of Religious Liberty: Theology and Criticism in Nineteenth-Century England," 137.

like Elizabeth Gaskell, was deeply "biblicist" and "is persistently marginalized, ignored, underrepresented, or minimized because scholars have found it uninteresting, if not an embarrassment."[41] Unlike Ward, who wants to divide the ethical teachings of Christianity from the stories of Jesus's life and miracles, "old" Unitarians insisted on the centrality of the Bible and particularly the gospel narratives to all matters of doctrine and practice, spending a great deal of intellectual energy in answering questions regarding the apparent discrepancies between the gospel accounts and affirming Jesus's miracles, particularly the bodily resurrection and ascension into heaven.[42] Clearly, this emphasis on textual integrity and the miracles of Jesus is opposed to Robert's revised faith, which specifically rejects these traditions as unnecessary, even obstacles, to the moral ideals of Jesus's teachings enacted in human relationships.

Just as Robert's conversion leads to a demythologized faith that emphasizes the imitation of Christ, so too does Joshua undergo a conversion of sorts leading him to imitate Jesus's moral teachings. After a failed attempt to perform miracles, Joshua questions the miraculous emphases of more traditional forms of Christianity, ultimately concluding that true Christianity must lie in its radical teachings about human community. Consequently, Joshua moves to London and begins teaching, working for social healing, and developing a community of followers. Likewise, Robert's conversion takes him to London's East End where he begins teaching the workers through public lectures, working for physical healing through improved living conditions, and establishing a community of believers. Although *Robert Elsmere* lacks the quasi-mystical alignment of Robert and Jesus suggested by Joshua's name and character, these activities of teaching, healing, and community building that govern both novels are a narrative shape drawn from the canonical Gospels. Within the Gospels, the sections detailing Jesus's ministry center around teaching and healing, activities which are frequently interrelated in a single episode or juxtaposed in alternating scenes. In response to these two activities, a community of followers develops around Jesus. That said, Robert and Joshua are markedly different from the Jesus of the Gospels because their work of healing is performed entirely through the salubrious effects of their teaching and the practical improvements their instruction brings. As a result, while their lives are patterned on Jesus, their very imitation of Jesus renders all of Jesus's notable acts prior to his passion and death

---

[41] Larsen, *A People of One Book: The Bible and the Victorians*, 148.
[42] Larsen, *A People of One Book: The Bible and the Victorians*, 147.

a subset of teaching. With all else subordinated to the apprehension of a moral vision and instruction in it, Jesus's character is circumscribed entirely by his role as a prophetic teacher, reducing him to an instructive model, a role to be played but not a character. It is through this disappearance of the characters of Joshua and Robert into the role of the moral teacher that unfolding narrative of each novel structurally undermines the purely ethical Christianity that both novels endorse.

In both *Robert Elsmere* and *Joshua Davidson* the overarching narrative form moves from engaging the historical Jesus and his role as a "Christ" to enacting the "Christ event" among the poor. While *Joshua Davidson* plays with the notion of Joshua as Jesus throughout the novel, *Robert Elsmere* never equates Robert's enactment of the Jesus narrative with Robert actually being Jesus: Robert follows a Jesus pattern, but he is not a Jesus character. In fact, while Robert's imitation of Jesus is part of his characterization, the replication that imitation involves always points to difference, to the separation between the copy and the original. As such, Robert's conscious imitation of Jesus serves to separate him from Jesus. Joshua, conversely, is always aware of his historical predecessor and similarly reflects on Jesus; but his very name, the ongoing plot details, and his re-enactment of famous scenes from Jesus's life blur this distinction between Joshua and Jesus. Rather than suggest the divinity of Joshua or allow the plausibility of Jesus being at all miraculous, the literalism with which Joshua's life reflects Jesus's life highlights the potential for a charismatic leader's identity to become confused with a prophetic moral ideal, overblown in both his own imagination and the minds of his followers.

This mimetic separation between Jesus on the one side and Robert and, to some extent, Joshua on the other is not the only significant narrative separation linked to the imitation of Jesus. Both novels present their protagonists as separate from the communities they form, with Robert gradually separating from others through a decrease in dialogue, whereas an air of separateness always surrounds Joshua. Such separation is significant in each novel's conclusion regarding the viability of Jesus's teachings. Other novels present Jesus intimately involved with the community surrounding him. Kingsley's Jesus is a mystical basis for human community whose ongoing ability to relate to believers is essential to their subject formation. While Adam Bede is not the basis for the Hayslope community, he is the preserver of its memory. The narrator repeatedly points to Adam as a primary source of community knowledge in his later years, thereby grounding the ongoing identity and coherence of the community for later generations in his stories about its earlier days. Yet, in *Joshua Davidson* and *Robert Elsmere* both protagonists stand apart from the communities they build, lacking ongoing intimate relationships with the community members and dying before they can serve as preservers of community memories.

In *Robert Elsmere* and *Joshua Davidson*, both men are positioned as fundamentally separate from other people. For Joshua, this separation is encoded through genre, which suggests not only the Gospels but the oriental tale that shapes *Rasselas*, and even the satire of a work like *Candide*.[43] Lacking Voltaire's humor and imitating the earnestness of the Gospel writers, *Joshua Davidson* is, thus, more in line with Johnson's tale of a young man's search for happiness. Linton uses the generic practice of separating the protagonist from society in order to comment on social structures and mores. However, unlike *Rasselas*, Joshua has no real companions, teachers, or mentors. He is in a class by himself, revered by his companions and, essentially, guided by no one (apart from his own literal application of Jesus's teachings).

To establish Joshua as holy, rather than simply disillusioned, the novel presents him in ethereal terms. Early on, he is described as "a beautiful boy, with a face almost like a young woman's for purity and spirituality."[44] He is also said to look like "a boy-saint" who is frequently "thoughtful," and "never out of temper" as a young man (although exceptions to this arise later in the novel).[45] When in his early fanaticism he attempts to "remove rocks by faith," the language reflects the transfiguration, with Joshua's "countenance glow[ing]" as he is "inspired, transported beyond himself, beyond humanity."[46] These early descriptions are reinforced through the course of the novel. Joshua is characterized repeatedly in terms of "sweetness" (or his "sweet sincerity") or as having a "quiet, mild face," all of which continue his characterization as the "boy-saint."[47]

While Joshua is set apart from others through his innate holiness, he is also set apart from others relationally. Joshua's friends include his small circle of followers as a young boy, Mary, Joe, and the narrator. Yet, these relationships are repeatedly cast within the power dynamics and inevitable separation found in relationships between leaders and followers. Mary is often filled with some

---

[43] For additional information on the genre and the Gospels, see Michael E. Vines, *The Problem of Markan Genre: The Gospel of Mark and the Jewish Novel* (Leiden: Brill Academic Publishing, 2002). Also Michael Wheeler, *St. John and the Victorians* (Cambridge: Cambridge University Press, 2011).

[44] Eliza Lynn Linton, *The True History of Joshua Davidson, Christian and Communist* (London: Bradbury, Evans, and Co., 1872), 4.

[45] Ward, *Elsmere*, 4, 13.

[46] Ward, *Elsmere*, 21.

[47] Ward, *Elsmere*, 25–6, 168, 211.

sort of awe, looking at Joshua with admiration, calling him an "angel."[48] Joe's anger and violence are subdued and he is reduced to tears by Joshua's "Christ-like" simplicity and exaltation "above common weakness."[49] And the narrator, who repeatedly remarks upon Joshua's holiness, positions himself as an observer but not participant in the events he relates. As a result, what relationship there is between Joshua and the narrator is implied rather than depicted—and that relationship is never presented as one of equals.

The ethereal, childlike, and feminized images combine with the repeated characterization of Joshua as a peerless leader, emphasizing the holiness of his personality. Such habits of characterization direct the reader's attention to Joshua's ideas, minimizing the structural space of free indirect discourse fostering sympathetic identification that one expects in even a satirical Victorian novel. As J. M. Rignall has commented, in *Joshua Davidson*, "it is the ideas that are important... not individuals."[50] The consequences of such narration are threefold. On the most basic level, Linton's narration "work[s]... against the tendency of the novel to create a primary interest in character," making the protagonist an "exemplary figure, significant not in his own right but for the views he propounds and the ideal he embodies."[51] Furthermore, such narration also minimizes any sense of Jesus, or Jesus-like characters, as real personalities with whom readers might sympathize; Joshua and Jesus are not so much people but a set of teachings that cohere around a common name in an almost allegorical fashion. Finally, such narration threatens to undermine the very set of teachings that the novel is testing. Joshua's Jesus-derived teachings are grounded in the equality of all people, manifest in loving relationships and practical care for others. Paradoxically, Joshua is characterized as "more equal" than the other characters. Joshua's teachings do not make him an actual part of the community he leads: he is over and above that community, not relationally integrated within it. As a result, the community is not a brotherhood of equals; it is a community under an idealistic leader.

While Joshua is depicted as set apart from the beginning of the narrative, Robert's character undergoes a gradual separation from other characters that is most significantly represented in the changing relationship between Robert and his wife Catherine. This marriage plot is particularly important in shaping Robert's imitation of Jesus. Robert's marriage to Catherine puts him in

---

[48] Ward, *Elsmere*, 116, 177.
[49] Ward, *Elsmere*, 164.
[50] Rignall, "Between Chartism and the 1880s: J. W. Overton and E. Lynn Linton," 38.
[51] Rignall, "Between Chartism and the 1880s: J. W. Overton and E. Lynn Linton," 38.

conversation with others and in a primary relationship that cannot be governed by simply imitating Jesus because Jesus, at least in the canonical Gospels and historical reconstructions derived from them, was never married. Perhaps unsurprisingly then, Robert emerges most fully as a sympathetic, dynamic character within this marriage. Moreover, through this marriage plot Ward eventually offers human romance as an alternative to Jesus for governing and structuring human life.

Early in the novel, the narrative tension between Catherine and Robert comes about because Catherine promises her dying father that she would care for her mother and sisters once he dies. Upon his death, Catherine believes this promise limits her freedom to marry Robert, since the marriage would take her away from the mother and sisters she has promised to care for. While Robert and Catherine disagree about her interpretation of this promise through much of the first volume, their relationship is characterized by active engagement with the other's opinions. Such lively conversation functions as a marker in Victorian novels of the ideal, companionate marriage, indicating to readers the suitability of a couple. To appreciate the developments in the Elsmere marriage, it is important to keep in mind that Victorian novels generally, and *Robert Elsmere* in particular, do not insist upon perfect agreement as the marker of a healthy romance but on engaged conversation in both agreement and disagreement as the foundation for a healthy marriage.

Following this logic, the trope of silence frequently marks some form of separation between Robert and others, be it separation growing from anger, illness, or impending death. After Robert's conversion, lively conversation ceases to characterize the Elsmere marriage. Catherine is repeatedly described as "silent," a descriptor that is emphasized as Robert wonders, "Over how many matters they would once have discussed with open heart was she silent now?"[52] While they disagree profoundly over the identity of Jesus and the historicity of his bodily resurrection, it is telling that this new disagreement is not met with the lively conversation of their earlier disagreement but with silence. It is not simply that they disagree about theology but that the dialogue and intellectual engagement that had characterized a good marriage have ceased. Thus, Catherine's "rigid" silence is emblematic of the couple becoming "more divided"; it is emblematic of the disintegration of the marriage.[53] Of course, the silence between Robert and Catherine is not one-sided. At times both "yield... to the impulse of silence"

---

[52] Ward, *Elsmere*, 344.
[53] Ward, *Elsmere*, 383.

or are "conquered by the same sore impulse to let speech alone."[54] Moreover, Robert's impending death is first marked by the loss of his voice; and in the final pages when death approaches and he becomes increasingly removed from earthly concerns, he is characterized as largely silent. His sentences are broken, and he "can only talk at rare intervals."[55]

The relational break between Robert and Catherine is not the only place in which Robert loses a key dialogue partner. For a variety of reasons not directly related to his conversion, Robert experiences the loss of many of his primary relationships after his conversion. Langbaum is removed from the story, chased away after his affair with Rose comes to an anticlimactic end. Robert's mentor, Henry Grey, dies. While these two friendships are replaced, to some extent, by Flaxman and Edwardes, both Flaxman and Edwardes present challenges as conversation partners. As long as Flaxman is "antipathetic" to Robert and pursuing Rose, their relationship is strained and their conversations are largely superficial. As Flaxman continues to associate with Robert, he becomes increasingly an interested observer, musing admiringly on Robert's power over his followers.[56] He is not, however, someone who advises, challenges, or otherwise engages Robert. Robert's relationship with Edwardes is also complicated as a friendship because the narrative positions Edwardes as his successor but not equal, despite the fact that Edwardes initially helped Robert establish his charity work in the East End.[57] Thus, neither Flaxman nor Edwardes represents new opportunities for dialogue; rather, they subtly reinforce Robert's otherness as they observe him with skeptical appreciation or place him on a theological pedestal.

Compounding the increasingly problematic nature of Robert's dialogue partners is the way in which the novel characterizes the East End's working-class. Rather than Robert's conversion leading to social engagement and deep relationships with the workers, Robert is separated from the working class through the narration. The workers are repeatedly discussed as a nameless, faceless group, a backdrop against which Robert's drama continues to unfold. When he first visits the East End school with Edwardes, the students are described as "a gang of young roughs," "pupils," and "shadowy demons."[58] Ward's habits of crowd or group characterization are particularly significant in this passage because they continue throughout the section of the novel set

---

[54] Ward, *Elsmere*, 385.
[55] Ward, *Elsmere*, 547.
[56] Ward, *Elsmere*, 435–6.
[57] Ward, *Elsmere*, 380, 434.
[58] Ward, *Elsmere*, 488.

in the East End. As Alex Woloch has argued, by highlighting representatives group characteristic through minor characters, novelists create a character field that both serves to represent the group and gives the minor character a more significant presence as a character. But Ward never depicts groups or crowds of workers in this typified manner such that a minor character's characteristics become representative of the group and a group's characteristics become particularized in a minor character. Because no individuals represent the group, no "grasping of a social characteristic—the analytic moment when we suddenly see a relationship between a large group of individuals"—takes place.[59] Unless we are to take "shadowy demons" as the unique and representative trait of all working-class schoolboys, then it is fair to say that Ward's crowd scenes give little more than generalized terms void of any group defining characteristics.

Vague characterization of this sort continues as Ward describes the working class in later sections. When Robert first visits the workers' club, the people outside, the very people whom Robert desires to help, are described only as "a knot of workmen."[60] During his lecture, "The Claim of Jesus on Modern Life," the audience members are, likewise, described repeatedly in terms of their group status, with no individuals emerging until the truncated speech of Andrews (marked through the novel only as "the Secularist") at the end of Robert's lengthy sermon. Apart from Flaxman, Rose, and Lady Charlotte, the "occupants" of the hall are "artisans—a spare, stooping, sharp-featured race," "dock-labourers," "watchmakers... potters" and "seamen."[61] The undifferentiated nature of the crowd has led Lynn Hapgood to conclude that Robert's preaching is "merely the articulation of his own thoughts" because the working class "remain[s] an amorphous mass, detached from the spiritual and intellectual drama which remains Robert's alone."[62] While sermons are always, to some extent, the articulation of the preacher's thoughts, the moments of audience response that punctuate Robert's lecture reinforce Robert's isolation. During Robert's speech, silence becomes the primary marker of audience engagement. In terms of the room itself, Ward initially depicts it as "full of noise" and finally as filled with "men scattered about... tugging silently at their pipes."[63] The workers' undifferentiated responses are described in terms of increasing silence in the room. Meanwhile,

---

[59] Woloch, *The One vs. The Many: Minor Characters and the Space of the Protagonist in the Novel*, 250.
[60] Ward, *Elsmere*, 497.
[61] Ward, *Elsmere*, 512.
[62] Hapgood, "'The Reconceiving of Christianity': Secularisation, Realism, and the Religious Novel," 399.
[63] Ward, *Elsmere*, 513.

Robert's "consciousness of his audience was passing from him" as "the world of ideas was growing clearer."[64] Readers do get particularized responses from Lady Charlotte, Flaxman, and Rose; but, as with the workers, these responses do not represent any form of dialogical engagement with Robert's preaching. Even years later, Flaxman "could not often be got to talk of the experience of this evening."[65] If dialogue is a key marker of robust relationships, then the silence fostered by Robert's preaching suggests that, while his ideas are appealing and even compelling, they are not producing actual relationships between Robert and those whom he longs to help.

A lack of dialogue also characterizes Robert's ongoing work in the East End. The narrator describes Robert's work in the East End, his ongoing lectures, the building and library he obtains for the New Brotherhood, and the services that the organization holds. Yet, through all these efforts, there is little dialogue between Robert and the working-class members of the community. Readers are told that Robert's followers are being "disciplined and moulded... [by] Elsmere's teaching and Elsmere's thought, show[ing] a responsiveness, a receptivity, even a power of initiation."[66] But none of these developments are presented through the lives of particular characters or through conversations with particular characters. What first appears as dialogue during one of Robert's sermons is immediately revealed to be an "appointed" litany of responses.[67] While Robert continues to have mundane conversations with Catherine, Flaxham, and others, even these are not the sort of vibrant intellectual tête-à-têtes that characterized his initial romance with Catherine or his intellectual affair with the Squire. In sum, while dialogue continues throughout the novel, it lacks intellectual intensity at the end of the novel, and it never really happens between the educated Robert and the workers of the East End.

To a large extent, Ward's inability to characterize the working class as a "knowable community" is the very issue Raymond Williams examines in George Eliot's work.[68] Robert's followers are distanced from Robert, Ward, and the readers by class and education. Consequently, Ward attempts to make them "knowable" through "inauthentic" means, giving them her own consciousness which is expressed through their reported response to Robert's

---

[64] Ward, *Elsmere*, 372.
[65] Ward, *Elsmere*, 371.
[66] Ward, *Elsmere*, 435.
[67] Ward, *Elsmere*, 438.
[68] See discussion of Williams's argument in chapter 4.

new religion.[69] Attributing her personal sensibilities to the working class is precisely why, as historian Timothy Larsen observes, "the thoughts of the urbane Unitarian thinker James Martineau [represented in Robert's New Brotherhood] mysteriously generate the results of [the Salvation Army's] William Booth."[70] While such inauthentic subjectivity may work to some extent in Eliot's novels (even if it marginalizes the working class), Ward's attempts to make working-class characters knowable through her own consciousness serve only to make the community separate from its leader and the success of Robert's ministry historically and sociologically inexplicable.

The Failed Prophet

Class and education aside, both *Robert Elsmere* and *Joshua Davidson* suggest that enacting Jesus's teachings and imitating his life may be an insufficient basis for building human communities because they keep their protagonists largely set apart from other characters. Indeed the conclusion of each work actualizes this ongoing suggestion, revealing that trying to enact Jesus's moral teachings is ultimately futile. Like the Jesus narrative, both Robert's and Joshua's narratives end in deaths characterized by self-sacrifice and even a sort of martyrdom. Robert dies from a protracted illness most directly linked to his attempt to save another man's life, whereas Joshua is beaten to death by an angry mob shortly after his return from Paris. On the surface, Robert's death literalizes the traditional idea that Jesus died to save others, whereas Joshua dies a martyr to his teachings, his senseless death an example of "the world... disown[ing] its Best."[71] Despite the potentially salvific effects of each man's death, both of their deaths are fruitless. Not only do Joshua and Robert die, but the communities they started eventually die, too. While these endings function as a disavowal of imitating Jesus and a disavowal of his claim on modern life, they also function as disavowals of character imitation as a way of producing new understandings within realism. Imitation does not lead to a better knowledge of Jesus's character, nor does it lead to innovative answers to contemporary social problems. Imitation leads only to the death of the self, to the death of the community each man initially inspired, and to the continuation of the social and economic status quo.

[69] Williams, *The Country and the City*, 170.
[70] Timothy Larsen, "Losing My Religion: Mrs. Humphry Ward's Robert Elsmere," http://www.booksandculture.com/articles/2015/janfeb/losing-my-religion.html?paging=off.
[71] Linton, *The True History of Joshua Davidson, Christian and Communist*, 275.

Joshua Davidson presents Joshua's death in the literal terms of martyrdom, and yet his death is not a generative event. Instead, his death provokes uncertainty. His lifelong friend and biographer confesses, "the death of my friend has left me not only desolate, but uncertain. For I have come round to the old starting-point again: Is the Christian world all wrong, or is practical Christianity impossible?"[72] Rather than a community empowered by Joshua's heroic self-sacrifice for the sake of his teachings, Joshua's death leads his friend, biographer, and only remaining follower to question if a life built on Jesus's teachings is even possible. The novel concludes with a prophetic call modeled on Elijah's challenge to the prophets of Baal on Mount Carmel. The narrator demands, "Let us have something definite. If Christ was right, modern Christianity is wrong; but if sociology is a scientific truth, then Jesus of Nazareth preached and practised not only in vain, but against unchangeable Law."[73] No answer is given; the challenge remains with the reader to "make the dark thing clear."[74] While the reader has the potential to be the ongoing, redemptive manifestation of Joshua's teachings, the rhetoric of science in the novel's conclusion precludes this possibility, casting Joshua's literal enactment of Jesus's teachings as sentimental and intellectually unsupportable. This conclusion—damning not only to the institution of Christianity but ultimately to Jesus himself—is perhaps why Charles Bradlaugh bought one thousand copies of the novel to hand out in support of his atheistic work.[75] The novel ends with no one carrying on Joshua's message because his death is the ultimate sacrifice of a kind, but delusional, fool. Thus, Joshua's appropriation of Jesus's life ends in obliteration: no redemptive presence—be it an extended community, a convinced witness, or Joshua himself—remains within the darkness.

The ending of *Elsmere* is less bleak but raises significant challenges to Robert's imitation of Jesus. As mentioned earlier, Robert dies because he catches a cold when he attempts to save a drowning man. The problem is that he fails—the man drowns and Robert himself dies shortly thereafter from the illness that set in after the rescue attempt. On the most literal level, Robert's death is not a generative event: he does not learn great truths from the effort, nor does the ongoing life of the drowning man bear witness to the salvation Robert purchased at the cost of his own life. Many critics have recognized the ambiguities created

---

[72] Linton, *The True History of Joshua Davidson, Christian and Communist*, 277.
[73] Linton, *The True History of Joshua Davidson, Christian and Communist*, 287.
[74] Linton, *The True History of Joshua Davidson, Christian and Communist*, 279.
[75] Anderson, "Eliza Lynn Linton: *The Rebel of the Family* (1880) and Other Novels," 127.

by this ending. Ilana Blumberg argues that Robert's death is not meant to be self-sacrificing but an instance to demonstrate that the community he started will live beyond his charismatic leadership.[76] Mildred Culp, recognizing the difficulties this ending creates, has explained it in terms of narrative closure, arguing that Ward, "dispenses with the whole apparatus of closure… to suggest that her spotlight is primarily upon idea, not character."[77] The problem with this analysis is that Robert's death (along with the swimmer's) offers closure in the most absolute sense. Because Robert dies just a few pages after his faith turned into a physical act (as opposed to his previous intellectual musing, teaching, etc.), the ending reinforces that Robert's life produced only silence. Once he is dead the novel ends and, consequently, the narrative universe he inhabits falls silent. Furthermore, while the narrator states that the community of the New Brotherhood "still exists, and grows," not "sink[ing]" with Robert, it remains an amorphous mass in Elgood Street Hall.[78] The only figure described is that of the silent, veiled Catherine who honors her husband's memory by attending the New Brotherhood's meetings, while continuing her commitment to and work with the Established church.

Any glimmer of hope for the community to be gathered from the silent Catherine among the masses is squelched in *The Case of Richard Meynell*, the sequel to *Robert Elsmere*. In this work Ward writes that, although there were "many" who "kept [Elsmere's] memory alive in [their] hearts," Elsmere's project was "a kind of landmark in the past" that had "in the course of time… begun to seem irrelevant."[79] Moreover, not only do Robert's followers lose faith in his mission; we also learn that they may have never fully believed in his mission in the first place. In one of the few mentions of Elsmere's new religion in *Richard Meynell*, we learn that Flaxman's "Supreme and tyrannical common sense had never allowed him any delusions as to the ultimate permanence of heroic ventures like the New Brotherhood."[80] While the two novels are separated by almost twenty-five years and Ward's own thinking clearly developed during that time, it is telling that, even in her own imagination, Elsmere's life and death are relegated to the past, martyrs to progress but largely irrelevant to the modern world.

The sense of separateness that characterizes both Robert and Joshua puts pressure on arguments that Victorian liberal theology produces a socially minded

---

[76] Blumberg, *Victorian Sacrifice: Ethics and Economics in Mid-Century Novels*, 209.
[77] Culp, "Literary Dimensions of *Robert Elsmere*: Idea, Character, and Form," 39.
[78] Ward, *Elsmere*, 458.
[79] Ward, Mary Augusta *The Case of Richard Meynell* (New York: Doubleday, Page, and Co., 1911), 17.
[80] *The Case of Richard Meynell*, 267.

gospel. Scholars like Lynn Hapgood have argued, "When Robert is able to accept that 'miracles do not happen' he is simultaneously accepting a materialist/rationalist standpoint" in which "the foundation of... religion becomes 'Dirt and drains.'"[81] Of course, Robert's actual obsession with "dirt and drains" comes during his time as a defender of Orthodoxy in his Surrey parish, not after his conversion and during his work in the East End. Similarly, Joshua is concerned with urban suffering after embracing a demythologized Christianity, but his concern also predates his conversion to communism. Moreover, while each man moves to the inner city to help the working class, both remain separate from those to whom they minister and neither leaves behind a lasting community. In both novels, this separation from others functions as a marker of Robert and Joshua's holy status, thereby aligning them with Jesus. However, it also undermines the very message of community that each preaches, calling the viability of Jesus's teachings into question. While Jesus's office as the moral prophet might emphasize lovely ideas, his teachings fail to produce rich relationships between those who embrace them and other members of society (particularly across class lines), they do not empower communities that outlive their founders, and they do not lead to redemptive deaths for either Robert or Joshua. *Joshua Davidson* ends on this note of disillusionment and confusion. *Robert Elsmere* offers more; it offers a constructive alternative through the domestic plot that Linton's thoroughly abstract and imitative vision of Jesus does not.

As Judith Wilt argues, Robert's death is "quiet and fruitful," citing the memory of the birth of his daughter as evidence of his death's productive nature.[82] Wilt's analysis draws attention to the domestic memories that are key to understanding what the novel presents as a replacement for Jesus's teachings. Rather than remembering Jesus in his dying moments, Robert remembers his daughter's birth, which is not a product of his death at all (*pace* Wilt)—it is a product of

---

[81] Hapgood, "'The Reconceiving of Christianity': Secularisation, Realism, and the Religious Novel," 377. While Hapgood and others associate the emphasis on social justice among Christians with a demythologized Christianity, the recent origins of such work were in the Christian Socialist movement headed by Kingsley and Maurice. Although Maruice's Christology was troubling to some, it was in no way "demythologized." Given Kingsley's sermons, and his participation in the committee for the defense of the Athanasian Creed (the longest and most forcefully stated of all the creeds), it is hard to consider his Christian faith or view of Jesus demythologized, or anything other than orthodox. Thus, the "material/rationalist standpoint" is clearly not what generally motivates Christian social action but something in the teachings of Jesus that apply to both traditional and demythologized versions of Christianity. Still, Hapgood's comment aptly sums up the scholarly narrative of thinkers like Perkins, Loesberg, and Judith Wilt who make "demythologized" or "liberal" Christianity synonymous with community and a concern for urban suffering.

[82] Judith Wilt, "The Romance of Faith: Mary Ward's Robert Elsmere and Richard Meynell," *Literature & Theology: An International Journal of Religion, Theory, and Culture* 10, no. 1 (1996): 35.

his life. As such, and juxtaposed with his death, it inscribes the fruitful nature of Robert's marriage as his last word, and not his particular brand of demythologized Christianity. Thus, the novel's conclusion suggests that Robert's legacy is not in his theology or in the New Brotherhood but in his love for his wife and daughter.

A New Hope

By pointing to Robert's wife and daughter in his dying moments, *Robert Elsmere* makes clear what the novel has been suggesting all along. Marriage functions within the novel as the means by which human sympathies are maintained and individual relationships are healed. A novel that champions romantic love and marriage as the ideal place for subject formation is nothing new. As Rachel Ablow demonstrates in *The Marriage of Minds*, Victorian novels frequently treat marriage as a "romantic and literary ideal" modeling sympathy, even as that ideal is revealed to be unattainable in later nineteenth-century fiction.[83] But *Robert Elsmere* does not present marital sympathy as an opportunity for subject formation so much as a source of forgiveness and human unity—the very ideals that Robert finds compelling in Jesus's teaching. Thus, romantic love becomes the true basis of human ethics and the ground of human sympathy and community, not a 2,000-year-old set of principles. As the novel divides ethical principles from loving human relationships, it suggests that, whereas Jesus's teachings have failed to build community, the lived experience of married love can produce reconciliation.

Throughout *Robert Elsmere* it is married love that repeatedly fosters sympathy for characters and heals relational breaches. At first glance, this sounds very much like *Adam Bede*, which literalizes the metaphor of the believer's marriage to Jesus through Dinah marrying Adam. The marriage in *Robert Elsmere* is different, though. Robert is aligned with Jesus by following the pattern of his life, but Robert is never characterized as Jesus within the narrative. He attempts to imitate Jesus's life, but he is not a representation of Jesus's character like Adam. As such, Catherine and Robert's married love for each other does not produce sympathy with Jesus, nor do Robert's Jesus imitations produce some sort of priestly mediation and reconciliation between Robert and Catherine, Robert and the community, or the reader and the characters. Rather, it is their marriage that

---

[83] Ablow, *The Marriage of Minds: Reading Sympathy in the Victorian Marriage Plot*, 16.

produces sympathy for each other within the novel's plot, which leads, in turn, to readerly sympathy. As readers identify with either spouse, they are carried along through married sympathy into an unintentional sympathy for the other partner. Robert's demythologized Christian teachings are never presented as the grounds for this sympathy, nor are Catherine's orthodox Anglican beliefs. In fact, Robert's and Catherine's different but equally dogmatic versions of Christian faith get in the way of sympathy. Rather than doctrines (traditional or demythologized) or even the inspirational spirit of Jesus's moral teachings, the ground of sympathy is always the romantic love and even sexual attraction underlying their marriage. As such, *Robert Elsmere* ultimately does away with Jesus as the moral prophet who offers a path toward sympathy and love.

Although Robert's and Catherine's different beliefs create a rift that severely limits their engagement with each other, the narrative never becomes a "peevish wife" plot largely because of Robert's love for Catherine. Often through free indirect discourse, Ward repeatedly aligns readers' sympathies with Robert's concern for Catherine—including his love for her, his appreciation of her beauty, and his sense of loss at any breach in their relationship. Thus, as "the sore silence between the husband and wife was growing, was swallowing up more of life," Robert's desire for Catherine ameliorates the potential animosity of the situation.[84] After one of their arguments, Robert remains "intimately conscious of her presence, of her pale beauty, which now at twenty-nine, in spite of its severity, had a subtler finish and attraction than ever."[85] He muses on her "old clinging dependence, that willing weakness of love, her youth had yielded him so gladly."[86] Such desire coupled with nostalgia prevents Catherine from becoming an unsympathetic character, particularly as Robert now thinks of Catherine as a "ghost and shadow" of her old self, emphasizing the death his conversion has caused in her.[87] Thus, even in his own longing to be understood, Robert continues to see Catherine as "the wife of his heart, of his youth," aware that her feelings of pain and desertion are his doing.[88] Such awareness of his own role in Catherine's suffering means that Robert "cannot speak without sympathy."[89] As a result of Robert's sympathy for Catherine, readers experience her through Robert's love and not simply through the narrator's

---

[84] Ward, *Elsmere*, 388.
[85] Ward, *Elsmere*, 385.
[86] Ward, *Elsmere*, 388.
[87] Ward, *Elsmere*, 388.
[88] Ward, *Elsmere*, 303, 360.
[89] Ward, *Elsmere*, 360.

characterizations of her as "rigid," or other character's comments that she is the "thirty-nine articles in the flesh."[90]

For Catherine, too, passion is what maintains her connection to Robert even as their religious ideals drive them apart. At the height of their estrangement, she "linger[s]... watching him, longing miserably, like any girl of eighteen, to throw herself on his neck and reproach him for their unhappiness."[91] Although her longing is, in part, to reproach, it is not simply reprimand that she is seeking. She is seeking to reprimand him in a passionate fit of love that ends in his arms. While she is miserable because of his new understanding of Jesus, her longing is for the emotional and physical union of marriage and not religious discourse. Just as free indirect discourse helps readers to see Catherine through Robert's love, so too free indirect discourse guides readers to sympathize with Catherine and to see Robert through her experiences. Thus, as she muses on Robert's "tender silence and consideration" as he "struggle[s] between love and intellectual honesty," readers are made aware of Catherine's appreciation for Robert's efforts on her behalf.[92] Readers also come to see that Catherine is not angry with Robert. Rather, she is "filled... with a dumb irritation and misery indescribable," leading to anger "not with Robert, but, as it were, with those malign forces of which he was the prey."[93] In this way the romance between Robert and Catherine functions formally to maintain readerly sympathy with each character even as it undergirds the pair's sympathy for each other.

Romantic love—not Jesus's teachings—is what ultimately frees Robert from his enmeshment in relationships that had been functioning as substitutes for discourse with his wife. In his near-affair with Madame de Netteville, it is the mention of Catherine that breaks the spell of Netteville's seductions and makes Robert aware of the connection between conversation and romance. Prior to the fateful night at Madame de Netteville's, Robert was frequenting Madame de Netteville's with Catherine on Friday evenings because he had, increasingly, become "socially... indispensable."[94] During these engagements, Madame de Netteville and Robert converse frequently and Robert is "grateful for her delicate social skill" as they discuss "literature, or politics, or famous folk."[95] When Robert finds himself alone with Madame de Netteville, he "proudly

---

[90] Ward, *Elsmere*, 125.
[91] Ward, *Elsmere*, 385.
[92] Ward, *Elsmere*, 361.
[93] Ward, *Elsmere*, 361.
[94] Ward, *Elsmere*, 386.
[95] Ward, *Elsmere*, 394.

endures" her advances, until he hears "Catherine's name coupled with some contemptuous epithet."[96] It is only then that "his self-control fail[s] him."[97] He immediately silences her propositions as "a passionate flood of self-reproachful love" overcomes him.[98] The threat of illicit sex makes his enduring passion for his wife clear to Robert, provoking a sense of shame at the intellectual affair in which he had been entangled already. At this point, Robert presents Catherine as the morally triumphant partner in the marriage, with Robert confessing that he is "doubly unworthy" of Catherine, both because "it has been possible for any human being to suspect for one instant that [he] was ungrateful for the blessing of her love" and because he "could ever forget and dishonour her."[99]

Not only does this affair revive Robert's awareness of Catherine's virtue, it instigates their reconciliation. Upon returning home, Robert confronts Catherine with " half-articulate words of amazement, of passion."[100] He "bends" over her, "kneel[s] before her" as he "make[s] her realise what was in his *own* heart, the penitence and longing which had winged his return to her," suggesting both his repentance and his resumed role as her lover, as his physical postures denote the roles of both protector and suitor.[101] Catherine will hear nothing of Robert's "self-reproach."[102] The chapter closes with an image of Catherine at once morally triumphant and emotionally dependent. She is literally upraised, "tower[ing] above him in the dimness, white and pure and drooping... lost in this new heavenly weakness of love."[103] At no time do Jesus's teachings motivate Robert's return to Catherine, but an awareness of illicit sexual desire that provokes the restatement of domestic bonds and romantic love. The chapter concludes by aligning marital romance with resurrection, declaring, "Paradise is here, visible and tangible by mortal eyes and hands, whenever self is lost in loving."[104] Although the narrator wants to align such love with "the narrow limits of personality [being] beaten down by the inrush of the Divine Spirit," there is nothing prior to this declaration suggesting religion or religious sensibility as the grounds for reconciliation.[105] Rather, Robert nearly denounces his own

---

[96] Ward, *Elsmere*, 398.
[97] Ward, *Elsmere*, 398.
[98] Ward, *Elsmere*, 398.
[99] Ward, *Elsmere*, 398–9.
[100] Ward, *Elsmere*, 400.
[101] Ward, *Elsmere*, 401.
[102] Ward, *Elsmere*, 401.
[103] Ward, *Elsmere*, 401.
[104] Ward, *Elsmere*, 401.
[105] Ward, *Elsmere*, 401.

theology while confessing marital love as the only guide of society: "Even his work seemed to have lost half its sacredness .... Of what worth is any success, but that which is grounded deep on the rock of personal love and duty?"[106]

In the end, for Catherine as for Robert, it is not Jesus's teachings in either a traditional or a demythologized context that provoke kindness or gentleness toward the other. It is their ongoing desire for each other and the memory of their early love that fosters sympathy both within the marriage and between readers and characters. A year after Robert's conversion, Catherine muses that "Love, and her husband, and the thousand subtle forces of a changing world had conquered," not just for Robert but also the breach between Robert and Catherine.[107] Although "she would live and die steadfast to the old faith," Catherine had "undergone that dissociation of the moral judgment from a special series of religious formulæ" that the narrator identifies as essential to the survival of Jesus's teachings.[108] The trouble with the narrator's analysis is that Catherine rejects the belief that moral judgment and religious dogma are separable, and she continues to look askance at Robert's teachings. It is not Robert's Christianity or Catherine's own interpretation of Jesus's teachings that soften her or repair the breach between them. In the end, it is Catherine's love for her husband, her desire for him to "get well and strong" physically and to live, that has triumphed over her concerns regarding his theology.[109]

Marital love and Victorian domestic ideology are what ultimately guide Robert and Catherine as they work to heal their relationship. This ending is set up in the novel's opening section. During their time in Westmoreland, when Robert is trying to win Catherine's love and overcome her sense of duty to the traditional authorities of father and faith, the narrator repeatedly appeals to feeling as the ground and authority for human morality. Readers are told that "This girl, brought up in the austerest school of Christian self-government, knows nothing of the divine rights of passion."[110] While Robert argues with Catherine that one must enrich old bonds with new relationships, foreshadowing his own religious journey, it is not this argument that wins her over.[111] She agrees to marry Robert because of his passionate pursuit of her, the "passion in his voice and touch" as he "pressed on remorselessly" for an answer, "clasp[ing] [her hands] with

---

[106] Ward, *Elsmere*, 399.
[107] Ward, *Elsmere*, 420.
[108] Ward, *Elsmere*, 420.
[109] Ward, *Elsmere*, 420.
[110] Ward, *Elsmere*, 78.
[111] Ward, *Elsmere*, 89.

rapture."[112] In the end, she is "helpless" and "impelled by a will not her own" as she embraces Robert.[113] It is passion and desire that lead Catherine to succumb to Robert's love, and passion and desire ultimately reunite them after Robert's conversion. It is, finally, the "divine rights of passion" that form the basis for sympathy and reconciliation, not Jesus or his prophetic moral teachings.

Robert Elsmere and *Joshua Davidson* inscribe the contrast between the experience of love in the intimate particularity of marriage and the moral teaching of love in the roles Joshua and Robert adopt. In both novels the teaching of ideals falls silent, but the encounter with another (even when disagreements remain) brings the nearest thing to an enduring community or relationship of love—something denied completely to Joshua's narrative. The incarnational justice of Kingsley, denied its supernatural grounding, turns from humanizing the divine to idealizing the human, elevating the charismatic moral prophet to a place removed from the realm of the human. This removal then undermines each moral prophet's ability to mediate reconciliation in the model of Adam's exultation in solidarity and sympathy. And after each prophet's death, both novels are left without a lasting human community that instantiates their teachings and the moral visions that motivate them. With no miraculous powers of prediction, the moral prophet of rational realism inspires some good but recapitulates a Jesus incompatible with either traditional Christianity or the modern world of nineteenth-century Britain. Ultimately, the prophet fails to project a future—unless it is a future where the abstracted ideals of Jesus or the literal re-enactment of his life serve as fading monuments to a fading fascination with a figure fading from view.

---

[112] Ward, *Elsmere*, 111.
[113] Ward, *Elsmere*, 112.

Conclusion

Although Victorian novelists wrestled with the character of Jesus, their attempts to reimagine his life through the novel were not projects of secularization exactly. Instead, many searched for new ways to imagine Jesus, new ways to understand the significance of his life, work, and teachings in light of a rapidly changing world. For Charles Kingsley, Jesus was an historical man and the cosmic king— and a problematic character who interrupts the narrative structure of his novels. But it is Kingsley's insistence on Jesus's role as the archetype for humanity generally *and* masculinity that anticipates Eliot's human Jesus figure in the man Adam Bede. However, as Eliot brings a masculine Jesus fully to life, she moves divinity into Dinah's ethereal Jesus, allowing for only the divine light of all human life to illuminate Adam. Similarly, Ward's Jesus is an intellectual and religious problem solved by separating the man Jesus from his teachings. Only Linton seriously challenges Jesus's status as a moral prophet, presenting instead a potentially delusional idealist. Yet both Ward and Linton ultimately leave Jesus and his teachings in the shadows of history. Linton rejects the possibility of Jesus's teachings as viable in light of modern political economy, whereas Ward displaces Jesus's teachings with an alternative moral vision formed by domesticity represented through the love Robert and Catherine have for each other.

These nineteenth-century attempts to understand and encounter the character of Jesus through the realist novel do more than help chart the changing understanding of Jesus in Britain. These novels demonstrate that the novel form is not inherently secular. If part of the realist endeavor is to represent not just the real but the experience of the reality, then part of that endeavor is to represent what believers experience in their complicated faith journeys and encounters with the divine. In Victorian Britain where religious experience formed a recognized and contentious aspect of human experience, Jesus must eventually make his way into the realist novel. Doing this in a way that is compelling to readers, particularly those from other religious backgrounds, is difficult.

But Kingsley, Eliot, Ward, and Linton each capture something of religious experience by attempting to narrate various sorts of encounters Jesus. As these novels demonstrate, narrating Jesus as a character or allowing characters to experience the character of Jesus does not always demand some sort of mystical salvation. Although Kingsley suggests a salvific religious experience and his denouements are not pretty, he captures the narratively disruptive force that Jesus introduces into believers' identities and lives. Insofar as readers believe in Kingsley's characters, they catch a glimpse of this generative and troubling force for themselves. Eliot captures Jesus as a human and, through Dinah, invites readers to fall in love with this human Jesus while also offering the Jesus Dinah almost sees during the Sermon on the Green, a suffering and compassionate savior always a little out of reach. Linton and Ward both ask readers to test Jesus's ideas. Linton confronts readers with the foolishness of Jesus, a folly that can only be embraced if one is willing to denounce empiricism. Ward represents of Jesus as a bringer of the sword, dividing husband from wife. While she admires Jesus's teachings, reconciliation lies within the bonds of domestic romance and not the imitation of Christ. Even in these novels where Jesus is found wanting, readers are still left with the experience of having confronted this elusive man through their imaginative sympathy with Ward's and Linton's characters.

What all these literary attempts to represent Jesus have in common is that their success is directly proportional to their willingness to cheat at the material and historical particularity that constitute the formal basis of realism. The novelistic portrayals of Jesus that are most compelling are those that prioritize the "beautiful story" over the facts and details of time and place, without reducing the story of Jesus to the self-sacrificing Christ figure or the idealized moral exemplar. These novels demonstrate what most sensitive novel readers already know: novels are true because of the stories they tell and the experiences they recreate, not because of the details through which those stories are told. As such, the problem of Jesus in the novel highlights the problem of realism as a narrative mode. Realism can only be real insofar as it is willing to be fictional. Thus, in their common quest to bring Jesus into realist-inflected novelistic discourse, these Victorian novels anticipate the magical realism, reworked epics, and genre fiction of the twentieth century, all of which sacrifice high realism in favor of narrative shape and human experience.

Despite Jesus's apparent demise at the end of *Robert Elsmere* and *Joshua Davidson*, fiction taking up the character of Jesus explodes in the late nineteenth and twentieth centuries. Oscar Wilde writes his fifth gospels "The Master" and "The Doer of Good" in 1894, and over the next hundred years novelists throughout the world like Thomas Mann, Nikos Kazantzakis, Jose Saramago, and Shusako Endo grapple again and again with Jesus in their novels. In the early twenty-first century, Jesus novels of all sorts enjoy a particular renaissance, including Colm Tóibín's *The Testament of Mary*, Richard Beard's *Lazarus Is Dead*, Philip Pullman's *The Good Man Jesus and the Scoundrel Christ*, and J. M. Coetzee's *The Childhood of Jesus*. These novels tend to approach Jesus in history, as opposed to modern incarnations of Jesus, and typically raise cries of "heresy" in direct proportion to their literary acclaim.

Realism, historical or otherwise, is not the only novelistic form to engage Jesus in the twentieth and twenty-first centuries. Writers often loosely known as the "Catholic Revival" (despite including Protestants) take up the possibilities of Jesus in the novel by abandoning history altogether, which allows them to remain largely within the good graces of traditionally minded Christians. Writers like G. K. Chesterton, C. S. Lewis, Dorothy Sayers, and J. R. R. Tolkien turn to epics, allegory, fantasy, science fiction, and crime fiction in order to follow Eliot in emphasizing rescue and romance, but all sacrifice her realism in the process, preferring genre fiction in a move similar to that of Linton. Others like Evelyn Waugh and Graham Greene continue within realism, engaging Jesus through their characters' experiences of him, often in increasingly mystical moments akin to Kingsley's endings.

As fascinating and significant as these later trajectories are, the particular strain of Victorian novels examined here offers their own commentary on theology and theological trajectories. Engaging the sentimental piety that dehumanizes Jesus, the religious individualism that strives for a self-centered wholeness, and the empiricist challenge to demythologize the emotionally utilitarian god of evangelicalism, these novels resort to the traditional Christological characterizations of prophet, priest, and king. Although characterizing Jesus as a moral prophet seemed a promising way to preserve his cultural and moral authority for many Victorian thinkers troubled by epistemic stakes of miracles and therefore their place in realist representations of Jesus, this path may well render his character irrelevant. Jesus as king and Jesus as priest both offer modes in which his person, and by extension his teachings, might maintain cultural authority. But as both *Robert Elsmere* and *Joshua Davidson* demonstrate, Jesus's morally prophetic teachings alone may prove more disruptive than helpful in scientific, urbanized, capitalistic, middle-class culture. As we learn from Linton's work, if Jesus's teachings are tried and found wanting—if the social, economic, and political disruptions are too much for a sensible person to bear, if his teachings are at odds with other deeply held truths about the nature of love, marriage, family, and the social order—then perhaps he is not a prophet for today's society. Perhaps his teachings are best rejected altogether.

Yet because they use Jesus to work out a representational aesthetics, the Victorian novels considered in this book do more than rework traditional Christology. The epistemological stakes of the Victorian culture wars pitted an orthodoxy like Kingsley's against the individualistic sentimentality of evangelicalism on the one hand and the equally self-centered projection of epistemic coherence promised by empiricist reconstructions of human history, life, and the cosmos on the other. Christology had long served European Christendom as a site of engaging epistemic tensions and imagining epistemic coherence, particularly tensions around identity, by insisting on the resolution of the human and divine within Jesus, the reconciliation of humans with the divine through Jesus's work, and the reconciliation of humans with themselves and each other through a religious encounter with him. Evangelical atonement with its emphasis on reconciliation of the individual to God and empiricist historiography with its appeal to authentication by any person with access to the same facts did not simply pit traditional belief against scientific investigation as a theological challenge, but it cast the self in the role of epistemic protagonist. Knowing, interpreting, and making sense of the world, oneself, others, God—in short, epistemic coherence—came to reside in the religious experience of the believer, or in the rational capacity of the empirical observer, that is, in the self.

The selection of Jesus to serve as the site of experimenting with the characterization of the realist self in these Victorian novels suggests parallels between the structures of novel characterization and the structures of Christology. Both require an empirically absent other to be instantiated in the real world of the reader's mind or believer's experience; both require this absent other be enmeshed in the material and relational webs of a human life different from that of the modern reader or believer; and both promise self-understanding to the reader or believer who properly apprehends this elusive other. Whether the other is fully divine, fully human, or both matters less than the anthropological challenge both realist character aesthetics and Christology face. How does a formless other dwell among humans? How are any beings recognizable to each other? And how do individuals become reconciled to themselves, others, and the divine? The theological questions that suggest the attempt to present Jesus as a novel character are at once genuine theological questions in the Victorian age and a pattern for thinking about representational aesthetics. In contrast to other novels, in which a character stands in for the reader's own desire for epistemic coherence, these Victorian novels present characterizations of Jesus as a solution to individual and social longings for coherence. Although not every representation succeeds in making Jesus incarnate within the material world of the novel, the popularity of these attempts speaks to the Victorian longing for an aesthetics capable of representing epistemic coherence, reconciliation, and salvation.

Bibliography

Ablow, Rachel. *The Marriage of Minds: Reading Sympathy in the Victorian Marriage Plot.* Stanford: Stanford University Press, 2007.

Abrams, M. H. *Natural Supernaturalism.* New York: Norton, 1973.

Adams, James Eli. *Dandies and Desert Saints: Styles of Victorian Masculinity.* Ithaca: Cornell University Press, 1995.

Adams, Kimberly VanEsveld. *Our Lady of Victorian Feminism: The Madonna in the Work of Anna Jameson, Bargaret Fuller, and George Eliot.* Athens: Ohio University Press, 2001.

Alderson, David. "The Anatomy of the British Polity: *Alton Locke* and Christian Manliness." In *Victorian Identities: Social and Cultural Formations in Nineteenth-Century Literature.* New York: Macmillan, St. Martin's Press, 1996.

Alexander, J. H. "Christ in the Pilgrim's Progress." *Bunyan Studies* 1, no. 2 (1989): 22–30.

Alford, Henry. *Psalms and Hymns Adapted to Sundays and Holidays Throughout the Year: To Which Are Added, Some Occasional Hymns.* London: Francis & John Rivington, 1844.

Anderson, Misty G. *Imagining Methodism in Eighteenth-Century Britain: Enthusiams, Belief and the Borders of the Self.* Baltimore: Johns Hopkins University Press, 2012.

Anderson, Nancy Fix. "Eliza Lynn Linton: *The Rebel of the Family* (1880) and Other Novels." In *The New Nineteenth Century: Feminist Readings of Underread Victorian Fiction*, edited by Barbara Leah Harman and Susan Meyer, 117–34. New York: Garland, 1996.

Armstrong, Neil. *Christmas in Nineteenth-Century England.* Manchester: Manchester University Press, 2010.

Arnold, Matthew. "Literature and Dogma." In *Dissent and Dogma*, edited by R. H. Super. Ann Arbor: University of Michigan Press, 1968.

Ashton, Rosemary. "Doubting Clerics: From James Anthony Froude to *Robert Elsmere* Via George Eliot." In *The Critical Spirit and the Will to Believe: Essays in Nineteenth-Century Literature and Religion*, edited by David Jasper and T. R. Wright, 69–87. New York: St. Martin's Press, 1989.

Aulen, Gustaf. *Christus Victor: An Historical Study of Three Main Types of the Idea of the Atonement.* Translated by A. G. Herber. New York: Macmillan, 1969.

Bakhtin, M. M. *The Dialogic Imagination: Four Essays.* Translated by Vadim Liapunov and Kenneth Brostrom. Edited by Michael Holquist. Austin: University of Texas Press, 1982.

Bebbington, David. *Evangelicalism in Modern Britain.* Boston: Unwin Hyman, 1989.

Berry, Wendell. "The Gift of Good Land." In *The Art of the Commonplace: The Agricultural Essays of Wendell Berry*, edited by Norman Wirzba, 293–304. Washington, DC: Counterpoint, 2002.

Blumberg, Ilana M. *Victorian Sacrifice: Ethics and Economics in Mid-Century Novels*. Columbus: Ohio State University Press, 2013.

Boase, T. S. R. "Biblical Illustration in Nineteenth-Century English Art." *Journal of the Warburg and Courtauld Institutes* 29 (1966): 349–67.

Bodenheimer, Rosmarie. *The Politics of Story in Victorian Social Fiction*. Ithaca: Cornell University Press, 1988.

Bradley, Ian C. *The Call to Seriousness: The Evangelical Impact on the Victorians*. New York: Macmillan, 1976.

Brooks, Peter. *Reading for the Plot*. New York: Alfred Knopf, 1984.

Brown, Colin. "Jesus in the History of the Debates on Miracles." In *Cambridge Companion to Miracles*, edited by Graham H. Twelftree, 273–90. Cambridge: Cambridge University Press, 2011.

Burstein, Miriam Elizabeth. *Victorian Reformations: Historical Fiction and Religious Controversy, 1820–1900*. Notre Dame: University of Notre Dame Press, 2014.

Calvin, John. *Institutes of the Christian Religion*. Translated by Henry Beveridge. Edinburgh: Calvin Translation Society, 1845.

Carlyle, Thomas. *On Heroes, Hero-Worship, & the Heroic in History*. London: James Fraser, 1841.

Chadwick, Owen. *The Victorian Church, Part 1, 1829–1859*. 2 vols. London: Oxford University Press, 1966.

Chadwick, Owen. *The Victorian Church, Part 2, 1860–1901*. 2 vols. Oxford: Oxford University Press, 1970.

Childers, Joseph W. *Novel Possibilities: Fiction and the Formation of Early Victorian Culture*. Philadelphia: University of Penn Press, 1995.

Clapp-Itnyre, Alisa. "Dinah and the Secularization of Methodist Hymnody in Eliot's *Adam Bede*." *Victorians Institute Journal* 26 (1998): 41–68.

Colley, Linda. *Britons: Forging the Nation, 1707–1837*. New Haven: Yale University Press, 1992.

Collinson, Patrick. *The Religion of Protestants: The Church in English Society, 1559–1625*. Oxford: Oxford University Press, 1982.

Colón, Susan E. *Victorian Parables*. New York: Bloomsbury, 2012.

Cragwall, Jasper. *Lake Methodism: Polite Literature and Popular Religion in England, 1780–1830*. Athens, OH: Ohio University Press, 2013.

Culp, Mildred L. "Literary Dimensions of *Robert Elsmere*: Idea, Character, and Form." *The International Fiction Review* 9, no. 1 (1982): 35–40.

Cunningham, Valentine. *Everywhere Spoken against: Dissent in the Victorian Novel*. Oxford: Clarendon Press, 1975.

Davies, Horton. *Worship and Theology in England, Vol 1: From Cranmer to Hooker, 1534–1603*. Princeton: Princeton University Press, 1970.

Davies, Horton. *Worship and Theology in England, Vol 3: From Watts and Wesley to Maurice, 1690–1850*. Princeton: Princeton University Press, 1961.

Davies, Horton. *Worship and Theology in England, Vol. 4: From Newman to Martineau, 1850–1900*. Princeton: Princeton University Press, 1962.
De Groot, Christiana, and Marion Ann Taylor. *Recovering Nineteenth-Century Women Interpreters of the Bible*. Society of Biblical Literature Symposium Series. Leiden; Boston: Brill, 2007.
DeWitt, Anne. *Moral Authority, Men of Science, and the Victorian Novel*. Cambridge: Cambridge University Press, 2013.
Dickens, Charles. "Old Lamps for New Ones." *Household Words* 1, no. 15 June (1850): 265–7.
Dodd, Valerie A. "Strauss's English Propagandists and the Politics of Unitarianism, 1841–1845." *Church History* 50, no. 4 (1981): 415–35.
Doody, Margaret Anne. *The True Story of the Novel*. New Brunswick, NJ: Rutgers University Press, 1996.
Doyle, Mary Ellen. *The Sympathetic Response: George Eliot's Fictional Rhetoric*. Teaneck, NJ: Fairleigh Dickinson University Press, 1981.
Edersheim, Alfred. *Life and Times of Jesus the Messiah*. London: Longmans, Green, and Co, 1906.
Eliot, George. *Adam Bede*. Oxford: Oxford University Press, 2008.
Eliot, George. *The George Eliot Letters, 1836–1851*. 9 vols. New Haven: Yale University Press, 1954.
Eliot, George. *The George Eliot Letters, 1852–1858*. 9 vols. New Haven: Yale University Press, 1954.
"Exhibition at the Royal Academy." *The Morning Chronicle*, May 4, 1850.
Farrar, F. W. *The Life of Christ*. New York: E.P. Dutton & Co, 1894.
Feuerbach, Ludwig. *The Essence of Christianity*. Translated by Marian Evans. London: Trübner & Co., 1881.
"Fine Arts: The Eighty-Second Exhibition of the Royal Academy." *The Examiner*, May 25, 1850.
Fraser, Hilary, and Victoria Burrows. "The Feminist Theology of Florence Nightingale." In *Reinventing Christianity*, edited by Linda Woodhead, 199. Aldershot: Ashgate, 2001.
Freed, Mark M. "The Moral Irrelevance of Dogma: Mary Ward and Critical Theology in England." In *Women's Theology in Nineteenth-Century Britain: Transfiguring the Faith of Their Fathers*, edited by Julie Melnyk, 133–47. London: Garland Publishing, 1998.
Gallagher, Catherine. *The Industrial Reformation of English Fiction: Social Discourse and Narrative Form 1832–1867*. Chicago: University of Chicago Press, 1985.
Gallagher, Catherine. *Nobody's Story: The Vanishing Acts of Women Writers in the Marketplace, 1670–1820*. Berkeley; Los Angeles: University of California Press, 1994.
Gallagher, Catherine. "What Would Napoleon Do: Historical, Fictional, and Counterfactual Characters." *New Literary History: A Journal of Theory and Interpretation* 42, no. 2 (2011): 315–36.
Garratt, Peter. *Victorian Empiricism: Self, Knowledge, and Reality in Rusking, Bain, Lewes, Spencer, and George Eliot*. Madison: Fairleigh Dickinson University Press, 2010.

Gatrall, Jefferson J A. *The Real and the Sacred*. Ann Arbor: University of Michigan Press, 2014.

Gibson, Richard Hughes, and Timothy Larsen. "Nineteenth-Century Spiritual Autobiography: Carlyle, Mill, Newman." In *A History of English Autobiography*, edited by Adam Smyth, 192–206. Cambridge: Cambridge University Press, 2015.

Gilley, Sheridan. *Newman and His Age*. London: Darton, Longman, and Todd, 1990.

Gladstone, William. "Robert Elsmere and the Battle of Belief." *The Nineteenth Century* 23 (May 1888): 766–88.

Graziano, Anne. "The Death of the Working-Class Hero in *Mary Barton* and *Alton Locke*." *JNT: Journal of Narrative Theory* 29, no. 2 (1999): 135–57.

Gregory, Rabia *Marrying Jesus in Medieval and Early Modern Northern Europe*. Abingdon: Routledge, 2016.

Greiner, Rae. *Sympathetic Realism in Nineteenth-Century British Fiction*. Baltimore: Johns Hopkins University Press, 2012.

Hale, Piers J. "Darwin's Other Bulldog: Charles Kingsley and the Popularisation of Evolution in Victorian England." *Science And Education* 21, no. 7 (July 2012): 977–1013.

Hanson, Ellis. *Decadence and Catholicism*. Cambridge: Harvard University Press, 1997.

Hapgood, Lynne. "'The Reconceiving of Christianity': Secularisation, Realism, and the Religious Novel." *Literature & Theology: An International Journal of Religion, Theory, and Culture* 10, no. 4 (1996): 329–50.

Hartley, Allan John. *The Novels of Charles Kingsley: A Christian Socialist Interpretation*. Folkstone: The Hour-Glass Press, 1977.

Hempton, David. *Methodism: Empire of the Spirit*. New Haven: Yale University Press, 2005.

Herringer, Carol Engelhardt. *Victorians and the Virgin Mary: Religion and Gender in England, 1830–85*. Manchester: Manchester University Press, 2008.

Hill, Christopher. *Society and Puritanism in Pre-Revolutionary England*. New York: Schocken Books, 1964.

Hilton, Boyd. *The Age of Atonement: The Influence of Evangelicalism on Social and Economic Thought, 1785–1865*. Oxford: Oxford University Press, 1988.

Hindmarsh, D. Bruce. *The Evangelical Conversion Narrative: Spiritual Autobiography in Early Modern England*. Oxford: Oxford University Press, 2005.

Hope, Norman V. "The Issue between Newman and Kingsley: A Reconsideration and a Rejoineder." *Theology Today* 6, no. 1 (1949): 77–90.

Hughes, Jessica Ann. "Dickens's *The Life of Our Lord* and the Problem of Jesus." In *"Perplext in Faith:" Essays on Victorian Beliefs and Doubts*, edited by Julie Melnyk and Alisa Clapp-Itnyre, 268–303. Cambridge: Cambridge Scholars, 2015.

Hume, David. *Philosophical Essays Concerning Human Understanding*. 2nd ed. London: M. Cooper, 1751.

Hymns Ancient and Modern for Use in the Services of the Church with Accompanying Tunes. London: Novello and Co., 1861.

Jenkins, Ruth Y. *Reclaiming Myths of Power: Women Writers and the Victorian Spiritual Crisis*. [in English] Lewisburg, PA: Bucknell University Press, 1995.

Jones, Paul Dafydd. "Jesus Christ and the Transformation of English Society: The 'Subversive Conservatism' of Frederick Denison Maurice." *Harvard Theological Review* 96, no. 2 (2003): 205–28.

Keen, Suzanne. *Victorian Renovations of the Novel: Narrative Annexes and the Boundaries of Representation*. Cambridge: Cambridge University Press, 1998.

Ker, Ian. *The Catholic Revival in English Literature, 1845–961*. Notre Dame: University of Notre Dame Press, 2003.

Keuss, Jeffrey F. *A Poetics of Jesus: The Search for Christ through Writings in the Nineteenth Century*. [in English] Aldershot: Ashgate, 2002.

Killick, Tim. *British Short Fiction in the Early Nineteenth Century: The Rise of the Tale*. Hampshire: Ashgate, 2008.

King, Joshua. *Imagined Spiritual Communities in Britain's Age of Print*. Athens, OH: Ohio University Press, 2015.

Kingsley, Charles. *Alton Locke, Tailor and Poet; an Autobiography*. New York: Oxford University Press, 1983.

Kingsley, Charles. *Charles Kingsley: His Letters and Memoreis of His Life; Edited by His Wife*. London: Henry S. King & Co., 1877.

Kingsley, Charles. *Hypatia*. The Works of Charles Kingsley. 2 vols. Philadelphia: J. F. Taylor and Co., 1899.

Kingsley, Charles. *Letters and Memoirs*. The Works of Charles Kingsley. 2 vols. Philadelphia: J. F. Taylor & Co., 1899.

Kingsley, Charles. *Sermons on National Subjects*. London: Macmillan, 1890.

Kingsley, Charles. *Town Geology*. New York: D. Appleton and Company, 1873.

Kingsley, Charles. *Yeast; Poems*. The Works of Charles Kingsley. Philadelphia: J. F. Taylor and Co., 1899.

Klaver, J. M. I. *The Apostle of the Flesh: A Critical Life of Charles Kingsley*. Edited by A. J. Vanderjagt. Boston: Brill, 2006.

Knight, Mark. *Good Words: Evangelicalism and the Victorian Novel*. Columbus: University of Ohio Press, 2019.

Knight, Mark, and Emma Mason. *Nineteenth-Century Religion and Literature: An Introduction*. Oxford: Oxford University Press, 2006.

Knoepflmacher, U. C. *George Eliot's Early Novels*. Berkeley and Los Angeles: University of California Press, 1968.

Krueger, Christine L. *The Reader's Repentance: Women Preachers, Women Writers, and Nineteenth-Century Social Discourse*. Chicago: University of Chicago Press, 1992.

LaMonaca, Maria. *Masked Atheism: Catholicism and the Secular Victorian Home*. Columbus: Ohio State University Press, 2008.

Landow, George P. "Aggressive (Re)Interpretations of the Female Sage: Florence Nightingale's Cassandra." In *Victorian Sages and Cultural Discourse: Renegotiating Gender and Power*, edited by Thais E. Morgan, 32–45. New Brunswick: Rutgers University Press, 1990.

Landow, George P. *Images of Crisis: Literary Iconology, 1750 to the Present*. 2nd ed. New York: Routledge, 2014.

Lane, Christopher. *The Age of Doubt: Tracing the Roots of Our Religious Uncertainty*. New Haven: Yale University Press, 2012.

Langland, Elizabeth. *Nobody's Angels: Middle-Class Women and Domestic Ideology in Victorian Culture*. Ithaca: Cornell University Press, 1995.

LaPorte, Charles *Victorian Poets and the Changing Bible*. Charlottesville, VA: University of Virgina Press, 2011.

Larsen, Timothy. *Crisis of Doubt: Honest Faith in Nineteenth-Century England*. Oxford: Oxford University Press, 2006.

Larsen, Timothy. *George Macdonald in the Age of Miracles: Incarnation, Doubt, and Reenchantment*. Hansen Lectureship. Downer's Grove: IVP Academic, 2018.

Larsen, Timothy. "Losing My Religion: Mrs. Humphry Ward's *Robert Elsmere*." http://www.booksandculture.com/articles/2015/janfeb/losing-my-religion.html?paging=off.

Larsen, Timothy. "The Nineteenth Century." In *Oxford Handbook of Christmas*, edited by Timothy Larsen. Oxford: Oxford University Press, 2020.

Larsen, Timothy. *A People of One Book: The Bible and the Victorians*. Oxford: Oxford University Press, 2012.

Lawrence, Anna M. *One Family under God: Love, Belonging, and Authority in Early Transatlantic Methodism*. Philadelphia: University Penn Press, 2011.

Lecourt, Sebastian. *Cultivating Belief: Victorian Anthropology, Liberal Aesthetics, and the Secular Imagination*. New York: Oxford University Press, 2018.

Lecourt, Sebastian. "Prophets Genuine and Spurious: The Victorian Jesus Novel and the Ends of Comparison." *Representations* 143 (Spring 2018): 33–55.

Lee, Susanna. *A World Abandoned by God: Narrative and Secularism*. Lewisburg: Bucknell University Press, 2005.

Levine, Caroline. *The Serious Pleasures of Suspense*. [in English] Charlottesvillle: University of Virginia Press, 2003.

Levine, George. *The Realistic Imagination: English Fiction from Frankenstein to Lady Chatterley*. Chicago: University of Chicago Press, 1981.

Linton, Eliza Lynn. *The True History of Joshua Davidson, Christian and Communist*. London: Bradbury, Evans, and Co., 1872.

Loesberg, Jonathan. "Deconstruction, Historicism, and Overdetermination: Dislocations of the Marriage Plots in *Robert Elsmere* and *Dombey and Son*." *Victorian Studies* 33, no. 3 (1990): 441–64.

Ludlow, Elizabeth. *The Figure of Christ in the Long Nineteenth Century*. Palgrave Studies in Nineteenth-Century Writing and Culture. Edited by Elizabeth Ludlow. London: Palgrave Macmillan, 2020.

Lukács, György. *The Historical Novel*. Translated by Hannah Mitchell and Stanley Mitchell. Lincoln: University of Nebraska Press, 1983.

Lynch, Deidre Shauna. *The Economy of Character: Novels, Market Culture, and the Business of Inner Meaning*. Chicago: Chicago University Press, 1998.

MacDonald, Tara. *The New Man, Masculinity and Marriage in the Victorian Novel*. New York: Routledge, 2016.

McKelvy, William R. *The English Cult of Literature: Devoted Readers, 1774–1880*. Victorian Literature and Culture Series. Charlottesville: University of Virginia Press, 2007.

McKeon, Michael. *The Origins of the English Novel, 1600–1740*. 2nd ed. Baltimore: Johns Hopkins University Press, 2002.

Menke, Richard. "Cultural Capital and the Scene of Rioting: Male Working-Class Authorship in *Alton Locke*." *Victorian Literature and Culture* 28, no. 1 (2000): 87–108.

Miller, Andrew H. *The Burdens of Perfection: On Ethics and Reading in Nineteenth-Century British Literature*. Ithaca: Cornell University Press, 2008.

Miller, J. Hillis. *Reading for Our Time: Adam Bede and Middlemarch Revisited*. Edinburgh: Edinburgh University Press, 2012.

Montgomery, James. *The Christian Psalmist, or Hymns, Selected and Original*. Glasgow: Chalmers and Collins, 1825.

More, Hannah. *Cœlebs in Search of a Wife: Comprehending Observations on Domestic Habits and Manners, Religion and Morals*. Edited by Patricia Demers. Peterborough, ON, Canada: Broadview Press, 2007.

Moretti, Franco. *The Way of the World: The Bildungsroman in European Culture*. New ed. New York: Verso Press, 2007.

Morgan, Susan. *Sisters in Time: Imagining Gender in Nineteenth-Century British Fiction*. Oxford: Oxford University Press, 1989.

Morris, Jeremy. *F. D. Maurice and the Crisis of Christian Authority*. New York: Oxford University Press, 2005.

"Mr. Kingsley's Imaginative Writings." *The Scottish Review*, April 1856, 97–112.

"Mr. Kingsley's Literary Excesses." *The National Review*, January 1860, 1–24.

Nettles, Tomas J. *Living by Revealed Truth: The Life and Pastoral Theology of Charles Haddon Spurgeon*. Fearn, Scotland: Mentor, 2013.

Newman, John Henry. *Apologia Pro Vita Sua and Six Sermons*. Edited by Frank M. Turner. New Haven: Yale University Press, 2008.

Newman, John Henry. "Ecce Homo." *The Month* 4, no. 56 (1866): 551–73.

Noll, Mark. *Protestantism: A Very Short Introduction*. Oxford: Oxford University Press, 2011.

Noll, Mark. "Romanticism and the Hymns of Charles Wesley." *The Evangelical Quarterly* 46 (1974): 195–223.

O'Malley, Patrick R. *Catholicism, Sexual Deviance, and Victorian Gothic Culture*. Cambridge: Cambridge University Press, 2006.

Oliphant, Margaret. *Salem Chapel*. Edinburgh: W. Blackwood and Sons, 1865.

Pals, Daniel L. *The Victorian "Lives of Jesus"*. San Antonio, TX: Trinity University Press, 1982.

Panek, Jennifer. "Constructions of Masculinity in Adam Bede and Wives and Daughters." [In English]. *Victorian Review: The Journal of the Victorian Studies*

Association of Western Canada and the Victorian Studies Association of Ontario 22, no. 2 (1996): 127–51.

Parker, Joseph. *Ecce Deus, Essays on the Life and Doctrine of Jesus Christ. With Controversial Notes on "Ecce Homo"*. Boston: Roberts Brothers, 1867.

Parris, Leslie. *The Pre-Raphaelites*. London: Tate Gallery, 1984.

Pecora, Vincent P. *Secularization without End*. Notre Dame: University of Notre Dame Press, 2015.

Perkin, J. Russell. *Theology and the Victorian Novel*. Montreal and Kingston: McGill-Queen's University Press, 2009.

Poovey, Mary. *Uneven Developments: The Ideological Work of Gender in Mid-Victorian England*. [in English] Chicago: University of Chicago Press, 1988.

Prystash, Justin. "Rhizomatic Subjects." *Nineteenth-Century Literature* 66, no. 2 (2011): 141–69.

Rauch, Alan. "The Tailor Transformed: Kingsley's *Alton Locke* and the Notion of Change." *Studies in the Novel* 25, no. 2 (1993): 196–213.

Rauch, Alan. *Useful Knowledge: The Victorians, Morality, and "the March of the Intellect."* Durham, NC: Duke University Press, 2001.

Reed, John R. "Soldier Boy: Forming Masculinity in *Adam Bede*." *Studies in the Novel* 33, no. 3 (2001): 268–84.

Renan, Ernest. *Vie De Jésus*. Translated by Charles Edwin Wilbour. New York: Carleton, 1867.

"The Rev. Charles Kingsley." *Blackwood's Edinburgh Magazine*, June 1855, 625–43.

Richmond, Leigh. *The Dairyman's Daughter: An Authentic Narrative Containing an Account of Her Extraordinary Conversion, Godly Exercises, and Happy Death, with Serious Reflections on Death*. Kilmarnock: H. Crawford, 1817.

Rignall, J. M. "Between Chartism and the 1880s: J. W. Overton and E. Lynn Linton." In *The Socialist Novel in Britain: Towards the Recovery of a Tradition*, edited by H. Gustav Klaus. New York: St. Martin's Press.

Rivers, Isabel. *Reason, Grace, and Sentiment: A Study of the Language of Religion and Ethics in England, 1660–1780: Whichcote to Wesley*. 2 vols. Vol. 1. Cambridge: Cambridge University Press, 1991.

"Royal Academy." *The Standard*, May 9, 1850.

Salmon, Richard. *The Formation of the Victorian Literary Profession*. Cambridge: Cambridge University Press, 2013.

Salmon, Richard. "'The Unaccredited Hero': *Alton Locke*, Thomas Carlyle, and the Formation of the Working-Class Intellectual." In *The Working-Class Intellectual in Eighteenth- and Nineteenth-Century Britain*, edited by Aruna Krishnamurthy, 167–94. Surrey: Ashgate, 2009.

Sanders, Elizabeth M. *Genres of Doubt: Science Fiction, Fantasy, and the Victorian Crisis of Faith*. Jefferson, NC: McFarland & Co. Press, 2017.

Sanders, T. C. "Reviews: Two Years Ago." *The Saturday Review*, 1857, 176–7.

Sandys, William. *Christmas Carols Ancient and Modern*. London: Richard Beckley, 1833.

Schramm, Jan-Melissa. *Atonement and Self-Sacrifice in Nineteenth-Century Narrative*. Cambridge: Cambridge University Press, 2012.

Schramm, Jan-Melissa. *Censorship and the Representation of the Sacred in Nineteenth-Century England*. Oxford: Oxford University Press, 2019.

Seeley, John Robert. *Ecce Homo: A Survey of the Life and Work of Jesus Christ*. Boston: Roberts Brothers, 1867.

Sharpe, Eric J. "'Gentle Jesus, Meek and Mild': Variations on a Nursery Theme, for Congregation and Critic." *Evangelical Quarterly* 53, no. 3 (1981): 149–65.

Shaw, Harry E. *Narrating Reality: Austen, Scott, Eliot*. Ithaca: Cornell University Press, 1999.

Simeon, Charles. *Horae Homileticae*. 21 vols. London: Hodsworth and Ball, 1832–3.

Smiles, Samuel. *Self-Help, with Illustrations of Character, Conduct, and Perseverance*. Oxford: Oxford University Press, 2002.

Smith, Adam. *Theory of Moral Sentiments; to Which Is Added a Dissertation on the Origin of Languages*. London: T. Cadell in the Strand, 1767.

Society, Religious Tract. *Christian Biography; Containing the Lives of John Bunyan, John Owen, Rev. Thomas Halyburton, Rev. George Herbert*. 15 vols. Vol. 13. London: Religious Tract Society, 1832.

Sopher, R. E. "Gender and Sympathy in *Adam Bede*: The Case of Seth Bede." *George Eliot - George Henry Lewes Studies* 62/63 (2012): 1–15.

Southey, Robert. *The Life of Wesley; and the Rise and Progress of Methodism, in Two Volumes*. Vol. 1. London: Longman, Hurst, Rees, Orme, and Brown, 1820.

Stark, Ryan. *Biblical Sterne: Rhetoric and Religion in the Shandyverse*. New York: Bloomsbury, 2021.

Stevens, Jennifer. *The Historical Jesus and the Literary Imagination: 1860–1920*. Liverpool: Liverpool University Press, 2010.

Strauss, David Friedrich. *The Life of Jesus, Critically Examined*. Translated by George Eliot. 2nd ed. New York: Macmillan & Co., 1892.

Sutherland, John. *Mrs. Humphry Ward: Eminent Victorian, Pre-Eminent Edwardian*. Oxford: Clarendon Press, 1990.

Taylor, Charles. *A Secular Age*. Cambridge: The Belknap Press of Harvard University Press, 2007.

Taylor, Charles. *Sources of the Self: The Making of the Modern Identity*. Cambridge, MA: Harvard University Press, 1989.

Tennyson, G. B. *Victorian Devotional Poetry: The Tractarian Mode*. Cambridge: Harvard University Press, 1981.

Tomko, Michael. *Beyond the Willing Suspension of Disbelief: Poetic Faith from Coleridge to Tolkien*. New York: Bloomsbury, 2015.

Tosh, John. *A Man's Place: Masculinity and the Middle-Class Home in Victorian England*. New Haven: Yale University Press, 2007.

Vance, Norman. "Kingsley's Christian Manliness." *Theology* 78, no. 30 (1975): 30–8.

Vance, Norman. *Sinews of the Spirit: The Ideal of Christian Manliness in Victorian Literature and Religious Thought*. Cambridge: Cambridge University Press, 1985.

Vanden Bossche, Chris. *Carlyle and the Search for Authority*. Columbus: Ohio State University Press, 1991.

Vanden Bossche, Chris R. *Reform Acts: Chartism, Social Agency, and the Victorian Novel, 1832–1867*. Baltimore: Johns Hopkins University Press, 2014.

Vines, Michael E. *The Problem of Markan Genre: The Gospel of Mark and the Jewish Novel*. Leiden: Brill Academic Publishing, 2002.

Walker, Stanwood S. "'Backwards and Backwards Ever': Charles Kingsley's Racial-Historical Allegory and the Liberal Anglican Revisioning of Britain." *Nineteenth-Century Literature* 62, no. 3 (2007): 339–79.

Ward, Mary Augusta (Mrs. Humphry). *The Case of Richard Meynell*. New York: Doubleday, Page, and Co., 1911.

Ward, Mary Augusta. "The New Reformation: A Dialogue." *The Nineteenth Century* 25 (1889): 454–80.

Ward, Mary Augusta. *Robert Elsmere*. Project Gutenberg, 2008.

Watson, J. R. *The English Hymn: A Critical and Historical Study*. Oxford: Oxford University Press, 1997.

Watt, Ian. *The Rise of the Novel*. 2nd ed. Berkeley: University of California Press, 2001.

Watt, James. "The Origin and Development of the Oriental Tale." In *Orientalism and Literature*, edited by Geoffrey P. Nash, 50–65. Cambridge: Cambridge University Press, 2019.

Webb, R. K. "The Limits of Religious Liberty: Theology and Criticism in Nineteenth-Century England." In *Freedom and Religion in the Nineteenth Century*, edited by Richard J. Helmstadter, 120–49. Stanford: Stanford University Press, 1997.

Webb, R. K. "The Unitarian Background." In *Truth, Liberty, Religion: Essays Celebrating Two Hundred Years of Manchester College*, 1–30. Oxford: Manchester College, 1986.

Wee, C. J. W. L. "Christian Manliness and National Identity: The Problematic Construction of a Racially 'Pure' Nation." In *Muscular Christianity: Embodying the Victorian Age*, edited by Donald E. Hall, 66–88. Cambridge: Cambridge University Press, 1994.

Welsh, Alexander. *The Hero of the Waverley Novels, with New Essays on Scott*. Princeton: Princeton University Press, 2014.

Wesley, Charles and John Wesley. *Hymns and Sacred Poems*. 4 ed. Bristol: Felix Farley, 1743.

Wesley, John. *Explanatory Notes upon the New Testament*. New York: J. Soule and T. Mason, 1818.

Wesley, John. *An Extract of the Rev. Mr. John Wesley's Journal from His Embarking for Georgia to His Return to London*. London: Printed for G. Whitefield, 1797.

Wesley, John. *A Pocket Hymn Book, for the Use of Christians of All Denominations*. London: J. Paramore, 1787.

Wheeler, Michael. *St. John and the Victorians*. Cambridge: Cambridge University Press, 2011.

Whitefield, George. *Sermons on Important Subjects*. London: Thomas Tegg, 1841.
Wilberforce, Robert and Samuel. *The Life of William Wilberforce*. 5 vols. London: John Murray, 1838.
Williams, Raymond. *The Country and the City*. New York: Oxford University Press, 1973.
Wilt, Judith. "The Romance of Faith: Mary Ward's *Robert Elsmere* and *Richard Meynell*." *Literature & Theology: An International Journal of Religion, Theory, and Culture* 10, no. 1 (1996): 33–43.
Winn, William E. "*Tom Brown's Schooldays* and the Development of 'Muscular Christianity'." *Church History* 29, no. 1 (1960): 64–73.
Woloch, Alex. *The One vs. The Many: Minor Characters and the Space of the Protagonist in the Novel*. Princeton: Princeton University Press, 2003.
"Yeast." *The Christian Remembrancer*, October 1857, 391–456.
Yonge, Charlotte Mary. *The Daisy Chain, or, Aspirations: A Family Chronicle*. London: Virago Press, 1988.
Zebedee. "List of the Improper Phrases Sometimes Used in the Pulpit." *Evangelical Magazine*, December 1795.
Zemka, Sue. *Victorian Testaments: The Bible, Christology, and Literary Authority in Early-Nineteenth-Century British Culture*. Stanford: Stanford University Press, 1997.
Ziolkowski, Theodore. *Fictional Transfigurations of Jesus*. Princeton, NJ: Princeton University Press, 1972.

Index

Adam Bede 34, 50, 101–30
    Arthur 106, 112, 114, 117–18, 120, 123–4, 129
    Dinah 106–11, 121–3, 129–30, 136, 148, 162
    Hetty 106–7, 110, 117–18, 120, 123–4, 129
    marriage 106–7, 110–11, 121, 129
    and *Robert Elsmere* 136, 139, 141, 148, 151, 162, 169
    Seth 112–14, 118–19, 124, 129
    Thais 119–20, 129
Alton Locke 67–99, See also Bildungsroman
    Eleanor 87–8, 91–2, 94–7, 111, 148
    Mackaye 74, 84, 90
Anglicanism, *See under* Established Church
Arminianism 18, 40
Arnold, Matthew 70
    Literature and Dogma 139–41
Arnold, Thomas 69–70
atonement 8, 30–1, 36, 39, 52, 75, 87, 99
    in *Adam Bede* 102, 105, 113–17, 124, 128, 130, 139
    history of 11–15
    and Jesus 25–7, 31, 36, 39, 52, 75, 87
    narrative implications 11, 18–19, 23–7
    penal substitution 15, 18–19
    ransom 12–13
    substitutionary 15
autobiography 19, 23, 82, 87
    see also Conversion Narrative

Bakhtin, M. M. 15, 17, 50
Bible 41–4, 56–61, 78, 80, 139–40
    Biblicism 7–8, 40
    criticism 4–5, 8–9, 11, 60, 70–1, 137
    illustrated 57–8
biblical characters
    Mary, mother of Jesus 59, 94, 105
    Mary Magdaline 94
    Mary and Martha 94

bildungsroman 21, 23, 35, 128
    in *Alton Locke* 80–3
biography 5, 7, 25
    fictionalized 3, 20, 60
Blackwood's Edinburgh Magazine 68
Book of Common Prayer 47–8, 50, 104
Bradlaugh, Charles 159
broad church 8, 43, 69–71, 85
Bunyan, John 29, 40
    The Pilgrim's Progress 1–2

Calvinism 13–15, 18, 22, 40, 42, 88–9
Catholicism, Roman 13, 39, 78, 111, 149
    anti-catholicism 19, 36
    catholic emancipation 42, 70
    eucharistic theology 5–7, 15
characterization
    in Conversion Narratives 32
    and the realist novel 32–6, 64, 80 n.37, 91, 153, 156
    and theology 8, 18–20
characterization of Jesus
    friend 29, 35, 49, 99, 103–5, 110, 121, 124, 129, 135
    husband 30, 106, 108, 110–11, 121
    infant 54–6, 78, 105, 107, 124
    king 67–8, 72, 74, 79, 99, 101
    lover 16, 29–31
    priest 8–9, 101–5, 128–31, 137, 145, 147
    prophet 8–9, 75–6, 134–7, 145–7, 159–67
    savior 1, 4, 17, 55, 59, 98, 170
    teacher 3, 90, 105, 130–2, 144–7, 151–2
Christian manliness 73–4, 80 n.37, 113
Christmas 8, 19, 52–6, 59, 78
Christology 4, 43, 45, 62, 71, 75
    Alexadnrian 75
    demythologized 105, 128, 132, 134–5, 146, 150, 161–6
    in *Robert Elsmere* 132, 144
Church of England *See under* Established Church

Coleridge, Samuel Coleridge 4, 70
conversion narrative 18–29, 32, 40–1, 122, 146
  in *Alton Locke* 79–91, 97–9
  Evangelical 21–3
  Puritan 19–21
  class 21–2, 80, 82, 84

Darwin, Charles 2, 44, *See also* Kingsley
dialogue 33, 84, 95–7, 136, 144, 151, 154–7
Dickens, Charles 53, 58–9
  A Christmas Carol 53
  The Life of Our Lord n 59
dissent 40, 42, 47, 69, 71, 78, 89
domesticity 47, 52–4, 56, 59–60

Edersheim, Alfred
  Life and Times of Jesus the Messiah 63–4
election (doctrine of) 14, 19, 40, 88
Eliot, George 4, 65, 131, 133, 138–41, 147–9, 157–8, 169–71
  Adam Bede (*see Adam Bede*)
  aesthetics 34, 50
  and biblical scholarship 102 (*see also* Feuerbach and Strauss)
  religious background 102–04, 107 n.17
  translations (*see under* Feuerbach and Strauss)
epistemology
  and David Hume 44, 138
  and John Locke 19, 23, 77
Essays and Reviews 7, 137
Established Church 7, 40–3, 69, 160
Evangelical Novels 5, 7
Evangelical Revival 8, 11, 15, 18–19, 22, 27, 40–1, 56
Evangelicalism 26–9, 40–9 See also conversion narrative
  and Charles Kingsley 69, 75, 85, 99
  and George Eliot 102, 122
  Reformed 22, 40
  Wesleyan 18, 27, 40
Examiner 59

Farrar, F. W. (Frederic William)
  The Life of Christ 62–4
Feuerbach, Ludwig 44, 113
  Das Wesen des Christentums (*The Essence of Christianity*) 102–5

  Eliot's translation 103–4
  in *Adam Bede* 128, 130, 138
fiction 3–6, 170–1, 31–6, 64, 162
  historical 20, 32, 35, 51, 60, 125 n.65, 139
  Oriental Tale 135–6, 142, 152
  realist 6, 8, 31, 34, 81, 91, 133, 135, 139
  speculative 5
Fifth Gospels 4, 64, 170

Gaskell, Elizabeth 4, 150
Gladstone, William 133, 149
God 85–6, 136–9
  character of 11–24, 101–5
  characterizations in theology 28–30, 130–2
  image of 76–8
  son (*see under* Jesus)
Guardian 140

high church 40–1, 43, 71
Hume, David 44–5, 138–40
  On Miracles 44, 138
Hunt, William Holman 58
hymnody 15–18, 23, 28–30, 85, 109–10
  Christmas carols 52–6
  Hymns Ancient and Modern 56

identity
  narrative construction of 22–6, 33
  in *Alton Lock* 75–87, 91, 97
incarnation, *See also* Jesus
  in *Alton Locke* 70–80, 101–5
  theological developments 39, 43, 101, 105, 137–41
  and Kingsley 70–5, 87

Jesus
  ascension 150
  Christ 4–6, 150–1
  demythologized 105, 128, 132–5, 145, 150, 161–6
  gender 58, 73–4, 111–14, 122–3, 130
  gospels 3–4, 50, 60, 64, 105, 118, 122–4, 136–7, 150–4
  imitation of 3–5, 132–6, 140–4, 150–3, 158–9, 162
  incarnation 5–7, 53–8, 124, 132, 137–40
  Judaism 63–4

see also characterization of Jesus
Jowett, Benjamin 70

Keble, John 42–3, 47–50, 70
  The Christian Year 42–53
Kingsley, Charles 101–5, 111–14, 131–2, 143, 147–8, 151
  and Darwin 69
  Hypatia 74, 79
  religious affiliation 68–71
  Yeast 67–8, 77, 79
  see also incarnation
  see also Alton Locke
  see also christian manliness

Linton, Eliza Lynn 142–3, 152, 161, 169–71
  see also Joshua Davidson
lives of Jesus 3–4, 59–64
low church 40–3, 71
Lukács, György 3, 6, 20 n125
Lyell, Charles (*Principles of Geology*) 2, 43

Martineau, Harriet 60, 64
Martineau, James 158
Martineau family 149
masculinity 58, *See also* Christian manliness
  and Jesus (*see under* Jesus and gender)
  and Kingsley 73–4, 111–14, 124, 169
  and the military 123
Maurice, Fredrick Denison 69–70, 75–6, 143 n161
Methodism 15–16, 22, 29–30, 40, 107, 109–10
middle-class 33, 58, 71, 74, 81–4, 96, 113
Millais, John Everett 58–9
Montgomery, James 55–6
More, Hannah (*Coelebs in Search of a Wife*) 46–7

narrative
  annex 91
  closed 15, 17, 36
  closure 160
  open 18
  structure 12, 20, 32, 35, 50
narrative atonement 22–6
National Review 68
Newman, John Henry 43, 45, 51, 62, 70

novel
  Catholic 5, 7
  history of 20–5, 50–1
  marriage-plot 35, 106, 121, 153–4
  realist (*see* fiction, realist)
  romantic 50–2, 59

Oliphant, Margaret (*Salem Chapel*) 47, 143 n.23
Oxford movement 42–3
  Tracts for the Times 42

Parker, Joseph (*Ecce Deus*) 62
Pater, Walter 132–3, 149
Priestley, Joseph 4, 149
Protestantism
  and national identity 15, 39–43
Puritanism
  atonement 13–15, 18–19, 22, 36
  Bible 3, 20
  see also conversion narrative

realism 34–5, 91, 97–9, 124–6, 133–6, 170–1
  high 7, 126 n.69, 170
  prescriptive 1
reformation 15–16
Renan, Ernest
  Vie de Jésus 3, 61–2, 147
resurrection 12–13, 15–16, 27, 31, 75, 94, 132, 137–9
  bodily 43–4, 69–70, 139, 145, 150, 154, 165
Richmond, Leigh
  The Dairyman's Daughter 46
Robert Elsmere 2, 9, 131–67, 170–1
  Catherine 134, 153–5, 157, 160, 162–7
  (De)conversion 140, 144–5, 150, 154–5, 161, 163, 166–7
  marriage 133, 135, 142, 153–4, 162–7
  Robert 3, 50, 65, 132–4, 136–8, 142, 144–67
Romanticism 40, 46–52, 64

sacraments 27, 40–3, 45
  baptism 27, 74
  eucharist 5, 7, 15, 27, 41, 43, 51
sacrifice 13, 15, 19, 48, 101–2, 124–5, 130, 139
  self-sacrifice 4, 52, 59, 105, 158–9

salvation 14, 16–19, 27, 31, 56, 86 n.54
sanctification 16, 19
Sanders, T. C. 112–13
Sandys, William 52–4
Scott, Walter (Sir) 129
   Waverley Novels 51, 125
Scottish Review 68
Seeley, John Robert (*Ecce Homo:*
   A Survey of the Life and Work of Jesus
   of Nazareth) 2, 63
secularization 2–3, 8, 49, 102, 133, 140
Simeon, Charles 28
Smiles, Samuel 125, 120
Smith, Adam 114–16
Southey, Robert 30
Standard 59
Strauss, David 2, 43–4, 49, 130, 138
   in *Adam Bede* 105, 110, 113, 118, 122
   Das Leben Jesu 49, 60–1, 90, 102–5,
      118, 138
   translations 49, 60–1, 103–4

three-fold office 8, 92, 131, 153, *See also*
   Jesus (King, Priest, and Prophet)
Tractarian, *See under* Oxford movement

The True History of Joshua Davidson:
   Christian and Communist 9, 132–67
   Joshua 65, 132, 135–6, 141–4, 150–3,
      158–61
   Mary 135–6, 144, 152
   narrator 132, 135, 144, 152–3, 159

Unitarianism 40, 43 n.14, 135, 149–50, 158
   new 149
   old 149–50

Ward, Mary Augusta (Mrs.) 8–9, 50, 131,
   139–41
   The Case of Richard Meynell 134, 160
   New Reformation 141
   Robert Elsmere (*see Robert Elsmere*)
Watts, Isaac 39–40
Wesley, Charles 16, 28, 30, 40, 46, 54, 85
Wesley, John 17–18, 27–31, 40, 46, 85, 107
Whitefield, George 17, 29–30, 40, 54, 111
Wilberforce, William 46
Wilde, Oscar 3, 5, 144, 170
Wordsworth, William 46, 50
working class 42, 49, 113 n.36, 144, 155–8
   in *Alton Locke* 71–6, 80–4, 88, 90, 95–6